MW00896469

Homicide: The View from Inside the Yellow Tape

Cloyd Steiger

©2018

https://cloydsteiger.com

To the secondary victims of homicide;
the loved ones left behind.

Acknowledgements

There are a lot of people to thank for a project like this. First, I'd like to thank Casey McNerthney, who spent years as a local Seattle reporter watching me from outside the yellow tape, for his enthusiasm, and editing skills.

I'd also like to thank all the partners I worked with in Homicide: John Nordlund, Greg Mixsell, Donna O'Neal, Mike Ciesynski, Jason Kasner, and Sonny Davis, (yes, even Sonny).

I'd like to thank my sons, Casey, Landon and Dylan for all the times I had to leave to go to work for long hours, sometimes missing family events.

All my friends and family, who repeatedly over the years have told me, "You should write a book!"

My six favorite people in the world; my grandchildren, Keaton, Kai, Kenley, Reese, Wyatt, and Dakota.

My wife Doreen, who when we first met, told me, "I could never be married to a police officer," and not only married one, but has two sons who are cops now, for all the times that damned phone rang in the middle of the night, sending me away for hours, and sometimes days, usually at very inconvenient times.

Finally, the Seattle Police Department, who hired a 21-year-old kid and made my dream come true.

1

My job's been murder lately.

I mean that literally; the blood, and the gore. And don't even get me started about the smell; the metallic scent of blood, usually mixed with alcohol, the putrid odor of decaying human flesh, the maggots, and blood spatter. It's not the clean, tidy murder like you see on CSI or several other television dramas that think they got it right.

They didn't.

My work life is about depravity; about asshole gang-bangers to whom life is some gangsta rap song advocating pulling out your gat at the slightest provocation, about sexual psychopath serial killers, domestic terrorists, the criminally insane, and a whole bunch of just stupid people who kill other people for no damned good reason.

At home, my life is PG-13, but my work life is definitely MA-17.

It's not a job for people who don't want to get their hands dirty.

This morning was no exception.

I drove the downtown Seattle streets, usually bustling with pedestrian and vehicle traffic, abandoned at that hour, except an occasional street sweeper or transient sifting through ashtrays, seeking out cigarette butts discarded with tobacco enough to roll their own.

The red and blue lights at the top of my windshield pierced the streetlight-lit night, I paused only briefly at each red light before driving through, eventually pulling my unmarked Chevy Impala detective car up to the scene, a gas station off Denny Way in the shadow of the Space Needle. Well, it would have been in the shadow if it wasn't four in the morning.

Another homicide.

Yellow crime scene tape encircled the lot, a dead black male lying near a gas pump, his head surrounded by a large pool of blood, his eyes in the fixed cloudy stare of death I'd seen hundreds, if not thousands of times in my career.

A young patrol officer stood at the edge of the tape, a clipboard in his hands logging everyone entering the crime scene, his uniform immaculately clean and pressed; obviously a rookie.

"Can I get your name, sir?"

"Steiger," I told him, "from Homicide."

"Serial number?"

"Four-three-one-three."

I saw the look in his eyes; he was looking at a dinosaur. His serial number was probably in the mid-eight thousands.

Two of my sons are patrol officers. He'd consider them old guys with seven and a half and eight years on respectively.

Johney Stevens was the Patrol Sergeant at the scene. I knew him well. I was a patrol officer with several years on when he was the rookie holding the clipboard.

"What's going on here, Johney?"

"The clerk inside heard a bunch of shots. He ducked and called 911. My guys got here and found this dude obviously dead," he said, gesturing to the body. "We found four guns; two in the car, and two outside. The thing is, all the shell casings are in the car, none outside. It looks like these guys were all sitting in the car when the shooting went down."

"Wow," I smiled. "The shootout at the OK Corolla."

I walked up to the car and looked in, the scent of cordite and blood in the air. A semiautomatic pistol lay just outside the front passenger door. Another was in the backseat. The magazine was inserted backward. It couldn't have fired in that condition.

Sucks to be that guy.

Another gun lay on the ground near the dead guy.

This wasn't my case. I was there to help the primary detectives, in this case Tom Mooney and Jeff Mudd.

Bob Merner, the Chief of Investigations pulled up in his car.

Chief's rarely show up at "routine" murder scenes. Bob isn't like a normal Chief. He'd recently come to Seattle from Boston PD, where he'd spent most his career as a Homicide detective or supervisor. He shot up the ranks late in his career to Superintendent of Investigations, Boston's equivalent of Assistant Chief.

I met Bob a couple years ago. He was a lieutenant with Boston Homicide when I attended a Homicide conference in New York.

I was glad to have him in Seattle.

"How is it I live in the suburbs, twenty-five miles from here, and you live just a few blocks away, but I beat you to the scene?"

"My phone only rang twenty minutes ago!"

I explained the scene to him.

"It looks as though these mopes shot it out in the car," I said. "It's amazing only one of them was killed. Most likely, it's a drug rip. A thinning of the gene pool."

It's what we sometimes referred to as a Misdemeanor Murder.

Later that Saturday morning, my contribution to this case was complete. Because of this case, the next murder would be mine. My partner, Jason Kasner, was out of town on vacation, so I'd be on my own. I went home at eleven AM.

By eight o'clock that night, my ass was dragging. I'm too old for this shit, and my years in Homicide has taught me, always assume you'll get called right back in. Get sleep when you can.

I went to bed.

My instincts were correct.

I woke to my cellphone ringing. I looked at the clock on my nightstand. Three-thirty in the morning again; two nights in a row.

Within a few minutes, I was in my car, red and blue lights flashing, heading up I-5 on my way to another murder. I'm definitely too old for this shit. This case is mine. I'll be at work for fifteen or sixteen hours.

At least it's my day off.

I'd been thinking of retiring. I'd been a cop thirty-six years. That's a long time. Twenty-two in Homicide.

I'd seen a lot during that time that someone not in this business wouldn't believe.

It's been a long road.

My telephone rang just before six in the morning on August 11, 1994. I was already up getting ready for work.

A seven-year-old girl was dead, reportedly shot while she slept at an address on South Chicago Street in Rainier Valley.

4

It would be my first case as a primary detective in a homicide. I'd transferred from Sex Crimes a few weeks earlier. I had fifteen years on the Seattle Police Department and had been a detective for four years, working as a precinct detective before my stint investigating rapes and child molestation cases. I'd wanted to be a homicide detective since before I got on the police department.

Walt Maning was my partner on the case. Walt and I had worked patrol together in Rainer Valley. I liked Walt a lot and knew we would work well together.

I met Walt in the Homicide office. The little girl, Angelica Robinson, had been taken to Harborview Medical Center, just a few blocks from Police Headquarters, where she was pronounced dead. Her mother was there with her.

We drove up the hill to the hospital.

We entered the Emergency Room and to a side room there. A patrol officer waited with Angelica's mother, Artina Robinson. Needless to say, she was a complete mess. There's nothing worse that can happen to a person than to lose a child.

Through her sobs, she told us she'd been renting a "room" at the Chicago Street address for a month. She rattled off the names of others staying there, but said that people came and went all the time.

The landlord was John Koby.

She said she'd been drinking with some of the other residents last night. When she went to her room, she saw that one of them, a guy named Garrison, was passed out on her bed. She slept on the floor.

She was awakened in the early morning hours by the sound of several gunshots. She heard Angelica moan. She looked down and saw blood.

She said she ran through the place asking people to call 911. She hadn't seen the shooter.

She denied that she'd been in any kind of an argument with anyone there.

We called Greg Mixsell, a detective at the scene. He said that neighbors reported seeing a gray Honda occupied by three black males flee the scene.

Four people were brought into the office just after ten AM. Garrison Sanders was among them.

He said that he had been drinking and playing cards with people in the building, including Artina, Angelica's mother.

He fell asleep and was awakened by the sound of gunshots. Next he heard Tina screaming that he daughter had been hit and asking people to call 911.

A little after four PM, we went to the scene.

Old sliding-glass doors were fashioned into a structure in the yard of a house, cordoned off into rooms, in which otherwise homeless people payed John Koby to stay in.

He charged each person several hundred dollars a month per "room," pocketing a tremendous amount of money, despite his claim he was only doing something to "house the homeless."

We interviewed a woman whom Greg Mixsell had interviewed earlier in the day. She lived down the street from the scene and had seen the Gray Honda pull up with three black males in it. Two got out and went to the house. She heard several gunshots, and then saw those two run back and get in the car before it drove away.

"How old do you think these guys were," I asked.

"They were between eighteen and twenty-five," she said.

She described the car as newer and clean.

We spent the next day running down leads that seemed promising at first, but all of them petered out.

The day after the murder, I was finally able to sneak away to meet my family for dinner. It was about eight-thirty PM when my pager went off. I recognized Maning's number. I called him.

"East Precinct officers stopped a stolen car tonight," he said. It was a gray Honda. They got in a foot chase, but have two in custody. They think it may be related to our murder. They're booking them into the Youth Center." (The Juvenile Detention Facility).

I left the restaurant to head back downtown.

In the Homicide office, Maning called the owners of the car.

Their fourteen-year-old daughter had apparently loaned the family car, (without authorization) to a group of young men who'd been to her house while the parents were in Las Vegas. They put their daughter on the phone.

"One of the boys is Tony Combs," she said. "There were two other guys. One goes by 'Stinky' or 'Stanky'. I don't know the third guy.

"On Thursday," (the morning of the shooting), "TC wanted to use the car again. I tried to hide the keys, but he found them. They left at about five in the morning. They came back an hour later. TC washed his clothes and they all went to sleep. I got up at eleven, but they slept until about five in the afternoon."

They took the car and left again.

"Do you know what they were wearing?" Maning asked.

"TC was wearing a white tee shirt, brown or corduroy pants and white shoes.

"Stinky or Stanky was wearing a dark hooded sweatshirt, had a nose ring, and brown cords or pants. He has frizzy hair.

"The third guy was wearing black jeans, and a black and red striped hooded jacket."

Maning called the officers who were in the process of booking the two suspects from the stolen car.

"Change of plans," he said. "Fingerprint and photograph them, but then bring them to the Homicide office."

It was just after two in the morning, when the officers arrived with Tyra Thompson and Royce Hendrix. We placed them in holding cells.

We took Tyra to an interview room.

"We're investigating a murder," we told her. Up to that point, she thought this was about a stolen car.

She was cooperative.

"Tony Combs used to be my boyfriend," she said. "On Friday, he showed up at my house driving a Honda.

"He's only fifteen years old," I said. "Did you ask who's car it was?"

"He said he bought it. He's a drug dealer, so I believed him."

"Scrappy had a gun," she said, identifying Scrappy as Royce Hendrix, the person she was arrested with, also fifteen-years-old.

"He fired one shot in the air," she said.

"I didn't know anything about a murder," she continued, "but we were in a park, and someone mentioned a little girl getting killed. They all laughed. I didn't know what was so funny."

We asked the officers who'd brought these two in to go to Combs' residence and arrest him, and then bring him to the Homicide office.

They arrived with him a little after three in the morning.

We interviewed him.

After advising him of his rights, he agreed to talk.

"Where'd you get the car?" Maning asked.

"I got it from my girl," he said.

"Who was in the car with you?"

8

"Scrappy and Little P," he said. He said that Little P's first name is Lavell.

"Little P told me to drive to a house in the Valley on Chicago Street," he said. "I was there a couple weeks ago. A white dude lives there who drives a black car. He ripped us for some cocaine.

"They got out and I was going to go with them, but they told me to wait in the car. They put they hoodies on and went in.

"I hears some shots, and they came walking out and get in the car. I didn't know anybody was hit until the next day."

Next, it was Royce Hendrix' turn.

"Why do you think you're here?" I asked after advising him of his rights.

"Because I was in a stolen car," he said.

"No," I said. "This is about a shooting. We've already talked to a lot of other people, and we know what happened. We know you were one of the shooters. We think this was just an accident, but it's really important you tell us the whole truth."

He told us he would. (I'm sure.)

"I was pretty drunk," he said. "I drank two forties," (40 oz bottles of malt liquor).

"Little P asked if I remembered the white dude that ripped us the other day. That dude told us we could stay there for a few weeks if we gave him some rock." (Crack cocaine).

"The dude took the rock, then went out the back. We got kicked out of the place.

"Little P", (whose first name, he said, was Lavell) "said we need to go back there and shoot up the place.

"I got my .38, and Little P got a .38 from the girl we got the car from.

"We gets there. Little P and me go in, while Tony stays in the car."

"What were you wearing?" I asked.

"I had on these same pants I'm wearing now, and a ballcap and a hoodie. I pulled the hoodie up over my ball cap.

"When we went in, I started shooting. We each fired four to five shots. We went back out and got in the car. We told Tony what happened and went back to the girl's house and crashed there."

By the time we got them booked, it was after seven in the morning.

Norm Stamper was the Chief of Police. He'd come to Seattle from the San Diego Police Department. He was a touchy-feely kind of guy, unabashedly Politically Correct. Though I liked him personally, I didn't think he was much of a leader.

He thought everyone involved in a child murder investigation needed to seek counselling. A group meeting was set up for that morning. Maning and I were ordered to attend.

I was annoyed.

We'd worked on the case all night long. I was tired and just wanted to go home. Instead, we had to go to this bullshit meeting.

I walked in; people sat in a circle. A bearded guy ran the meeting. I plopped my butt in a chair.

"How do you feel about being involved in this case?" bearded guy asked.

"I feel like if I have to talk to someone like you every time something like this happens, I'm in the wrong fucking line of work and need to think about a career change."

I got up and walked out.

We were back to work at noon. Lavell Cotten, (Little P) was in custody at the Youth Services Center. Cotten was fourteen-years-old.

We brought him into a room and advised him of his rights.

"We're investigating a murder," I told him. "We have reason to believe you're involved.

He was upset.

"I ain't talking to you!" he said. "I want a lawyer.

We stood up to leave.

"Fine," I said. "We gave you a chance to tell your side, but if that's what you want, we're out of here."

"Fine," he said. "I'll talk to you."

We showed him photos of Hendrix and Combs. He pointed to Hendrix and referred to him by a different name. He denied knowing who Combs was.

"I was at the Spruce Motel with my girlfriend," he said. in room 106. You can ask her."

We hadn't mentioned when the murder we were talking about had occurred.

We went to the house of the people whose car had been taken. They handed over a .38 pistol. We also had the pistol Hendrix had used.

We sent them both to the crime lab, who matched them ballistically to the fired bullets recovered at the scene.

All three were charged as adults for Murder in the First Degree.

The murders came fast and furious in my first months in Homicide. Most were drug and/or gang related.

One weekday morning we were called to a Rainier Valley address. A woman was leaving for work. When she exited her house, she found a dead body in her front yard.

Such a discovery can sometimes alarm the unrefined.

As we worked the case that day, we developed two suspects.

When you identify suspects in a murder case, it's imperative you find the weak link and go after that person. You then work your way up the food chain to the main guy.

We identified our weak link and brought him to the office for an interrogation. Our supposition proved correct; this guy wasn't a tough nut to crack.

"I was there, but I didn't do it!" he said. "He's crazy. He shot that guy for no reason!" He gave us the name of the shooter.

We picked up the guy he named; he was eighteen-years-old and a real punk. He thought he was a real tough guy.

During the interrogation, I played the understanding fatherly type. I put my hand on his shoulder.

"Look," I said. "I know this was all a big mistake. You didn't mean to kill the guy. It just got out of hand."

"Take your hand off my shoulder," he said.

By that time, I'd pretty much had it with this punk.

I whispered into his ear.

"I'll tell you what, tough guy. Why don't you take my hand off your shoulder?"

He stared at me, making no attempt to move my hand away.

We booked him into jail for Investigation of Murder.

An Investigation charge is used to hold a suspect for up to three business days. At the end of that time, the prosecutor needs to either file formal charges against the suspect, or he has to be released.

The only evidence we had linking him to the crime was his friend's statement. The prosecutor wouldn't charge based solely on that statement, so after three days, he was released.

A couple weeks later, my phone again rang in the middle of the night. Off to another homicide. (They never seemed to happen during business hours).

The scene was at the Happy Valley restaurant in Rainier Valley. A body laid under a police blanket in the middle of the parking lot.

A patrol officer briefed me.

"The owner of the restaurant was closing for the night. This guy walks in and sticks a gun in his face, trying to rob the place. The owner had a gun of his own. He pulled it and shot the guy. The suspect ran out the door, but dropped dead in the parking lot."

I walked up to the body and lifted the blanket.

There was the punk who'd killed the guy for no reason that I'd had to release earlier. I smiled.

Karma's a bitch

2

I was home watching the news in January of 1995. The lead story reported a large fire in Seattle, not far from the Kingdome at the Mary Pang Chinese Food warehouse. It had been a huge, multi-alarm fire, with hundreds of firefighters attacking the blaze.

There were four firefighters missing.

What do you mean, four firefighters are missing, I thought?

By the next morning the firefighters were presumed dead.

By the time the alarm sounded about the Pang Warehouse fire that Thursday night, the tinder-box of a building, built in 1908, was already an inferno.

Several firefighters entered on the main floor to attack the fire. As they fought the fire from within, the floor collapsed. Lt. Walter Kilgore, Lt. Greg Shoemaker, Firefighters Randy Terlicker and James Brown fell to a lower floor they didn't know existed. Trapped, they broadcast a mayday over the radio. No one knew where they were or how to get to them.

Their bodies were recovered the next morning, huddled in the basement. They weren't burned; they ran out of air and suffocated or died of smoke inhalation. It was the worst disaster in the history of the Seattle Fire Department.

Fire Marshals determined that an accelerant had been used. It was arson. That made it a quadruple murder.

I was one of seven detectives, along with a sergeant, assigned to a task force to investigate the crime.

We set up an office in a conference room at the end of the hall on the 5th floor of police headquarters. We worked eighteen hour days, seven days a week early in this investigation.

We met each morning to discuss what needed to be done to advance the case.

Early on, we focused on Martin Pang, the adopted son of Mary Pang, who owned the business. He'd told employees in the days before the fire that they needed to get their personal belongings out of the warehouse.

Mary Pang was a member of a very prominent local family. Her sister, Ruby Chow, sat on the King County Council. Ruby's son was a District Court judge, and her daughter was on the Seattle City Council. Confidentiality in this case was paramount.

Hundreds of tips came pouring in to our office about the case.

The problem is, those tips have to be sorted as to their usefulness, and the likelihood that they'll advance the case.

Every day those tips came in. They were sorted by administrative staff, and reviewed. The ones that seemed like they may be useful where assigned to detectives for follow-up.

I was assigned an intriguing tip that came to us by way of the Fire Marshal's office. The person calling the tip in claimed to have important information about the case. It instructed that we take a personal ad in the Seattle Times with the words "ET phone home", and a phone number. The tipster would call.

I grabbed a copy of the Times to check the personal ad section. There was already an ad there. It said, "ET phone home." with a phone number on the ad.

I called the number. I got the voicemail of a reporter for the Times. I was pissed. Someone was leaking tips before we even got them.

I went to Al Gerdes, the Homicide lieutenant, and told him what I'd found. The usually quiet and soft-spoken Gerdes erupted.

We'd only received the tip that morning from the Fire Marshal's office, so the leak had to be there.

We tracked the leak to an investigator in the Fire Marshal's office, who'd given it to a reporter.

The tip ended up being nothing, but it highlights the problem with high-profile cases when shit like that happens.

We continued our focus on Martin Pang; he was one weird dude.

We interviewed several of his ex-wives. We learned that he had a quick temper and had been abusive. He saw himself as a playboy. He had what seemed to be a narcissistic personality.

One of his ex-wives recounted their honeymoon. He took her to the concentration camp at Krakow, Poland.

Even family members described him as dangerous.

I went to interview a close friend of Pang who worked at a scuba shop in Lynnwood in Snohomish County, fifteen miles north of Seattle.

I walked into the shop on a Friday night at about seven PM. The guy I needed to speak to was with a customer. I watched for a few minutes. He was effeminate, with long blonde hair. When he was finished with the customer, I approached.

"I'm Detective Steiger with the Seattle Police Department," I said, holding up my badge. "I need to speak with you about Martin Pang."

He became defensive.

"I'll need to speak to a lawyer before I talk to you."

I'd been working long hours several days in a row. I was in no mood for this bullshit.

I leaned in close.

"Listen closely: Fuck your lawyer."

He was wide-eyed.

"You're a witness," I told him. "You have no right to a lawyer."

I thought he was going to cry.

"Here's the deal," I said. "You're either going to sit down and answer the questions I have for you, or I will drag your ass downtown, where you'll sit for several hours before it's convenient for me to speak with you."

He answered my questions. Smart choice.

We worked closely with prosecutors on the case. We decided it would be best to conduct and Inquiry Judge Proceeding for the case.

An Inquiry Judge is the closest thing to a grand jury in the State of Washington. It's a secret, closed-door proceeding before a judge where the witnesses are compelled to testify. We prepared subpoenas to serve on the witnesses we would call before the Inquiry Judge.

Another detective served one on my dive shop friend

"He doesn't like you", he told me when he got back.

I smiled.

"Good."

Greg Mixsell and I went to Mercer Island to serve Mary Pang with a subpoena. It was a Saturday morning when we got to her house.

We knocked on the door, but got no answer. There was a window in their garage. Their car was parked inside. We left to grab breakfast.

When we were finished, we went back to the Pang's house. There was still no answer. I knew they were inside.

I had a police flashlight. I tapped on the door. Continuously.

After about ten minutes, the door flew open. Mary Pang stood there, and exasperated look on her face.

17

"What?!" she yelled.

"Good morning Mary," I said. "I have something for you." I handed her the subpoena.

I heard later that she didn't like me either.

Martin Pang was charged with four counts of Felony First Degree Murder. (He committed a felony, in this case, Arson in the First Degree, and people died because of it. It's the same as if he'd intentionally killed the four firefighters.)

Shortly afterward, he disappeared. We had information he'd fled to Los Angeles. Greg Mixsell and Dale Tallman went there looking for him, but couldn't find him.

We found out he'd used his passport to flee to Rio De Janeiro, Brazil. That caused a problem; The United States didn't have an extradition treaty with Brazil.

We asked the FBI to issue an Unlawful Flight to Avoid Prosecution, (UFAP) warrant. That afforded us federal resources to hunt for Pang.

I attended meetings at the FBI office where we discussed ways to get him back to the US. We even talked about just kidnapping him off the street and taking him to Uruguay, with whom the US did have an extradition treaty. There had been a recent US Supreme Court case where something similar had happened. The court ruled that a person is not protected by the constitution when they're not on US soil.

The FBI director at the time, Louis Freeh, offered the use of his jet to fly Pang back to the US.

There were representatives of the State Department at the meeting. They were fearful of offending Brazil. Me, I could give a shit. Pang wasn't a Brazilian national, he was a US citizen. It was none of Brazil's business.

We needed to send someone to Rio. It would be an open-ended trip. Most of us didn't want to be away from our families for an extended period.

Steve O'Leary was single. He would go. The only problem, was O'Leary was deathly afraid of flying. He agreed to go, along with two FBI agents.

I had no doubt in Steve's ability to self-medicate on the flight down there.

Pang was arrested in Brazil by local authorities and held in a Brazilian jail. I'm certain the conditions there were much worse than the jail here.

When they got to Brazil, O'Leary and the FBI agents had to wait for a diplomatic solution to the Pang problem. Steve sent photos of the three of them poolside, a foo-foo drink in hand. They spent a month there, after which a diplomatic solution was reached.

Brazil had no felony murder rule. They would extradite as long as Pang was charged with Manslaughter, the equivalent crime in Brazil.

Again, Pang was a US citizen, and not Brazilian. It was none of their business which crime he was charged with here.

The federal government agreed to that condition. I thought they should have agreed, and then once Pang was in the US, give Brazil the proverbial finger and keep the murder charge; four firefighters died while doing their jobs because of his greed.

I guess that's why I'm not a diplomat.

O'Leary and the FBI agents, Pang in tow, flew back to the US.

Ultimately, Pang pled guilty to the four manslaughter charges with an agreed sentence of thirty years. I wasn't thrilled, but it was more than the standard sentence for the manslaughters.

Pang was an ultimate manipulator, doing whatever gave him gratification, either financial or emotional. He succeeded in manipulating the rule of law through the government of Brazil. Four brave firefighters lost their lives fighting a fire he started for reasons of greed. He should have been convicted on four counts of First Degree Murder, and should have spent the rest of his life in prison. Instead, he'll soon be released.

3

In April of that year I was working late on a Thursday afternoon. I was about to go home when a call came in to the office. A woman was found murdered in her condo near 135th and Lynden Avenue North in North Seattle. I was next-up for a murder, so I headed to the scene.

I arrived at the relatively new condo building. A patrol officer briefed me.

"Constance Murray lives alone in the unit," he said. "Her friends hadn't seen her for a few days. The newspapers were piling up on the porch. A neighbor got a key from another neighbor, and went in. He smelled her right away. She's in the bedroom on the bed. It looks like she's been stabbed.

"The Fire Department responded and checked on her, but she was obviously dead.

"She has a car that's missing from the parking lot. It's a 1987 Chevy Cavalier. It hasn't been seen since Saturday."

I walked inside and was met with the same unmistakable odor I had experienced many times before, and would for the rest of my career: The sickly-sweet scent of death.

The light was on in the bedroom, but all the other lights in the unit were off.

I stood at the foot of her bed and took in the scene.

She wore a nightgown and laid on her back. There were stab wounds on her chest, and one stab wound through her upper lip and palate. There was a book on the bed, *The Magic Bullet;* it had a notch in the top of its spine. From that, and the wound to her upper lip, I surmised she'd been lying in bed reading the book, when the killer attacked her, the knife nicking the top of the book before plunging into her upper lip and palate.

She had deep stab wounds to her hands and arms, likely defensive wounds as she tried in vain to ward off her attacker.

She wore only a blood-stained tee-shirt.

Two pillows covered her head, obviously placed there after she'd been killed. This could be a psychological act by the killer, trying to "undo" the crime, and not wanting to see her dead face.

Her bed had no headboard, and the wall at the head of the bed was covered with medium-velocity blood spatter. The spatter indicated a direction of the attack from right to left, with some vertical spatter. The killer was probably right handed.

This had been a violent attack.

There was a folding-blade Buck knife on the bed next to her body covered in blood; a perfect bloody fingerprint on the handle.

This was going to be easy.

A woman's purse sat on a makeup table near the bed; a blood stain was on upper left corner of that purse. It was empty. The table top was covered with items that had probably been in the purse, but had been dumped out.

A bathroom was just off the bedroom where the victim laid. The sink had watery blood in and around it. There was a Power Rangers watch lying on the sink; the type that would normally be worn by a thirteen-year-old boy.

On the floor below the sink was a pair of men's size 33 blue jeans stained with blood spatter. A pair of white athletic socks, also spattered with blood, lay nearby.

I looked closely at the socks. There were brown dirt spots on the toes of both. The killer had holes in the toes of his shoes.

After the clothing was photographed, I picked up the jeans. The pockets were empty, except the right front. Inside that pocket was copper mesh. The type crack addicts used to smoke crack in glass pipes.

Her killer is a crack head.

I went in to the living room. There was laundry with clean, folded men's clothing.

She was supposed to live here alone.

There were several pairs of rolled white athletic socks in the basket. I picked up a pair and unrolled them. There it was: A faint stain where there'd been dirt spots before they'd been laundered.

She was doing the laundry of the person who killed her.

There was a VHS tape atop the VCR near the television. It was the movie *Reservoir Dogs*.

I put the cassette in the VCR. It was at the closing credits.

I spoke to the neighbor who'd discovered her.

"What do you know about men in her life?"

"She has a boyfriend," he said, piquing my interest, "and two sons."

"Tell me about the boyfriend," I said.

"He's older, seems like a nice guy. He's around here from time to time, but I haven't seen him lately."

"What about the sons?"

"One manages a supermarket somewhere. The other, I don't know much about."

In these cases, it's almost always someone close to the victim who does this. It's Occam's razor: The simplest answer is usually the correct one.

I asked a patrol officer at the scene to do an Auto Theft report for her missing car. That way we could get it in the computer systems as being related to this murder. We asked the Communications Section to send notifications to the King County Sheriff, Stata Patrol and Snohomish County agencies, (since the scene was only a few miles from the Snohomish County line) to look for the missing car.

We found the boyfriend. He was devastated; I quickly erased him from my suspect list.

"Her son has a drug problem." He told us. "He's been staying with her for the last couple weeks. She's been trying to get him back on his feet."

No more calls, we have a winner! That son was likely the killer.

While we were at the scene, the phone rang. Gene Ramirez answered.

The caller identified herself as the victim's daughter-in-law. Ramirez got her Green Lake area address, and told her we'd stop by.

The Medical Examiner arrived. It was Dr. Don Reay, the Chief Medical Examiner of King County at that time, along with his investigator Bill McClure.

Reay did his initial examination of the victim.

When he removed the pillows from her head, he found a pair of eyeglasses.

The ambient temperature in the room was 62 degrees. He took a body core temperature by inserting a probe into her liver. It was also 62 degrees.

She'd been here awhile after death.

After the ME removed the body, Gene Ramirez and I went to her son and daughter-in-law's house. and knocked on the door. A young man answered, his very pregnant wife stood behind him. We identified ourselves, and he invited us in.

"I'm afraid I have some very bad news," I said. "Your mother's been murdered."

"My brother killed her," he said.

I stared at him a moment.

"Why do you think that?" I asked.

"I just know. My brother has a serious drug problem. He showed up at her house and wanted to stay there. I told her not to, but she let him."

His brother was Daniel Murray.

"Do you know where Daniel is?"

"I don't know," he said. "If he contacts me, I'll call you."

We gathered what information we could find about Daniel. We'd already put out the bulletin for the car. We added his photo, and again, distributed it within the region..

Karen Tando was a Latent Print Examiner at SPD. She examined the buck knife with the bloody fingerprint on it. She came to the Homicide office at about ten-thirty that night.

"I've made a tentative ID of the print. It matches Daniel Murray."

A couple hours later, we got a call from the Edmonds Police Department. Edmonds is a suburban city north of Seattle in Snohomish County.

The victim's car was parked in a motel parking lot in their city.

We raced up Interstate 5 to Edmonds.

The Edmonds officers were watching the car when we arrived.

A Korean couple owned the motel. I went to speak with them. I asked which room the car was associated with. The man told me.

"We're going to need a key to the room," I said.

The man balked.

"You can't have a key."

"Fine," I said, turning to walk away. "We'll just break the fucking door down."

The woman spoke to him in Korean, her voice loud and animated.

He gave us the key.

We approached the room, our guns drawn. I stood to the side of the door and pounded. "Seattle Police," I yelled. "Open the door!"

The door opened. Daniel appeared in his stocking feet. Six feet tall, with graying brown hair, with blue eyes, unshaven and somewhat disheveled.

I could see dirt stains on the toes.

"You have dirt spots on your socks," I said.

"Yeah, my shoes have holes in them."

"We just came from your mom's house."

"Oh," he said, staring at the floor.

We put handcuffs on him, and took him down to the Chevy Astro van that we'd driven up there. I put him in the back seat.

We sped back down Interstate 5 toward downtown. Just as we entered the north city limits, smoke poured out of the back of the van. I pulled to the shoulder.

"I'm a mechanic," Murray said. "I can look at it for you."

I smiled.

"No, we'll call a tow truck."

Another detective car stopped and picked us up. We left the van on the freeway and went back to headquarters.

We put him in an interview room.

"I was in the living room watching Reservoir Dogs on TV." Murray said. "I thought, 'I should kill my mother'.

"I went into the bedroom. She was lying in bed reading. I started stabbing her. She said, 'Why are you doing this? I love you!' I didn't want to hear that shit. I just kept stabbing the fuck out of her."

The next day, I went back to the condo. I recovered the *Reservoir Dogs* video from atop the television and put it in evidence.

Daniel Murray was charged with Aggravated Murder for the death of his mother.

He ultimately pled guilty.

4

I was called to a murder later that month at two o'clock in the morning. The scene was in South Park, a neighborhood in Seattle southwest of downtown.

South Park is a mix of residential and industrial, and the closest thing to a barrio that exists in Seattle.

I pulled my car up behind marked patrol cars at the house in question. An old faded yellow Victorian house sat atop a knoll looming in the darkness, its macabre façade reminded me of the Munster's house.

A makeshift boardwalk led up to the cinder block walkway.

Paul Kloss was the patrol sergeant in charge of the scene. Paul and I were good friends, having worked together in patrol early in our careers, and we were on SWAT together. We hung out off duty, and our families often vacationed together.

"A group of guys share the house," he told me. "Brian Rowe lives here. He got home at about one o'clock in the morning. He found the front door to the house standing open. He went in and saw that his roommate Paul's bedroom light was on. The drawers were open in his dresser, and it looked like they'd been gone through. His room was fine, so he went downstairs to get a beer. He passed James Overlord's room, and saws him in bed. He assumed he'd been sleeping.

"Paul works at the Ernst Hardware store in Ballard at night. So does James. Paul called and asked Brian if he knew why James hadn't come to work. Brian went in James' room to wake him. He touched James' hand and it was cold. He lifted the blanket and saw some blood. He immediately called 911. The call came in at 1:51 AM."

Kloss led me up to the bedroom. The body of a white male in his twenties laid on a bed nude, flat on his back, a blanket pulled to his waist. His right arm was outstretched. There was a gaping wound in his left breast area, but with no corresponding blood that would have been present if he'd suffered the wound while alive. A brass marijuana pipe was pushed into the wound. Just below the wound was a "pound sign" in blood. It looked like it was intentionally drawn on the body.

The wound was obviously post-mortem.

In an adjacent room, on the floor was a Smith & Wesson Model 19 .357 revolver. The cylinder was partially opened. The gun was unloaded.

A pager on a nightstand went off three times while we were there, each of the phone numbers displayed were long distance numbers.

There were six empty 40 ounce malt liquor cans next to the bed.

Other detectives, prosecutors and eventually the Medical Examiner arrived at the eerie scene.

Dr. Terri Haddix a forensic pathologist from the Medical Examiner's office examined the body. She agreed: The gaping wound occurred after death.

We rolled the body over; there was a small lump just under the skin.

"I think that's a bullet," she said.

The temperature in the room was 68° Fahrenheit. Haddix took a body core temperature liver at 6:12 AM. The core temperature was 92°. In a controlled environment like the interior of a house and the victim covered by a blanket in bed, it was consistent with the death occurring at around midnight, give or take.

She and her investigator removed the body and the scene was processed.

I left the scene at about 7:30 in the morning, and went to the Homicide office to complete paperwork.

This wasn't my case. Gene Ramirez and John Nordlund were the primary detectives, so once I was finished with that, I was done with the case.

Not so much.

A few days later, I was in the office, working night shift, writing a report at eleven-forty-five.

Just before midnight I was gathering my things to leave, when the main phone line into the Homicide office rang.

"Homicide," I said into the phone.

It was Jim Rice. Rice was a Reserve Officer on SPD, and I knew him well.

"Is Ramirez around?" he asked.

"Gene's out of town," I told him. "Can I help you?"

"Paul Paulinkonis is a friend of mine," he said., "He's at my house now, and just confessed to killing James Overvold."

Rice gave me his address in Ballard, a neighborhood in northwest Seattle. I called Communications and had them dispatch a car to his house.

Once the patrol officers arrived at Rice's house and had Paulinkonis in custody, I asked them to bring him downtown to headquarters and the Homicide office.

The officers arrived with Paulinkonis and Rice at 12:35 AM. I put Paulinkonis in an interview room.

Paulinkonis had written his statement to Rice on a yellow legal pad.

"I told him to tell the truth about what happened," Rice said to me.

I read the statement Paulinkonis had written.

30

In it, he said that Overvold was involved in a stolen credit card scam. He wanted Paulinkonis to get in on it with him, and to allow products to be shipped to the house. Paulinkonis claimed in his statement not to want anything to do with it.

Paulinkonis said that he went on vacation, and returned the day of the murder. Overvold asked if he'd allow packages to be shipped to the house. Paulinkonis alleged that he said no, and Overvold became angry.

Paulinkonis said he went to his room and retrieved the gun. He was fearful that Overvold was going to kill him, so he went near Overvold's room and fired a shot, fleeing the house. He said he returned later to find Overvold dead.

He tried to make it look like a drug-related murder by cutting into the wound and inserting the pipe. He then left and went to work.

Paulinkonis signed each page of the statement.

Tom Pike and I entered the interview room. Paulinkonis appeared calm and collect, smoking a cigarette and drinking a can of Coke.

I had him go through the story, and he recounted what he'd written in his statement.

"I went to my room," he said. "I got the gun. I was sure he was going to kick down the door."

"Did he?" I asked.

"No," he said.

"Did he even try to turn the knob?" I asked.

"No," he said.

"I heard him down the hall, go into his room and close the door," he said. "I wanted to get away.

"When I opened my door, I saw his bedroom door was open. I went to his door, and I saw his silhouette on the bed. I fired a shot and ran out of the house."

When he talked about the shooting, he shook and looked like he was about to cry.

"I came back to the house later, and found him dead," he said. "I took a knife and cut into the bullet wound. I shoved the pipe in there and went through drawers and messed the place up. I wanted it to look like drug dealers or someone had come in the house."

I drew a diagram of the floor of the house the bedrooms were on.

"James was in bed," I said, "dressed only in his underwear. If you were afraid of him, why would you go into his room? You walked right past the front door of the house to get to there. You could have just left and called the police. Instead you went to his room, where he was obviously sleeping and shot him in the chest. He wasn't armed and was no threat to you."

I arrested him for murder and booked him into jail.

Months later, the case went to trial. The prosecutors assigned to the case were Jeff Baird and Lisa Marchese.

We discussed the case before my testimony. They were concerned about an old gun found under Overvold's bed.

"It's inoperable," I told Baird.

"How do you know it's inoperable?"

"Give me a pencil," I said.

I inserted the pencil down the barrel of the gun, eraser first. I cocked the gun and pulled the trigger.

Nothing happened.

Next, I took my own pistol, carefully unloading it, and put the pencil in the barrel, eraser-side down. I pulled the trigger. The pencil shot up to the ceiling.

They gasped.

A firearm uses a firing pin to work. For center-fire cartridges, there's a small round cap with a small amount of gun powder in it. That's called a primer. When the pistol is pulled on a cocked or double action weapon, the firing pin strikes this primer. The collision between the primer and the firing pin causes a small spark inside the cartridge. This spark ignites the much larger cache of gun powder in the casing, which explodes. The explosion sends the bullet down the barrel.

If there is no firing pin, or if it doesn't work for some reason, there is no impact between the pin and the primer, so nothing happens.

The pencil eraser was a surrogate for the primer. There was no impact on it from the weapon in question. In my own weapon, it struck with such force as to shoot the pencil out of the barrel.

"I'm going to have you do that on the stand!" Baird said.

Just as in my demonstration to the prosecutors, the pencil didn't move in the gun found under the bed when I repeated the demonstration on the stand, but shot to the ceiling from my gun

Paulinkonis was convicted.

His mother and sister were already in prison for killing his father.

Maybe they could be cellmates.

Irvin Charat was a retired dentist. His daughter, Barbara, lived at Roxbury House, a Housing Authority tower in West Seattle. Barbara had manic depressive issues. She'd told her father that she wanted to move out of the building. Her boyfriend, who also lived in the building, had been abusive.

Charat arrived to take her to a dental appointment. When she didn't meet him in the lobby, which was her normal practice, he went upstairs to her apartment. He found her lying on her bed. She was dead; her throat had been cut.

Patrol officers were called to the scene. They confirmed Dr. Charat's worst nightmare; his daughter had been murdered. They called for Homicide.

We arrived to a scene teeming with patrol officers. Yellow tape enclosed the hallway leading to her apartment.

We examined her body; she was dressed in only panties and a blood-soaked tee shirt. She'd been stabbed multiple times, and her throat was cut, and laid open in a gaping wound. She had defensive wounds to her arms. There were petechial hemorrhages in her eyes. That is a sign of strangulation.

The veins carrying blood from the brain back to the heart are shallower in the neck than the arteries that take freshly oxygenated blood from the heart to the brain. Pressure on the outside of the neck, either with hands or ligature often obstructs the blood returning to the heart, but not the blood going to the brain. There is a back-up of blood in the head, and with nowhere to go, blood pressure increases, causing the small vessels, the petechiae, in the eyes, face, and inside the lips to burst. That's petechial hemorrhage.

There were several knives in and around the apartment, but we were drawn to one in a box that had been packed with various items. There was a blood stain on one of the box flaps and a kitchen knife with about a four inch blade was inside. The knife had red staining that appeared to be blood on the blade. This was very likely the murder weapon.

The Medical Examiner arrived. The ME investigators were Bruce Lyle and Don Marvin. Two pathologists responded, Dr. Raquel Fortin, along with Dr. Nick Hartshorn. Dr. Hartshorn was British, and had been the attending pathologist who, several months earlier, had performed the autopsy on Kurt Cobain after he committed suicide. (Yes, it was a suicide).

Dr. Hartshorn found at least three incised wounds to the neck during his scene examination, running from right to left.

The ambient temperature was eighty-two degrees. The core temperature of the victim is taken by inserting a temperature probe into her liver, and it read ninety-five degrees.

The Medical Examiners removed the victim's body from the scene.

Dr. Charat told us that he knew his daughter was seeing another resident of the building named Alvin, though Dr. Charat said he's never met Alvin.

There was a note in the living room. It read, "WE ARE DEAD. 401+ 403."

We were in apartment 401. Detectives checked apartment 403 and found the woman resident there fine.

Her boyfriend, Alvin Phillips, lived in apartment 303. We went there with the manager.

We knocked on the door.

"Alvin, Seattle Police! Open the door!"

There was no answer. I looked at the manager.

"Open the door."

He used a pass key. Alvin was lying, unconscious on a bed there. He had blood on his hands and feet.

He was breathing, but barely. He'd tried to kill himself. We had our suspect.

Medics took him to Harborview Hospital.

The next day, Tom Pike and I went to Harborview Medical Center. Phillips was still unconscious and unresponsive.

I went to the Medical Examiner's office on the south side of Harborview. I attended the autopsy of the victim, along with King County Prosecutors Patty Eakes and Roger Davidheisier.

A day later, I returned to Harborview. Phillips had regained consciousness. Two police officers guarded his room. They confirmed to me that he'd been conscious and had been communicating all day.

He was hooked to telemetry, so the nurses could monitor his vital signs from the nurse's station electronically.

I spoke with Phillips for a few minutes, making sure he was completely lucid before I got into the meat of the matter.

I advised him of his rights and he said he understood.

I asked him to tell me his side of the story.

He said that he and Barbara hadn't been getting along, and she was moving out. He was helping her pack. They got into an argument after he accused her of sleeping with another resident of the building.

He was on the verge of confessing to murdering Barbara, when the door to his room burst open. A nurse stood in the door.

"What the hell is going on?" she demanded.

I looked at the officer.

"Get her the hell out of here!" I said.

"No one comes in; not even staff!"

He pushed her out the door and posted outside.

Luckily, Phillips was unaffected by the interruption and continued where he left off. He said Barbara had punched him in the shoulder. They got into a shoving match for a few minutes. He claimed she grabbed a knife she'd been using to pack and came at him. He was able to get the knife away, and told her, "I'll stab you if you don't get back!"

He said he tried to hit her, but stabbed her in the neck. He tried to hit her again, and stabbed her in the side.

After that, he went downstairs to his room to take an overdose.

When I left the room, the nurse stood there, along with her supervisor.

They weren't happy.

"His heart rate was way over the top." She said. "What makes you think you can keep us out of our room?"

I had a photo of Barbara's murdered body with me. I held it up to them.

"This is the only person whose welfare I give a fuck about," I said, and walked away.

Several months later, Alvin Phillips pled guilty to the murder of Barbara Charat.

5

84-year-old Bodegard Mitchell led a miser's life in an apartment in Seattle's Central Area. Battling dementia, he kept to his apartment. In September of 1996, Timothy Coghlin a, a 40-year-old maintenance man who worked for the apartment complex came by to repair a fan and a vent in Mitchell's apartment.

Mitchell apparently thought the maintenance guy was there to evict him. He pulled out a pistol and fired, grazing Coghlin's forehead. Coghlin fled the apartment and called 911.

The patrol officers who responded contained Mitchell's apartment. They tried to coax Bodegard out, but he was having none of it.

They called the SWAT team.

After a five-and-a-half-hour stand-off with no progress, SWAT team members decided to make a slow and deliberate approach to the apartment using a ballistic shield.

They were a few feet from the door, when it opened. Mitchell appeared, still armed with the pistol. He fired at the SWAT officers, striking sergeant Brian Kraus in the arm with what ended up being a shot round, sometimes referred to as a varmint round. Kraus and Officer Pete Sicilia fired back. Mitchell was hit. Medics took him to the hospital, but he died.

I was in the Homicide office with my partner, Sonny Davis when the phone rang, summoning us to the scene.

Davis had been in Homicide several years when I started working with him. He was a good detective when he wanted to be, which wasn't often, particularly if the case was a "routine" homicide like a gang-bang or doper murder.

He'd been a Captain in the Army in Vietnam. He had a serious alcohol problem. In retrospect, I'm pretty sure he suffered from Post-Traumatic Stress Disorder.

I liked Sonny a lot. When we had a "good" murder, one that is unusual or interesting, as opposed to the majority of the murders we investigate, which are "routine" from a detective's perspective, he was great to work with. The other times, I was pretty much on my own.

We arrived at the shooting scene. It was late afternoon on a weekday, so there were news crews everywhere, setting up for their "Live at Five" shots.

Back in those days, we didn't have CSI, or anyone else to process our crime scenes; we did them ourselves.

I was photographing the inside of Mitchell's apartment, while Davis was looking through things, trying to identify what may be evidence. He picked up Mitchell's wallet.

"Ooh!" he said. I looked over and saw him take a wad of cash and stuff it in his pocket. I thought he was joking, and chuckled. He looked up at me, and I could see on his face, this was no joke.

You've got to be fucking kidding me.

"Don will be watching you," he said to me, "to see how you handle this. It's a squad thing."

The Don he was referring to was Don Cameron, our sergeant. "Mr. Homicide," as he was known around the police department, mostly since he'd been in Homicide since dirt was new.

My head was spinning. What the fuck am I supposed to do now? I didn't know how much money Davis had taken, but it didn't matter. No amount of money was worth my career.

Then I got pissed.

I walked out of the apartment without saying anything. I got in our car and drove back to the office.

I sat at my desk and seethed.

A couple hours later, Cameron and Davis came back

"I need to talk to you," Cameron said.

He went to an interview room. I followed him in.

He closed the door and sat in a chair.

"This hasn't come up in quite a while," he said. "I need to know how you want to handle this."

I couldn't believe my ears. This guy, purportedly the guru of Homicide, someone I'd looked up to since before I worked here was asking me if I was good to go with this.

"I don't know what you're talking about," I said.

"You know what I'm talking about," he said.

Now I was really pissed. I got up from my chair. I walked right up to him, and leaned in. My face was inches from his face. I poked his chest with my finger.

"You're not listening to me, sergeant. I don't know what the fuck you're talking about!"

Big, tough, Mr. Homicide's face turned red. His eyes were saucers. I turned and stormed out of the room.

I went home.

That night, I was obviously upset. Doreen knew something was wrong, but at first I didn't tell her.

What am I going to tell my sons, I thought, when I get fired, or answer them when they ask why their dad wasn't a policeman anymore.

No matter how much money it was, it was nothing compared to how much money I would make in the rest of my career, not even counting the reputation I'd tried to build as a good cop.

I was livid that they'd not only jeopardized my well-being, but that of my family.

Doreen kept asking me what was wrong. Finally, I told her.

She was shocked.

"You have to confront them," she said.

I knew she was right, but it was the last thing I wanted to do.

The next morning when I got in, I went to coffee with other guys in Homicide. I told them what happened. They were shocked. Whatever I decided to do, they said they were behind me.

I went back to the office. Cameron and Davis had gone to coffee somewhere else. I looked out the window and saw them walking to the front of the building.

When Cameron came in the office, I walked up to him.

"In the interview room. Now."

We entered the room. I closed the door.

He had a reputation as a tough-as-nails, old-school cop. I found the truth that day: He was a paper tiger.

"I'm not putting up with this bullshit, Don!" I said. "You're not only threatening my future, you're threatening my family's future. I can't believe you'd risk your own reputation for something like this!"

"Calm down, Cloyd," he said, knowing that my booming voice could be heard through the walls of the interview room. "I'll take care of it. Actually, I feel better handling it this way."

I walked out and went up to Davis,

"Your turn." I walked back to the room.

Davis walked in, a sheepish look on his face.

"How dare you?" I said. "You can mess with me all you want, but you don't fuck with my family. You said Don wanted to see how I'd handle this. Well guess what? Now he knows."

"Calm down," he said. "I didn't mean to put your family at risk."

I realized he didn't get it. He didn't have a family. He'd been married and divorced several times, and had a son he was estranged from. It sound's funny, but I actually felt bad for him.

"I'll take care of it," he said.

John Boatman and Gene Ramirez were another team of detectives in my squad. I told them what happened. When I mentioned the remark about the "squad thing," they were outraged.

"What squad thing?" Boatman said. "I've never seen anything like this." He'd been in Homicide a long time too. "If this is a squad thing, someone owes me a hell of a lot of money."

I smiled.

I left the office, going out on the street. I didn't want to be around Davis or Cameron.

Later that afternoon, I came back. There was an evidence sheet and a page of a follow-up report on my desk.

The report said that Cameron and Davis had returned to Mitchell's apartment. They'd made up some excuse to get back in there. While they were there, according to the report, they came across cash.

Ten thousand dollars.

I was shocked. I thought we were talking about a couple hundred dollars. Not that it mattered how much money it was.

Bodegard Mitchell was a senile man who didn't use banks, but hoarded money in his apartment. What a coincidence that the money they put into evidence was a nice round figure like ten thousand dollars.

At least they put that much back.

Sonny and I continued to work together, but it was different; I didn't trust him. I also continued working for Cameron.

People asked me if I thought Cameron was in on taking the money. I don't. He didn't need the money. The problem was he was a weak supervisor, despite his reputation as a tough-as-nails cop. He let people like Sonny Davis walk all over him. Davis obviously felt comfortable telling him what happened with the cash.

Eventually, the story got out. It was quite a media sensation.

Davis was charged with theft. He was tried twice, the jury hung on both occasions. I was good with that. I didn't really want him convicted of a crime. Sonny had a lot of personal demons. He retired into oblivion, drinking himself to death at 69 years old.

Don Cameron lost something much more valuable; he lost the reputation he'd worked his whole career to build. He retired in disgrace.

Sad.

6

I was working nights in December, 1996. We were called to a murder scene in an apartment building in Rainier Valley. An elderly, wheelchair-bound woman was found dead.

Patrol officers met us at the scene. One of them was a young officer I didn't know. He introduced himself as Rolf Norton. Norton would later himself become a Homicide detective, and I would work around him for several years.

Norton's partner was Zsolt Dornay.

"We were here on an unrelated disturbance," Dornay said.

"While we were handling that, this guy comes running up. There was blood on his cheek. He told us his mother had been murdered. He led us to the apartment and we found her."

I looked in the door of the apartment.

Mildred Simmons wedged between the bed and a chest of drawers in her bedroom. A white bathrobe was covering her face. This is consistent with a psychological "undoing" by the killer, not wanting to look at her face after he's killed her.

She wore an adult diaper. It and panties she had been wearing were pulled down to her ankles. She suffered several stab wounds to her chest, hands and head. Her throat was also cut from ear to ear; her head hung like an open Pez container. A grapefruit-sized ball of foam protruded from the wound in her throat.

She had several stab wounds to her face, and one in the center of her forehead. There were also several stab wounds around her vaginal area, clearing showing a sexual motivation for this murder.

The bathroom door was open and water was running in the sink. A brown paper bag was on the floor just inside the door. Inside

44

was an empty 22 ounce bottle of "211" malt liquor. There was a "GPC" brand cigarette butt floating in the open toilet. That's a cheap cigarette that a lot of down and out people smoke.

There was a blood smear on the phone. The phone had a redial button on it. Gene Ramirez, his hands gloved, picked up the phone hit the redial button. It went to 911. Mildred's son had likely used it upon finding his mother.

A glass laid on the kitchen counter, a small amount of what looked like water in the bottom. There was what appeared to be a blood stain on the rim of the glass.

There was a plastic step stool in front of the closet in the bedroom near Mildred's body. There are two burned wooden match sticks atop it.

There was another GPC cigarette butt on the carpet, crushed, as though someone stepped on it to extinguish it. A corresponding black scorch mark was under it on the carpeting. There was another unburnt wooden matchstick lying nearby.

In the bedroom, papers were laid out on the bed. These were the kind of papers one would keep in a purse. It appeared as though someone had dumped the purse contents on the bed to go through them.

There was a blood-saturated pillow sticking out from under the bed.

A metal cabinet was on a wall adjacent to the bed. There was low velocity blood spatter on the cabinet and the wall behind it.

There was a portable toilet on the floor, with a small amount of urine inside. The toilet was smeared with blood, and there was spatter around it too.

A large pool of blood had formed on the floor next to Milred's body. Floating atop the blood were several more wooden matchsticks. They'd obviously been dropped there after the blood was present.

Crack smokers sometimes use wooden matchsticks. Crack has to have a continuous flame held to it while it's smoked. It doesn't ignite like tobacco or marijuana. Cardboard matches burn too quickly and burn the fingers of the person using them, so crackheads use either butane lighters or wooden matches.

There were also GPC cigarette butts on top of the blood pool.

Whoever did this had hung around, smoking crack and cigarettes after he'd raped and killed Mildred, admiring his work.

Mildred's son didn't seem to be a crackhead.

In cases like this, it's always prudent to first focus on the son. It's usually someone close to the victim that commits a crime like this.

He'd been taken to the South Precinct, which covered this area of town. Mike Ciesynski went there to interview him.

"I was at the apartment earlier," he told Ciesynski. "My friend came over with her daughter and another girl. We all went to the movies at the Lewis and Clark Theater. We went to the 4:10 showing of 'Daylight'."

He showed Ciesynski ticket stubs from the movie.

"Afterward, I stopped by to get a video. My mom was on the phone, so I didn't talk to her.

"I went to Thompson's Point of View restaurant up on 28th and East Union. I saw a couple friends there. Then I went to the Hook Line, and Sinker Lounge in the 9200 block of Rainier Avenue South. I played darts with friends there. I came back at 10:15. When I got here there were two police officers at the door. I let them in. I asked if there was a problem, and they said they were there for a disturbance.

"I went upstairs and found my mom dead. I could see her throat was cut. I went into the living room and called 911.

"I went downstairs to find the officers I'd let in. I told them what I found."

"Do you or your mom smoke?" Ciesynski asked him.

"My mom doesn't smoke, and I haven't smoked in twenty years."

Ciesynski released him. He called us at the scene.

"This guy didn't do it, I'm sure."

Rick Ninomaya was at the precinct with Ciesynski. While they were there, Clayton Powell, a patrol officer, approached them.

"I made a domestic violence arrest at that same building earlier," he said. "The guy I arrested is Willie Haggerty. I arrested him for assaulting his mother. He had blood on his ankle when we arrested him.

Ninomaya and Detective Walt Maning went to the holding cell where Haggerty was being kept. They looked at him, but didn't see any obvious signs of blood. He had a scuff on one of his knuckles.

They looked at the clothing he'd been wearing when he was arrested. A pair of gloves had what could be blood stains on them.

They advised Haggerty of his rights.

"I want a lawyer," he said.

They photographed Haggerty and his knuckles.

They returned to the scene and spoke with the manager.

"I've seen Mildred with Willie Haggerty together in the day room," he said. "I know Willie sometimes goes up to Mildred's apartment."

There was blood in the stairwell between the floor Mildred lived on and the one Willie lived on with his mother.

Ninomaya and Maning went to Willie's mother's apartment. They knocked on the door. She answered. She was confined to a wheelchair. There was a phone off the hook. It was the noise phones do when that happens.

"Do you mind if I hang up the phone?" Ninomaya asked.

"Sure," she said.

He walked in and hung it up. He saw a pack of GPC cigarettes on top of the TV.

There was a wooden-handled knife, like one found in Mildred's apartment, on top of a refrigerator in the kitchen. Ms. Haggerty, in a wheelchair, could not have put it up there.

"We're going to seek a search warrant," Ninomaya told her. "I'll need you to go to the day room until we get one and come back."

He had a uniformed officer stand guard at the apartment until he got the warrant.

When they returned, they searched the apartment. They found a pair of men's dress shoes in a garbage can. They were covered in blood.

There were several blood drop stains on tile in the kitchen. They also found a box of wooden matches, and two bottle caps from 211 malt liquor.

They went to the jail to get a DNA sample from Willie.

"I want to talk to you about the case," he said.

"I don't assault women," he said. "That's not my style."

He told them he'd been released from Coyote Ridge prison a couple years earlier.

"I met Mildred at a bus stop across from the King County courthouse. She told me where she lived, and it was the same place my mom lived.

"She let me stay at her apartment. I was there about three days a week, on the couch.

"That night, I was playing dominos with other people in the building. I told Mildred I'd stop by.

"I went to her apartment, but the door was locked. Usually when she knows I'm coming by, she leaves the door unlocked.

"I was able to get in the apartment," he said. " I saw her on the floor. I thought she fell. I went up to her, and I could feel something hitting me. She looked at me. She was trying to talk to me with her eyes.

"I turned on the light, and I saw her throat was cut. Blood was spraying on my pants.

"I tried to call 911 from the bedroom, but it didn't work. I turned the lights off and went to my mom's apartment.

"The police were there when a man came and said his mom was dead."

Nice try.

Willie was charged with Mildred's murder. He was a third-striker, having been previously convicted of two other violent felonies.

Willie was a predator. Mildred, elderly and disabled, was probably a very lonely woman. Willie took advantage of that, ingratiating himself to her, and gaining her trust, until the predator came out again, and he raped and killed Mildred.

He was convicted at trial and sentenced to life without the possibility of parole.

Bart Foster was homeless. He slept under the Alaskan Way Viaduct, which runs along the waterfront in downtown Seattle. One night, while sleeping, Foster became another statistic of the dangers of living homeless. Someone crushed his head with a cinder block across from the downtown ferry terminal where tourists and commuters take boats to Bainbridge Island and Bremerton.

I was next-up for a murder. My partner was still the mostly-drunk Sonny Davis.

We weren't called to the scene of this murder; a very bad thing for a detective trying to solve a case like this. Tom Pike and Paul Suguro were the on-call detectives who went to the scene. Foster was taken to Harborview. They didn't think he was going to die, so they didn't call us out.

They were wrong.

After he died, I called Richard Harruff, the Medical Examiner, who had conducted the autopsy on Foster.

"He had injuries to the left side of his head," he said. "It's consistent with being hit with a large block. It caused a fracture to the base of his skull. There were also abrasions to his knees and his right cheek."

We, (actually I, since Davis had little to do with this case) were behind the eight-ball from the beginning, but I caught a break early on. Keith Kzmirski, a cab driver, was reportedly a witness to the assault. I tracked him down to a West Seattle address. He wasn't very cooperative at first, but I got him to tell me what he knew. I have a way with people like him. This is a murder, not a Goddamned car prowl. I let him know, I wasn't going away. If I had to drag him before a judge to tell me what he knew, I was going to do that, and I'd do it on my schedule, when it was convenient for me, with no consideration about imposing on him. He decided to cooperate.

I knew he would.

He was working for Pioneer Cab Company as a supervisor.

"Where were you between four fifteen and four twenty-five in the morning, on May 20th?" I asked.

"I was near the power plant," he said, "down on the waterfront."

50

"Is that across from the ferry terminal there?" I asked.

"Right."

"Tell me what you saw there." I said.

"Well, I was pulling right up by the power plant. I saw a black gentleman, twenty-five to thirty. He had a cinder block and he brought it down on something behind the dumpster."

"Was it a full cinder block?" I asked.

"No, a half cinder block."

"So, you saw it was up over his head?"

"I saw it up over his head," he said, "and then he was bringing it down."

"With both hands?"

"Both hands."

"Did he bring it down hard on something?" I asked.

"Well, he didn't bring it down soft," he said.

"Could you see where he was standing?" I asked.

"He was standing right behind the dumpster," he said. "I had a shot of him from the waist up. There's two couches there. I didn't realize at the time what he was doing, or I would have called the police myself.

"But then I realized that there's two guys sleeping on those couches and that he must have been doing something to one of them."

He'd gotten a good look at the suspect, so I had him help with the creation of a composite drawing.

Betty Kindcaid was the forensic artist I used. Betty was a civilian employee of the police department and a very accomplished artist. I'd had really good results from her before. It wasn't just because she was a good artist—she was. Her drawings always look like real people, not the alien-looking drawings I see other police departments put out. She was also an excellent interviewer. She had a hypnotic way about her that drew extra information from the witness she was working with. On several occasions when she developed a sketch of an unknown suspect, once the suspect was identified and arrested, the sketch looked just like him.

I set her up with the cab driver. After about three hours, she had a sketch. She gave it to me.

I made up a bulletin using the sketch. I walked it down to the SWAT office on the third floor of the old headquarters building.

SWAT officers, when not training, (which is most of the time) drive around in plain cars. I gave them the bulletin.

"Do you think you could grab this guy by seven?" I asked, jokingly.

I was back in the office at seven-thirty when my phone rang. An operator in the 911 center was calling.

"There's a Zebra Unit, (the designation SWAT uses) who have a person stopped at 2nd South and Washington Street that apparently matches a bulletin you put out tonight."

"I'll be right there," I told the operator.

I pulled up at that location. Officers Joe Fountain and Rudy Gonzales had two people stopped.

"We saw this guy," Fountain said. "He looks like the sketch you put out tonight. The guy he was with said he told him he'd assaulted a guy down on the waterfront a few days ago.

That was all I needed.

"Hook 'em up and bring them to my office," I said.

Once there, I put the guy that looked like the sketch, whom we had identified as Nathan Payne, in an interview room. I walked in and advised him of his rights. Then I took out the sketch and laid it on the table in front of him.

"Who's that?"

"That's me," he said.

After three hours of intense, but quiet interrogation, he'd confessed to the murder. I was getting ready to book him into jail when Sonny came in.

"Who's that in the interview room?" he asked.

"That's the killer in our latest murder. I'm about to book him."

Sonny had a sheepish look on his face.

"I wasn't' there to help you with this at all. Good job."

I appreciated the comment, at least.

Fifteen years later, after an appellate court decision that affected his case, I saw Payne again in court, where he was for a resentencing. He greeted me like we were old friends.

I get that a lot.

7

Greg Mixsell approached me in March of 1997.

"I got a call from a detective in Maryland," he said. "A guy there supposedly overheard a telephone call on his scanner. The people on the phone were talking about one of the guys flying to Seattle to kill someone. One of the people on the phone was the guy's neighbor, Todd Anthony Rogers. There was some talk about a hundred thousand dollars, but he didn't know more. He was just giving us a heads up. He'll call back when he knows more."

The next day I answered the phone. The caller was Rich Alban, a detective with the Ann Arundle County Police in Maryland.

"I found out a lot more since I called earlier," he told me. "The guy who intercepted the calls is Robert Colebank.

"He intercepted more calls since he first reported it. The guy calling from Seattle told Rogers that he was going to 'scope out' a dump site for the body. They talked about meeting the victim near a bar."

Alban said they never named the potential victim.

"They discussed their plan. Plan A was they would do it on Friday when Rogers gets there. Plan B, was they would do it Saturday, and Plan C was they would 'do Ruth' at the same time.

"The caller was concerned that someone would see them with the victim in the bar.

"It sounded like Rogers would be the shooter. Rogers said they'd shoot the victim in the chest and in 'the dome', presumably the head.

"The caller told Rogers to be careful not to 'splatter' him when he shoots the victim.

"They talked about putting the victim's body in a sleeping bag and then taking it to the place the caller had scoped out.

"The caller said he would get 'the honeymooners' out."

Alban told me he'd done some research since he last called.

"Todd Rogers is booked on a flight on TWA to Seattle next Friday out of Reagan National Airport in DC. There's a layover in St. Louis. He's scheduled to arrive in Seattle at ten forty-two PM local time.

"I ran Rogers for criminal history. He's been handled in the Seattle area in 1994."

He'd also done research on the airline ticket Rogers was flying on.

"The ticket was purchased by a guy named Aaron Lord," he said. "He listed an address of 2357 South 52nd Street in Tacoma."

"When the time comes," I asked, "can you put Rogers under surveillance and make sure he gets to the airport on time, and let us know what he's wearing?"

"No problem," Alban said. "Let me know if you want me to serve a warrant on his house."

"I may need you to put a trap and trace on his phone," I said.

A trap and trace is a device that records all incoming and outgoing calls on a land line, which unlike cell calls, are not itemized in records.

"I'll get started on that," he said.

I did research on Lord. He had an extensive criminal history of burglary, but no violent crimes. I got copies of his latest jail booking photos.

I put a game plan together.

I met with Chuck McClure, a sergeant in the Criminal Intelligence Unit. I'd need their assistance with this. They have undercover detectives and surveillance equipment that we may need to have available.

"I'll talk to the lieutenant and get him in the loop," McClure said. "We'll meet with you later to come up with a plan."

Next, I called Marilyn Brenneman from the Prosecutor's Office. She worked in the Special Investigations Section of the office. They handle wire authorizations. In murder-for-hire cases, that's a tool we often use.

Dave Ritter, a sergeant in Homicide, called the FBI to make sure they didn't have a parallel investigation going on in which we'd step on each other's toes.

They didn't.

I set up a meeting between Brenneman, myself and the Intel guys.

The lieutenant in Intelligence was a good guy, and I liked him a lot, but he had a way of doing things that was prevalent when I first came on the police department; do the least possible to get by. Don't make waves. I was infuriated by that attitude.

"I think we should just meet the plane when it arrives," he suggested, "and tell the guy to turn around and go back."

Really? That's what the fuck you're going to do in a murder-for-hire case? Like giving a guy who rolls through a stop sign an oral warning?

"That'd be really good," I said. "until the guy that hired him just hires someone else and the victim gets killed anyway. No, we're not doing that."

I was a detective and this guy was a lieutenant, but this was my case. We were doing it my way, even if I had to do it without the Intelligence Unit. Fortunately, Marilyn Brenneman spoke up.

"I don't think that's a good idea," she told him.

"If Rogers shows up and is met by Lord, I think that's the substantial step we need for a Solicitation for Murder charge," Brenneman said. "You can arrest them at that point."

When that happened, Davis and I would take Rogers downtown for an interrogation.

On Friday, March 14th, I was in the office early, getting everything set up for the operation that evening. Midway through the day, I got a call from the Maryland detective.

"He left the house. We followed him to the airport. It looks like a go."

He described the clothes Rogers was wearing.

Later, we got confirmation that Rogers had boarded his connecting flight in St. Louis.

A little after eight PM, Sonny and I headed for the airport. Several other Homicide and Intelligence detectives also went in separate cars.

We parked on an upper concourse set aside for police parking, and headed for the gate. This was pre 9/11, so we didn't have to check in with TSA. We met with the Port of Seattle Police, who patrol the airport. We gave them photos of Lord and Rogers. They were available if we needed backup.

We found out that his flight would be delayed. Now it wouldn't be in until after 11:30.

When we got to the gate we spread out in the seating area. We had newspapers, books and other things to make us look like we were just waiting to pick up a friend like everyone else.

Only one guy looked at us suspiciously. He looked at each of us, one by one, a curious expression on his face.

Finally, the plane arrived. We watched the passengers disembark. I recognized Rogers when he stepped off the plane.

I'd seen his photograph, and he was wearing the clothing described by the St. Louis detectives.

He walked from the waiting area toward baggage claim. I fell in a step behind him, the other detectives behind me.

As he passed a bank of payphones, he suddenly turned around, bumping into me.

"Excuse me," he said.

"No problem."

He picked up a phone. I pretended to use the phone next to him.

"I'm here," he said into the phone. "Okay, I'll be right there."

He hung up and walked toward baggage claim. I followed, this time about fifteen feet back.

When we got to baggage claim, I saw Aaron Lord. I'd seen his photo too. There was another man with Lord.

We'd originally planned to arrest them when they met. I signaled for the others to wait. I wanted them to lead us to their car. There could be incriminating evidence inside that we could get to with a search warrant.

We lingered for fifteen minutes or so until Rogers got his bag. Then Rogers, Lord and the third guy walked toward the parking garage.

All eight of us walked behind them. They were oblivious and didn't have a clue.

When we got into the garage, Lord walked diagonally across the parking area. It was obvious that he'd forgotten where he'd parked.

Surely they'd notice us now, I thought, following as they cut across rows in the garage, but they didn't.

Finally, they approached a gray 1987 Nissan Pulsar. As soon as Lord stuck the key in we pounced, our guns drawn.

"Seattle Police! On the ground!"

I walked up to the now-prone Todd Rogers and put handcuffs on him. I lifted him up.

"Come on, Todd. You're coming with us."

He had a look on his face that said, 'How do they know my name?'

Davis and I walked him to our car.

"What's this about?" he asked.

"You have some unpaid parking tickets," I told him.

Once at the car, I put him in the back seat on the passenger side. Sonny was driving. I sat behind him, next to Rogers.

"How should we handle this, partner?" I asked Davis. "I say Plan A, we talk to him tonight. Plan B, we wait until tomorrow, or Plan C, we wait until the third day."

I looked at Rogers. He looked like he was about to shit himself.

"Okay, I'll talk," he said.

Back in the Homicide office. We put him in an interview room.

He told us he'd known Aaron Lord for about twelve years.

"Our parents used to date," he said. "We lived together for a while."

"How long have you been in Maryland?" I asked.

"About two and a half years," he said.

"Do you speak with Aaron regularly?"

"Once about every few months," he said.

"Tell me how this whole thing came about," I said.

"Aaron called me last weekend," he said. "He said that a friend had ripped him off of a lot of money after a bank job," (Burglary). "He said he knew who did it, and wanted to take care of it."

"Did you know what friend he was talking about?"

"Yeah."

"Who was that," I asked.

"Andre."

Andre was the guy who accompanied Aaron to the airport to pick up Rogers.

"Do you know Andre?" I asked.

"Yeah," he said. "Just from hanging around Aaron."

"When he said, 'take care of it', did you know what he meant?"

"Yeah. Kill him," he said.

"Did Aaron tell you that?" I asked.

"Yes."

"Tell how he wanted it to go down," I said.

"He wanted to do 'a job' meaning a burglary job on a bank or ATM, and then go back to his house and kill Andre."

"What did he say about the job?" I asked.

"A lot of money."

He told us that Andre would help with the job, and the killing would occur after. He was supposed to collect about one third of the take, which he estimated at twenty thousand dollars.

"Aaron and Andre were going to do the job. I was going to be the lookout.

"After the job, we'd go to Aaron's house, and they'd be counting money. Aaron would go get a gun and shoot Andre."

It was very convenient that Rogers alleged that Lord would be the one to actually kill Andre, counter to what it sounded like in the calls, but at this point, it didn't matter to my case.

"What did Aaron want you to do?" I asked.

"Basically to help him bury the body."

Lord flew Rogers all the way out from Maryland to help bury a body? I didn't by it, but again: it didn't matter to my case.

"Where was he going to bury the body?" I asked.

"Somewhere out by a power line or something," he said.

"How was he going to get the body there?"

"With some ATV or four wheel vehicle or something," he said.

"Was he going to conceal the body somehow?"

"He was going to put it in a sleeping bag," he said.

"When was thing going to happen?" I asked.

"Tonight," he said.

Aaron Lord was in another interview room. I went in.

I played a few moments of the recording of our interview with Rogers for him.

"If that's what you think I did, then I guess I'm guilty," he said. He wouldn't answer any questions.

We tried to talk to Andre, but he wanted nothing to do with us.

Ingrate. If it hadn't been for us, his ass would be dead right now.

We served a search warrant on Lord's Tacoma house. We found evidence in the bank burglaries. There was a van in behind the house, with an ATV in the back and a tarp attached by rope.

We searched the woods near his house. Under some powerlines there, we found what looked like a pre-dug grave.

Lord was charged with Solicitation to Commit Murder. He went to trial. Rogers agreed to testify for the state in exchange for an agreed guilty plea to Attempted Conspiracy to Commit Murder in the Second degree, and a much-reduced sentence.

Lord was convicted and sentenced to thirty years in prison.

This case was a perfect example of the enigma that was Sonny Davis. He did good work on this case. He could be a very good detective when he wanted to. When he didn't, he was dead weight.

Sad.

8

In September, 1997, I partnered with John Nordlund; "Johnny Deuce" around the office.

I liked John a lot; he's a really good guy; friendly and fun to be around socially. But he had a different style than me. He was a checklist detective. Everything in its time. I think he attained this trait when he worked as a civilian employee of the FBI, before coming on Seattle PD. The FBI is hyper-regulated. The Federal Bureaucracy of Investigation. A brand-new officer right out of the police academy has much more discretion in handling a situation than a twenty-year FBI veteran.

I'm much more of a fly by the seat of your pants type.

We were called in the middle of the night to a homicide on the West Seattle Bridge. There were two dead at the scene and three others wounded and on their way to Harborview.

I pulled myself out of bed and off to work.

The West Seattle Viaduct is a raised highway that leads from West Seattle across the tide flats to Interstate 5.

I arrived to find the viaduct completely shut down. A Honda Accord stopped eastbound on the shoulder, bullet holes all through the front windshield and sides of the car, the deck of the roadway covered in shell casings. They were 7.62x39; the type fired by AK-47's and similar weapons.

A patrol sergeant briefed me on the scene.

"We've got two dead here, and three girls who were wounded. They said that they'd been out tonight, and were on their way home when they got a flat tire. They called someone to come help them, and were waiting, when a small red car, they thought it was a two-door Toyota with a spoiler on the trunk and Asian decals on the rear pulled up. An Asian male got out of the passenger side with a rifle and opened up on them. He killed the two guys who were outside, and shot at the girls in the car. They were hit, but it looks like they'll survive."

Behind the Honda on the ground laid the bodies of two Asian males. They'd been shot several times, including what appeared to be coupe de grace shots to the forehead.

I interviewed Colin Trask. He'd been driving up to the scene when the shooting happened.

"I was coming down about mid-span when I heard a popping sound," he said. "At first I thought I had a flat tire.

"About a hundred yards in front of me, there was a car stopped. Two people were out of the car shooting at another car. People were hiding behind the car. I backed up.

"There was a young woman running toward me. The people who were shooting at the other car took off, and the woman collapsed in front of my truck.

"I tried to console her and tried to flag people down to call 911."

"What did the car with the shooters in it look like?" I asked.

"It was red," he said. "I couldn't tell the make or model, but it was a smaller car, probably Asian or European. It was a two-door"

"Can you describe the shooters?"

"I just saw dark figures," he answered. "I couldn't see a face or a body.

"The car doors were open. I think the driver was firing a pistol. The passenger was firing an automatic weapon."

Nordlund and I went to Harborview to see if we could interview the surviving victims. Christina Chung and Suzie Park were in surgery. Jennifer Chung was still in the Emergency Room, but she had been intubated and was unconscious.

At 8:15 that morning, myself, Nordlund and Don Cameron went to the Medical Examiner's office to attend the autopsies of the two dead victims.

Dr. Paul Spence was the attending Forensic Pathologist.

The victims had suffered devastating wounds, having been shot by a high-powered rifle.

Jerry Webster was an investigator at the Medical Examiners. He told us that dead victims had been identified as Visa Khamvongsa and Son Le.

The next day, Suzie Park had regained consciousness and was able to talk, though she was under the influence of pain medications and was somewhat lethargic.

"We got two flat tires," she said. "We called for someone to come help us. I was sitting in the passenger seat. I was facing toward the back seat of the car talking to Christina. Jennifer was sitting in the driver's seat. Visa and Son were outside the car. We had the music on and were just waiting for our friends to come. We heard some gunshots. I ducked, and I got shot in one leg and then the other. The car door was open, and I fell out, and I got shot again. We were screaming and calling for help. Some guys came and helped us."

"Do you remember what the man who shot you looked like?" Nordlund asked.

"Oh, yeah, I looked over at the car before I fell out and all I remember was that he was kind of bald, and his hair was just starting to grow back. I'm pretty sure there was red somewhere. It was a red car and he was wearing red clothes, or something like that."

Next, we interviewed Jennifer Chung.

"We were going to Alki, but we got a flat. Son made a U-turn and we pulled up next to the exit. We were waiting there about thirty minutes when the car pulled up. The next thing I know, they're shooting at us."

"Do you know how many shots were fired?" Nordlund asked her.

"I just know it was a lot."

"Did you stay inside the car?" he asked.

"Yeah. I stayed in the car, because I didn't know what to do.

"When they left, I got out of the car. Suzy was on the ground beside the car. I saw Visa and Son. Son was dead, but Visa was still alive. I could find my sister. Suzy was bleeding from head to toe. She just kept saying, 'help me'.

"I found my sister down the street. She ran.

"I thought I'd been shot, but I got metal and glass in my eye. I'm blind in my left eye."

Jennifer's sister, Christine Chung, was much more lucid that the others. We questioned her.

"I saw a red sporty Honda Civic, or some sort of that type of car," she said, "and a guy coming out of the passenger seat. He was about five-two or five-three. He had a white tee shirt and some dark jeans or possibly some black dickies. He had partly shaved hair, I mean almost bald, but hair coming out. He had a gun that required two hands to hold. The gunshots were rapid and fast, and he shot for about five minutes.

"The car he was in had some sort of white writing on the right side near the rear.

"Do you know what the writing was?" I asked. "Was it writing or a symbol, or picture?"

"It could have been writing or a symbol. I don't know."

"Tell us where you were in the car," Nordlund said.

"Suzy was in the passenger seat, and my sister was in the driver's seat. I was in the back toward the passenger side, with my legs out when they shot.

66

"Son and Visa were sitting on the rail. They shot them first, and then the fire came toward us. I got shot in the leg. I wasn't sure about my sister or my friend. I ran down the street, and I fell. They were still shooting when I fell. A man came and helped me."

"What side of the car did the shooter come out of?" I asked.

"The right side," she said.

"Could you see the driver?"

"No."

"Did the shots sound all the same, or did some of the shots sound different from the others?" I asked.

"They all sounded the same."

We put a bulletin out, looking for information about possible suspect vehicles with a spoiler and stickers on the back, possibly a Honda. Dozens of possible vehicles were reported to us, none of which appeared to be related to this homicide.

Like any widely-reported murder, tips from the public poured in. The sheer volume of tips creates its own problem, most of them called in by well-meaning citizens, the information really having nothing to do with the case. A few of them however, contain important information. The wheat has to be separated from the chaff in order to root out the good tips; a labor-intensive job.

Shannon Sharpe was an Administrative Specialist in the Homicide unit, and was charged with organizing and filtering the incoming tips.

She divided the tips into three categories: Hot Tips, ones that seemed very promising, and should be followed up on right away, Interesting Tips, which could be good, and should be looked at as soon as possible, and "I was walking on Guam one day…" tips that obviously had nothing to do with this case.

Ironically, the name she gave for this category would turn out to be an interesting choice of words.

One early tip we received came from a resident of an apartment complex in Tukwila, a city just south of Seattle. A group of people lived in an apartment near the tipster. They seemed to match the description of the people involved in the murder, and had a car that was similar to the description that had been released.

I drove to the apartment complex the day after the tip came in. There was no one around. No car that matched the description was parked nearby, and I couldn't find an apartment manager. I left, intending to return in a few days for another look around.

I spent the next several days chasing down other leads, many seeming promising, only to lead down blind alleys and peter out.

On September 25th, I got a call from a patrol officer with the King County Police. He worked the Sea-Tac area. He stopped a guy, who told the officer he had information about the West Seattle Bridge murders.

I asked Mike LeBlanc, a Gang Unit detective, to meet with that officer and bring the possible witness to me.

When LeBlanc brought him in, he was very cooperative, but afraid. He asked to be treated as a confidential informant.

"These people have a car just like the one that was described," he said.

"Who are these people?" I asked.

"One of them is John Guest," he said. "The other people are Marvin, John and Kyle."

"Is that Marvin Francisco?" I asked.

"Yes."

"Describe Marvin," I said.

"He's a Filipino guy, nineteen years-old, with a dark complexion, with a bald head and a moustache, about my height."

"How tall are you?"

"Five-six of five-seven," he said.

"How much do you think he weighs?"

"Between one-fifty and one-seventy.

"A few weeks ago, they came into some money. I don't know how, but at first, they were broke, and then all of the sudden, they start flashing large amounts of cash.

"In the last few weeks, someone broke into John's house in West Seattle and stole their cash. They thought they knew who did it. They kidnapped and assaulted some of those people.

"Marvin has access to a couple red cars. One's a Nissan 240SX. It's got a big whale-tail on it."

"Where are these cars normally parked?" I asked.

"Up in Pyramid Point."

"In Tukwila?"

"Yeah."

"Do you know them to own rifles?" I asked.

"Yes. I think one was an SK, but I'm not sure."

An SK is the Chinese version of the AK-47. It fires 7.62 rounds, just like the ones used in this murder.

"I heard one of their family members talking very secretively about this case. They said Marvin did it."

The Pyramid Point Apartments is the same place we got the earlier tip about, that I'd driven out to, but found nothing.

When multiple tips come in about the same people from different sources, they need to be investigated right away. It's what we in the business call a clue.

I called Nathan Freeman, who'd phoned in the original tip about the Asian males at Pyramid Point.

69

"I was watching the news," he said, "when I saw the story of the shooting. They put out a description of the car, and said it was red, with a spoiler and writing on the behind the passenger door. Right away, I thought of the car that always parks here. It has a big spoiler. It didn't have writing, but had a 'bad boy' symbol."

"Did anything else make you think this car could be involved?" I asked.

"They said the suspect was an Asian male with a bald or shaved head. The guy that drives that car is Asian with a shaved head."

We received a call from a woman who wanted to remain anonymous. She asked if the murder weapon was a handgun or rifle.

"It was a rifle," Nordlund told her.

"Oh, my God!" she said. "The shooter is Marvin Francisco. He's been trying to get rid of a rifle since a couple days after the shooting.

"The car he was driving belongs to his girlfriend, Eleanor Yumul."

She was very frightened, and still refused to identify herself.

"Marvin is getting ready to leave the country," she said.

We drove to Tukwila.

Parking down the street from the apartment in question, I walked to the address. A small red coupe was parked in front. It didn't have a spoiler, or decals on it like the surviving victims described. I took a closer look.

There were holes on the trunk where the spoiler had been before being removed. On the rear window, there were adhesive marks; the decals had been scraped off. The appearance of this car had been altered so it didn't look like the description being widely reported in the media.

No more calls, we have a winner.

We went back to our car, keeping an eye on the suspect vehicle.

We called the office, and asked for SWAT officers in plain clothes to come sit on the car while I got a search warrant for the apartment. They arrived in several cars. Once they set up, we went back downtown.

I was writing an affidavit for search warrant for the apartment, when I got a call from the SWAT officers on surveillance. Two Asian male and one Asian female got in the car and drove off. SWAT was following them.

"Wait and see where they go," I said. "Once they're stopped, take them down."

A few minutes later, I got another call from the SWAT guys. They'd driven to an address in Allentown, just south of the Seattle city limits. They had all three in custody and were bringing them in. One of them was Marvin Francisco.

Other officers were sitting with the car and on the house they'd driven to.

We interviewed Tony Supnet, the other male that had been in the car.

"I've known Marvin about five months," he said. "Marvin is crazy, and doesn't talk about his business. I've seen Marvin with a .380 pistol and a rifle with a banana clip.

"I noticed that Marvin stopped driving the red car about the time of the shooting. He got real moody. When people talked about the shooting, he'd yell at them to shut up."

We found out from witnesses that the rifle was in a closet in Marvin's mother's house. Paul Suguro and Don Cameron went back. They found the rifle there.

We interviewed Eleanor Yumul. She was the Asian female who had been in the car when it drove from the Tukwila apartments to Allentown.

71

"The night of the shooting, Marvin called me at about 2:00 AM. He told me he was at the Skyway Bowl, and was going to the Tulalip Casino. Then he called at 2:20 and said he was at Tulalip."

"Tulalip is more than thirty miles from the Skyway Bowl," I said. "How could he have made it there in twenty minutes?"

"That made me suspicious too," she said.

We found out that Francisco had asked a friend to store the spoiler from the Nissan in the friend's car trunk. The friend agreed to give is the spoiler.

Eleanor told us that her brother, Emerson, had been with Marvin the night of the shooting.

"Emerson's a pussy," she said. "He wouldn't be involved in this."

"Where's Emerson now?" I asked.

"He's went to my parent's house. They live on Saipan."

We interviewed Marvin Francisco. He denied any knowledge of the shooting.

"Why did you remove the spoiler from the car?" I asked.

"It was damaged in a car prowl, so I took it off."

I called the Seattle FBI office, and asked if there was an FBI office on Saipan.

"Yes, there is," the agent told me and gave me the number.

I called the number.

"I want to see if Emerson Yumul is on the island," I told the FBI agent, Steven Stokes. Stokes was shouting in to the phone.

"Sorry," he explained. "We're in the middle of a typhoon."

I gave him the particulars about Yumul.

The next morning when I got to the office, there was a voice message from Stokes.

"He's here."

Emett Kelsie, who'd been my first patrol sergeant, was my lieutenant in Homicide. He was the prototypical big black burly boss often depicted in TV cop shows.

I walked in to his office.

"I need to go to Saipan."

Long pause.

"Where the hell is Saipan?"

"It's a little island in the South Pacific," I said.

"When do you need to go?"

"Tomorrow."

Another long pause.

"Okay."

There was one problem: I didn't have a passport. Once again, I called the Seattle FBI office.

"Who do you know at the passport agency?"

They gave me a name. I called her, and explained the situation.

"What state were you born in?" she asked.

"Washington."

"Bring me a copy of your birth certificate and a passport photo."

At that time, the Vital Statistics office was located in the King County Administration Building, across the street from headquarters. I went there, and got a copy of my birth certificate. Then I went to the police photo lab. They took a passport photo. I drove to the Passport office and dropped them off.

73

Three hours later, my phone rang.

"Come pick up your passport."

The next morning, Deuce and I were on the milk run to Saipan: Seattle to Honolulu—a seven-hour layover, with a cab to Waikiki, and lunch on the beach—then Honolulu to Guam, (and the incredible coincidence with Shannon's tip category), then Guam to Saipan. The trip took almost twenty-four hours.

We arrived on Saipan at about eleven PM local time on October 22nd.

As we disembarked the plane, a group of men waited.

"Are you guys from Seattle?" they asked.

"Yes," we replied.

Agent Stokes was there, along with two local cops from the Mariana Islands Department of Public Safety.

We'd walked off a DC-10 full of people, but they made us as cops. It's innate. I've done it myself, meeting planes with cops from other agencies coming to Seattle. It's the way cops look; the way they carry themselves. One cop can spot another in a second.

"We arrested Yumul at his grandmother's house," Stokes said. "He'll be in court tomorrow morning."

They buzzed us past Customs, and walked us out to their cars. When the automatic doors opened, it was like getting hit in the chest with a brick. Though it was after eleven in the evening, it was one hundred degrees with ninety percent humidity.

They took us to an ocean-front hotel and dropped us off.

"We'll be here to pick you up at eight in the morning."

It was an older hotel, probably built in the in 50s. It was situated on a beach. It was very nice. We were in a suite.

74

Across from our hotel was a bar. It looked like photos I'd seen of Manila; the Filipina girl standing outside looked very friendly.

I called home and spoke to Doreen. It was just after six in the morning there.

I tried to sleep, but I was wide awake. After an hour of tossing and turning, I got up, threw on a pair of shorts and a shirt, and went out to the beach behind the hotel.

There was a bar, closed at that hour. I grabbed a white plastic chair and sat on the beach. I waded into the ocean, warm as bath water.

The heat and humidity was oppressive. I thought of the Marines who had invaded this island during World War II, having no respite from the heat. I could just walk back into the air-conditioned hotel. I thought of my father, trapped on a beach just a couple hundred miles from here on Peleliu, under constant fire from the Japanese, the only water they had to drink warm and tainted with oil.

A medium-sized, mutt-looking dog walked up the beach. He didn't notice me at first. As he came closer, I called out to him.

"Hey, buddy."

He looked startled, and growled. A second dog appeared, and then a third, all growling. I sat in the chair, not reacting at all. After a few moments, they continued down the beach. They were wild dogs, I later learned. Descendants of dogs brought here during the war to root the Japanese soldiers out of the caves. When the war ended, the dogs were left behind, their feral relatives all over the island.

When the sun came up, I saw something in the water, directly out from where I sat; the turret of an American tank that had been here since the war. The Marines had landed on the beach I was sitting on.

I walked around to the front of the hotel. Truck after truck drove down the street, men crammed in the beds, on their way to the sweat shops.

At eight, I was showered, shaved and ready to go, having not slept a minute.

Saipan is part of the Commonwealth of the Northern Marianas, a territory of the United States. There's a federal courthouse on the island, part of the Ninth Circuit Court of Appeals.

Yumul had been arrested for the Unlawful Flight warrant before we arrived, his arrest apparently big news there. News crews were stationed outside the courthouse.

Because he had been arrested before we got there, he'd been appointed a lawyer. We couldn't talk to him. The judge ordered him extradited to Seattle.

We'd planned to take him back with us. There was also a US Marshal's office on Saipan.

I spoke about the extradition with the marshal in charge.

"We have a flight that'll come through here in a couple weeks. We can just put him on that, if you don't want to take him with you now."

Sweet. The thought of babysitting a murder suspect on a twenty-four-hour sojourn back to Seattle didn't sound appealing to me at all.

"Let's do that," I told him.

Once we were done with the business at hand, the FBI agents took us up into the jungle, to some of the historic war sites. I was all in.

We visited the Final Outpost, where the Japanese commander on Saipan committed Hari Kari when defeat was certain, and the suicide cliffs, where local Japanese civilians threw their children into the Philippine Sea, before jumping over themselves. They believed that the American military would eat their children and themselves if they were captured, as the Japanese military had told them. Japanese monuments covered the cliff edge; a very somber place.

Standing highest point on the island, about two hundred feet above sea level, I looked across at Tinian, and at the airstrip with bomb pits dug so the Enola Gay piloted by Colonel Paul Tibbets could be loaded with "Little Boy", the atomic bomb dropped on Hiroshima.

A couple days later, on that same strip, "Fat Man" was loaded on Box Car piloted by Charles W. Sweeney, to be dropped on Nagasaki.

Those bombings stopped the planned invasion of Honshu, the largest island of Japan.

My dad had been a Marine in War II and had taken part in the battles of Peleliu and Okinawa. He was slated to be in that invasion. Had those bombs not been dropped ending the war, there would have been millions of casualties on both sides, and I may never have been born.

It was time to return to Seattle. A local Chamorro police officer, a member of an FBI task force, picked us up at our hotel at four AM.

We flew from Saipan to Guam. Once there, we changed planes for the flight to Honolulu. Our scheduled departure time came and went, but we didn't budge.

More than an hour after we were supposed to leave, the pilot came over the intercom. We were waiting for late cargo, and we'd be leaving soon.

Finally, long after we were supposed to push off, the plane backed away from the gate. As we did, the engines stalled. The emergency lights came on, (the red lights really do lead to the green lights, marking the exit). We backed away again. Again, the engines stalled. That happened four times. I looked over at Deuce.

"We're not going anywhere."

We taxied toward the runway.

A 747 crashed there a month earlier. I laughed.

"You've got to be fucking kidding me."

We took off and began the long flight to Hawaii.

Again, the pilot came on the intercom.

"I apologize for the delay. To make it up to you, drinks are free for the entire flight."

The flight attendant came by to take our order. It was still before seven AM.

"I'll have coffee," I told her.

The Deuce jumped in.

"He'll have coffee and four screwdrivers, and I'll have four screwdrivers."

Really?

A few minutes later the flight attendant came back with my coffee and eight screwdrivers. Deuce and I had a center aisle of five seats to ourselves. He put all the tray tables down, and lined up the screwdrivers. He drank them all.

Later, the flight attendant returned.

"He'll have four more screwdrivers, and I'll have four more," Deuce told her.

"And another coffee," I added.

We arrived in Honolulu late that evening. Because of the delay on Guam, we'd missed our connecting flight.

"Let's stay here a day or two," I told Deuce. "We're in Hawaii."

"No, we have to get back," he said.

He booked the last two seats on a red-eye to San Francisco. We'd spent the last eighteen hours on a plane. We crammed into the last two center seats. It was miserable.

I can't believe I got on that plane. I was the junior detective at the time, but I should have said, "I'll see you in Seattle in a couple days," but I didn't.

We submitted all the shell casings and bullet fragments to the lab when we got back. They were forensically matched

A month later, I got a call from the US Marshal. The plane carrying Emerson Yumul was going to land at Boeing Field the next day.

We met the flight.

The Marshal's brought Yumul off the plane and turned him over to us.

Yumul was eighteen years old, with no prior criminal history. He was charged with Aggravated Murder, a charge carrying the possibility of the death penalty.

When we pulled up to the jail, he looked at me with doe eyes.

"Is this where I'm going to die?"

"No, that'll be at a prison somewhere else," I told him.

Ever the sensitive guy.

I walked him up to the booking desk.

"This is the nicest kid I've ever booked for Aggravated Murder," I told the booking officer.

Yumul had been the driver of the car, and hadn't fired a shot. As I said, he had no criminal history. He was afraid Francisco, the shooter, would shoot him too if he didn't go along with it.

"That's all fine," I told him. "But all you had to do, after you were no longer with Francisco, was to pick up a phone and call the police and tell them what happened. If you'd done that, you wouldn't have been charged with a crime. Instead, you fled to Saipan."

Ultimately, the prosecution made a deal with him. He testified for the state in exchange for a twenty-five-year sentence. He took the deal. Francisco was convicted and sentenced to life without the possibility of parole.

Time and again, I see how the wrong decision made in a second can affect the rest of someone's life.

9

On September 12th, 1997 the body of a black female was found bound and gagged in a wooded area east of downtown Seattle, known colloquially as "The Jungle". The Jungle is southeast of where Interstate 5 intersects with Interstate 90. It's the site of many homeless camps. Drug sales and use is rampant in the area. Finding a body back there is not particularly unusual.

Other Jungle residents came across the bound and gagged female body. They walked out to Interstate 90 and flagged down a state trooper. He and other troopers followed the men to where the body was. Once they found it, they notified the Seattle Police Department.

Mike Ciesynski and Dick Gagnon were the primary assigned detectives in the case. I didn't go to the scene of the murder, but I talked about the case with Gagnon and Ciesynski, and looked at the scene photos.

The victim had been tied up with her own shoelaces. She was lying adjacent to a homeless camp.

The medical examiner identified her as Denise Harris.

Ciesynski and Gagnon spoke to Harris' boyfriend, James Cooper. He told them that Denise was a preschool teacher, but was currently unemployed. She had a crack cocaine problem, he told them.

For the next few weeks, Ciesynski and Gagnon followed up on leads, and as is often the case, none of them had anything to do with her murder.

Saturday, January 10th, 1998 was an unusually cold day in the Seattle area. The normal temperature for that time of year is in the high thirties or low forties, but that day, it didn't get much above ten degrees. It's almost never that cold.

My oldest son, Casey was wrestling for Illahaee Junior High.
That day was the tournament for the district championship.
We'd just arrived there when my pager went off. I was next-up
for a murder, so I knew what to expect. I called the office.

Don Cameron was still my sergeant.

"I'm just giving you a heads up," he said. "We're headed to a
scene in the 1100 block of Airport Way South. There's a woman
there with her throat cut."

"I'm guessing she didn't cut her own throat," I told him. "I'm
on my way."

"I have to go to work," I told Doreen.

The district tournament is a pretty big deal in junior high, and
Casey was one of the better wrestlers. As so often happened,
the job got in the way of family events.

When I arrived, Cameron was there, along with John Boatman
and Gene Ramirez. They'd been working in the office when the
call came in. Everyone was bundled up and freezing their asses
off.

I walked up to Boatman. John had been in Homicide a long
time, and was a good detective. He pointed down the exterior
stairwell of a business.

The body of a Native woman lay at the bottom of the stairs,
surrounded by blood, severe cuts to her throat and hands, left
there with all the deference given a discarded soda can.

"Two local transients were walking by this morning. They were
going to go down the stairwell, but saw someone was already
down there. They walked away. When they came back by here
a couple hours later, they saw that she hadn't moved. They
looked closer and saw blood. They went over to William Booth
House," (a nearby Department of Corrections halfway house),
"and called the police. They say they didn't go down the stairs,
but one of them has blood on him."

I walked to a nearby patrol car. The transient with blood on him was sitting in the back seat. I talked to the patrol officer whose car it was.

"Take him to the Homicide office," I said. "I'll be there in a bit to interview him."

The victim's shoes were partially unlaced.

A young patrol officer guarded the scene. I'd never met him. He introduced himself as Al Cruise. Cruise later become a Homicide detective himself, and we would work in the same squad for years.

Richard Harruff is a Forensic Pathologist with the Medical Examiner's office. A small-statured man with thick glasses and an acerbic wit, death and dying is his life study. He holds both an MD and a PHD. He's a brilliant man.

He and Investigator Arlee Markey arrived, bundled against the chill.

Harruff began his preliminary examination at the scene, his eyes poring over the lifeless corpse of our as yet-unidentified victim, two deep slashes to her throat and right cheek, the wounds on her arms telling the story of her desperate, but futile attempt at survival.

Despite the bitter cold, her core body temperature was still pretty warm; she'd been killed overnight.

"We'll post her Monday," he told me as they loaded her body into the truck.

I looked across Airport Way, on the western edge of the Jungle.

"This is really close to where Ciesynski and Gagnon's victim was found," I said to Don Cameron. "Her shoe laces were partially undone. This could be a serial killer."

I went to the office to interview William Gilmer, the transient with blood on his clothing, and the palm of his hand. He also had a swollen lip.

"How'd you get the blood on you?" I asked.

"I was in a fight earlier this morning," he said.

"Did you go down the stairwell when you found the victim?" I asked.

"No, we just looked from the top. We didn't go down at all."

"So there's no way that's her blood on you?"

"No, there's no way," he said.

"I'm going to have to swab the blood on your skin and take your outer clothing," I told him.

"That's no problem," he said.

After completing those tasks, I gave him a jumpsuit to wear, and drove him back to William Booth Center, and then rushed back to the wrestling tournament.

As I walked into the gym, I saw Casey's hand being raised by the referee. I stood by the side of the mat. When he walked off, I told him how well he'd wrestled.

I hadn't seen a second of it.

On Monday morning, Nordlund and I went to the Medical Examiner's office. At that time, it was in the basement on the south side of Harborview Medical Center, the regional trauma center; it was a dark and dank place.

At the rear of the office, a stairway led up to the autopsy suite. By the first two steps, it was evident if there was a decomp case that day; you could smell it from there. On Mondays, there almost always was. The bodies were stacked like cordwood from the weekend.

The autopsy was well underway when we walked in. The victim had been cleaned up, so her wounds were much more visible. They were gaping and vicious. Harruff confirmed his scene findings; two slashes to the throat, with defensive wounds to her hands and arms. She also suffered seven stab wounds to her chest and buttocks.

She had a tattoo on her left hand. It said, "Forrest."

She was identified by fingerprints as Olivia R. Rocha, a known crack cocaine user with a history of prostitution. No surprise there. She was a little over a month short of her 28th birthday. She had a warrant out for her arrest.

Her last known address was 517 3rd Ave. That address is across the street from the King County Courthouse, and a block away from where police headquarters was at the time. It's the Downtown Emergency Services Center, a shelter and generic address used by many of Seattle's homeless population.

Crack-dependent prostitutes are ready-made victims, controlled by their addiction like a mouse in the talons of a raptor, on a glorious flight to certain doom.

We ran her name in the computer systems and found that she was the victim of an assault last year. The suspect was listed as Forrest Britt.

Her last known address was in West Seattle. I drove to her home and found a dysfunctional family who hadn't seen her in days. Devastated by her death, they had no idea who could have done this. They told us that her real name was Olivia Smith.

Forrest Britt had a felony warrant outstanding for his arrest. I put a bulletin out asking that he be arrested for the warrant, and that we be notified when that happened.

We contacted Britt's Community Corrections Officer. He told us the felony warrant out for Britt stemmed from an incident in which Olivia Smith alleged that Britt had threatened her with a knife.

I was intrigued.

I was in the office on Sunday, February 1st. At 5:44 PM that afternoon the main phone line rang. It was the Chief Dispatcher. East Precinct units were at the scene of a suspicious dead body on South Poplar Place, just south of Dearborn Street.

It was just beginning to get dark when I arrived; a fine mist of rain fell.

Greg McFadden, my academy classmate, was the primary patrol officer on the scene. The patrol sergeant was Fred Jordon.

"The guy who called is a transient," he said. "He was walking behind these buildings looking for cans and bottles, when he came across a skeleton."

He led me behind the warehouse that abutted Interstate 90. We got to the back, down a bank from the freeway. He shined his light on a spot.

"It's right there."

I looked at the spot lit by the flashlight.

"I can't see anything."

Skeletal remains are like camouflage. They're easy to miss, especially when enveloped in vegetation.

"See right there?" Greg asked. "There's the shirt, and there's the skull."

In the early nineties there were posters that became kind of a fad. When you first looked at them, you saw nothing but a pattern. But as you stared at the image, a three-dimensional picture suddenly appeared. That's what happened to me at this scene. The red plaid shirt came into view, followed by a skull, a gag through its gaping mouth, perhaps reflecting the silent scream that was the final moments of her existence on earth, the skeletal arms and legs tied behind her back with shoelaces.

I called other detectives to the scene. Don Cameron came, along with Nordlund, John Boatman and Gene Ramirez.

Dr. Paul Spence and Investigator Jane Jorgenson arrived from the Medical Examiner's Office.

Since it was a skeletal find, Kathy Taylor, a forensic anthropologist, also responded.

Taylor was nearing the completion of her PHD in Forensic Anthropology. She was, (and still is) the person for bones. She's now Dr. Kathy Taylor. She works out of KCMEO, but is the Forensic Anthropologist for the entire state of Washington.

When K.T., as we call her, is on a skeleton find, she is completely into it. This case was no different. She was on her knees before the skeleton, reaching underneath, feeling around, reaching back underneath, feeling around more. About the third time she stuck her arms under the victim and pulled them back out a huge rat scurried from the hole she'd been reaching in. She screamed, everyone jumped, and I almost pissed myself laughing. Cameron took her hand and counted her fingers.

"If that rat had bitten you," I said, "you'd be getting shots for the next two years."

Once all that excitement died down, I approached Don Cameron.

"This victim was tied up with her shoelaces, just like Ciesynski and Gagnon's victim," I said. "And Olivia Smith's shoes were unlaced. All three scenes are within one square mile. I'm telling you, this is a serial murderer."

This murder was originally assigned to Gene Ramirez and John Boatman.

The next morning, I met with Ciesynski and Gagnon. I told them my theory that the cases were related. They agreed.

Ciesynski and Gagnon agreed that we should join our investigations.

The skeletal victim was identified as Toinette Jones. She had a history of drug use and prostitution. Though she hadn't been seen for a month, and was the mother of small children, no one had reported her missing. Her friends and family just assumed she'd gone on another bender, like she had several times before, and that she'd eventually show up.

Ciesynski approached me in mid-April.

"I've got this guy calling from the jail," he said. "He's in custody for a robbery. He claims to have information on the Denise Harris case. His name is Dewayne Lee Harris."

Ciesynski and Greg Mixsell went to the jail and checked Harris out, bringing him back to our office.

I wasn't there when Ciesynski talked to Harris the first time. Mike told me what he'd said.

"He said he was there when Denise Harris, (no relation) was killed. He claims the killer is a guy named Mike Smith. He said Smith tied her up and strangled her in his presence.

"Harris mentioned that he'd hit his head on a branch with a beer can crushed on it. There was a can crushed on a branch right above where Denise was found, so he was definitely there."

"Mike Smith?" I said. "What a bullshit name. He's either lying about the killer's name, or he's the killer."

"I was thinking the same thing," Mike said.

A few days later, Harris called Ciesynski from the jail again.

"He said he knows where another one of Mark Smith's victims was," Ciesynski said. "He said it's near Goodwill off of Dearborn."

That was where Toinette Jones was found.

Mike and I went to the Regional Justice Center in Kent where Harris was housed. We checked him out. Without us saying anything, he led us directly to the Toinette Jones scene.

We took him to the rear of the warehouse. He pointed out that the fence had been cut, (we'd cut it away while processing the scene). He accurately pointed out where Jones' body was, and the position of the body.

We took him back to the Homicide office.

"I have to go to a doctor's appointment," I told Ciesynski. "I'll be back afterward to work this."

I drove to my appointment near my home in the suburbs. I was in the exam room. My doctor was taking my blood pressure when my pager went off. It was one of those text-pagers we carried back then, before cell phones and text messages. Shannon Sharpe, our administrative specialist was paging me.

"Get here quick! Mike's guy is confessing to killing Denise Harris!"

"Holy shit!" I yelled startling the doctor. "Sorry Doc, I have to go. I've got a guy confessing to being a serial killer!"

I grabbed my things and ran out of the office, buttoning up my shirt as I left, and raced back downtown.

When I got to the office, Harris was still in the interview room. Ciesynski was standing outside.

"He had his head down when I walked in," Mike said. "He told me, 'Mikey-Mike, I'm tired. I've been killing all my life. I killed that girl, the one off Dearborn and the girl in the stairwell. I killed some you don't even know about.'"

I interviewed him about Smith's murder.

"Tell me about the weather that night." I said.

"It was cold as fuck," he said.

"I didn't know that girl," he continued. "I told her I'd give her crack for sex, so she went down the stairs with me. Once she was down there, she was trapped. I had my baby-spot. I was gonna choke her ass out, but she pulls a knife on me, and cuts my fuckin' finger."

89

When Harris spoke, his normal tone was conversational; even pleasant. But when he started talking about his kills, he took on a guttural tone. His eyes flared, and he had a look on his face, like talking about the act he was reliving it.

"I took that fuckin' knife from her, and cut her fuckin' throat!"

"Did you cut her throat once, Dewayne?" I asked.

"I cut her fuckin' throat two times!" he said.

That's what I needed. Corroboration from him of what happened which matched the evidence that the Medical Examiner found. Now I knew he really did it, and wasn't just trying to confess to a crime he didn't commit to make himself sound like a bad-ass.

We drove Harris past the area of the Olivia Smith murder. As we passed the building, Harris gestured at the stairwell where Smith's body had been found.

"That's where I killed that bitch, right there," he said.

Later, blood we'd collected from the stair rail was matched by DNA to DeWayne, as well as semen from Smith's vaginal vault.

"What did you do next, Dewayne?" I asked.

"I had to go to the hospital, but I couldn't go here," he said. "So I took a Greyhound to Portland. Then I took a city bus to Vancouver. I flagged down a police car and told them somebody stabbed me in the finger. They took me to a hospital there, and they stitched me up. The weather was so bad; I was locked in the hospital for a long time."

We were later able to find the records of him getting his finger stitched up on Vancouver on January 10th, while we were at the murder scene, freezing our butts off.

Harris said that his "Nana", who ended up being his girlfriend's grandmother, drove him to the Greyhound station for the bus ride to Portland.

Prosecutors Jeff Baird, Roger Davidheiser, and I met with Nana, whose real name was Mollie McMillan. She admitted that Harris showed up at her house that morning with a cut finger. He told her he'd killed someone, and asked for a ride to the bus station. She gave him one.

She said her son, Timothy McMillan, was home at the time.

We tracked Timothy down.

"DeWayne knocked on my door that morning," he said. "He told me he'd killed someone, and cut his hand. He had a yellow glove on it. It was bleeding pretty bad."

"Did you believe him when he said he'd killed someone?" I asked.

"Yeah," he said. "He's told me he killed other people before."

"Did you ever consider calling the police when he told you things like that?" I asked.

"No," he said. "That never occurred to me."

Incredible.

Later, I interviewed Harris about Toinette Jones.

He described meeting her and telling us how he led her to the area along I-90. He was describing the process of finding the correct spot.

"She was like, in front of me. At this time here…"

"Again, all this time, you had a plan."

"What?" he asked.

"I'm just trying to clarify this. It wasn't like you were just wandering around looking for a place to do dope."

"Naw."

"You had a specific plan."

"Yup," he said laughing.

"Once again, what was that plan?"

"Murder, man! Murder, murder, murder, murder!"

I saved that audio clip. It's the most chilling statement I'd gotten in my entire career.

Harris told us that he had help with the Toinette Jones murder. He told us that he'd been with a guy who went by the street name, Wild, Wild Wes.

"Like the gunfighter," Harris told us.

Harris talked about killing Jones.

"I gets her over the fence, then I fucked her ass!" he said. "I was gettin' ready to choke her ass out, and she says, 'Y'all don't have to do this. I got babies at home!' but I didn't want to hear that bullshit. I told her, 'You tell it to Jesus when you see him in a minute.' Then I choked her ass out until her eyes bulged, and she pissed herself. Then I knew she was dead!"

As it turned out, we knew who "Wild, Wild Wes" was; an older, burned-out crackhead. We picked him up and brought him to our office, putting him in an interrogation room.

"Wes," I told him. "We have information that you were at the scene of a murder we're investigating."

Wes's eyes opened up wide. He wailed and fell to the floor in a fetal position.

"No! No! No! No!" he yelled.

Just as suddenly, he looked up at us from the floor, and in a conversational tone, said, "But I'll say I was, if you want me to."

We helped him up from the floor and led him out the front door of headquarters.

We ended up taping hours of interviews with Harris as we drove around, giving him the opportunity to show us other scenes where he claimed to have killed. He took us to a couple actual murder scenes, but didn't know enough about the murders to make us believe he did them.

During these road trips, he'd quote Frost.

"The woods are dark, and the woods are deep. Miles to travel before I sleep."

On one of those road trips, we put him in the back of the minivan we were in. I jumped in next to him. I had a sawed-off Remington 870 across my lap.

"Cloyd, why you got that shotgun?" he asked, laughing.

"Well, Dewayne," I said, laughing with him, "If you try to run, I'm going to kill you with it."

He laughed, and I laughed for a second, but then, serious as a heart attack, I said, "I'm not kidding.

The smile was instantly gone from his face.

"Oh."

Harris talked about killing up in the Jungle.

"Why do you take your victims to the Jungle?" we asked.

Harris got an evil look on his face.

"No one can hear you scream up there."

While this was going on, Don Cameron continued denying that this was a serial killer, even though we had confessions with corroborating information.

At one point, he walked up to me.

"When you're through with that bullshit case, I have other work for you."

By that time, I'd had it. Big, tough Mr. Homicide. I walked up to him.

"Look, Don. You're my supervisor. If you have a problem with the way I'm doing my job, maybe you should have the balls to call me on it, instead of making snide remarks. Do you have a problem with the way I'm handling this case?"

Like always, he put his hands up, a sheepish look on his face.

"No, Cloyd. You're doing fine."

He was a paper tiger.

He probably still made remarks behind my back, but he never said them to my face again.

Harris talked about searching for victims.

"I troll for prey," he said.

"Who was your prey," I asked.

"A human," he said.

"So you're out looking for someone to kill?"

"Yup."

"If I let you walk out this door right now…" I said.

"You'd have four more body bags."

"Who's the Grim Reaper," I asked.

"I'm the Grim Reaper," he said.

One Friday afternoon, other guys in the unit were investigating an unrelated murder. They asked if we'd pick up a sixteen-year-old prostitute who was a witness. She was at her grandparent's house in Redmond.

Mike and I drove out there.

The grandparents had a really nice place. We spoke with them for a while. They were very nice people. We picked up their granddaughter and headed for downtown.

It was a Friday, rush hour. We were on the highway 520 floating bridge across Lake Washington. I was driving, and Mike was the passenger, while she sat in the back seat. '

Mike was making small talk with her.

"You've got really nice grandparents who care about you. You should get off the street," he told her. "It's really dangerous out there. Have you had anything scary happen to you?"

"Yes I have," she said. "I got picked up by this guy named Chilly Willy. He tied me up with my shoelaces. I thought he was gonna kill me, but I was able to get away, and I ran naked down the street!"

I just about drove the car off the bridge. What the fuck?

This girl had been picked up by our serial killer, and had managed to escape alive! What are the odds that Mike and I would be the ones picking her up when she told this story?

The next day, we checked Harris out of the jail again. We asked about her. He admitted trying to kill her. In his guttural tone, he told us how frustrated he was that he didn't get the chance.

Harris was originally from Boston. He claimed to have killed people there before moving to Seattle.

We called Boston Police Homicide in an attempt to identify cases there he may have been responsible for.

We put Harris on the phone with the Boston detective. They spoke a few times over a couple days, but the Boston detective couldn't find cases Harris was talking about, though he admitted that the record keeping for the era Harris spoke of was not good.

Harris was all-in. He'd confessed to murders we could convict him of. He wanted to be a much bigger deal than he was. I thought he may be trying to embellish his kill number.

Finally, field trips with DeWayne came to an end. In the fall of 1998, it was time to go to trial.

The case was prosecuted by Jeff Baird and Barbara Flemming. Harris was represented by John Hicks.

Hicks is a private attorney who takes state-appointed cases. He's a soft-spoken, competent defense attorney.

The trial judge was Marsha Pechman. It was one of the last cases she tried in Superior Court before being appointed to the Federal bench.

For Harris, the trial was show time. He had frequent outbursts in the courtroom in front of the jury.

He claimed he was being persecuted for his Islamic faith. He told the court, "With Jesus as my witness, I'm a Muslim."

You can't make this stuff up.

I sat at the prosecution table, a few feet from Harris. When trial was in session one day, he picked up a chair and hurled it across the courtroom. The jail guards tackled him to the floor. As they were putting handcuffs on him, he glanced up at me and winked.

Another day, the court took a recess. Before the guards took him away, I saw him leaning in, having quiet, but animated conversation with Hicks, his attorney. Hicks' face turned red.

After he was taken away, only Hicks and I were in the courtroom.

"John," I said. "Did he threaten you?"

Hicks' face reddened again.

"That son of a bitch," he said. "If he comes anywhere near me, I have a gun!"

"Wow," I said. "That's like that movie, *Cape Fear*. You don't think that could really happen, do you John?"

I know how to pull Hicks' chain.

It was obvious that the jury was deathly afraid of Harris. Judge Pechman told him if there were any further outbursts, she would remove him from the courtroom. It didn't take long before he did it again.

True to her word, Pechman ordered him from the courtroom. A small storage room down the hall was set up with closed-circuit television. Harris was appointed a second counsel, Michael Danko, who sat in the room with Harris. Danko had a portable radio. Hicks wore an earphone, so Danko could relay anything Harris wanted him to know. I think Hicks liked the arrangement much more than Danko did.

When the jury left the courtroom, they passed this storeroom. One afternoon as they filed by, Harris yelled from inside, "Jurors! I'm being held against my will!"

Just before Christmas, the case went to the jury. He was quickly convicted of three counts of First Degree Murder, and one count of Attempted First Degree Murder.

The jurors were so disturbed by what they heard in the trial, they asked the court to appoint them psychological counselors. The court agreed.

After Harris had been lead away, and the jury was dismissed, Baird and Flemming were gathering their things. Baird suggested we go to the Merchant's Café, (the oldest bar in Seattle) for a beer. Ciesynski and I were all in. I looked over at Hicks, dejectedly putting his papers in a brief case.

"John, why don't you go have a beer with us?"

"What?" he said, a little surprised.

"Come on, go have a beer with us."

"Okay," he said.

We all walked three blocks to the bar. We were seated at a table.

"John," I said, "Mike and I appreciate the job you did; you vigorously defended Harris, but you didn't play any silly games. I got you something."

I handed him a wrapped gift. Instead of a bow, I tied it up with shoelaces.

Hicks looked surprised. He took the gift smiling, his face reddening again.

"Open it," I said.

He did. It was a video of the original *Cape Fear* starring Gregory Peck.

"Oh, shit!" Hicks said, laughing. He knocked his beer all over us.

Hicks and I are still friends today.

10

Greg Mixsell and I became partners in October of 1997. We'd asked to work together. We'd both come to Homicide at about the same time and knew we'd work together well. Late that month we were called to a murder about one in the morning.

The case had all the makings of a loser, with little or nothing to go on.

A security guard worked at a building in Pioneer Square downtown. He saw two people fighting on a corner. He thought one guy was punching another man. The man being punched fell to the ground. The other guy walked away.

The guy who'd gotten punched didn't get up. The guard thought he may have been seriously hurt, and called for medic.

The guard had been correct. The guy was seriously hurt. In fact, he was dead. He'd been stabbed repeatedly.

The guard had been more than a block away at night. He could only say that the person who stabbed the victim had been male. Nothing else.

A bus was stopped at a layover a block in the other direction. The driver also saw the fight, but didn't have any more to add.

We spent the first couple days trying to identify the victim. His name was Henry Burr, but we didn't find much more.

A couple days later, my phone rang. The caller wanted to remain anonymous.

"The killer is Mike. He hangs out at a hotdog stand near First Avenue South and Washington Street Friday and Saturday night after ten."

Guess where we were that Friday night?

We walked up to the hotdog stand. A guy stood behind the cart. He wasn't Mike. There was no one else there.

"Where's Mike?" I asked.

"He was around here a minute ago," he said, looking around.

"Oh, here he comes."

He pointed across First Avenue. A guy was crossing the street in the crosswalk. His head was down, not paying attention.

We waited on the corner until he reached our side of the street.

"Hey Mike!" I said.

He looked at us.

"Yeah?"

I held up my badge.

"Seattle Police. You don't have any weapons on you, do you?"

I patted him down. There was a glass crack pipe in his pants pocket, with residue in it.

"Gee, that looks like dope. You're under arrest."

I put handcuffs on him, and we put him in the back of our car, which had been parked at the corner. I got in the back seat next to him. Greg drove, heading to the office.

"What's this about?" he asked.

"Mike," I said, smiling. "You know what this is about! You're hoping it's not; but it is."

His face blanched.

In the office, we placed him in an interview room. After a few minutes, we went in.

"Mike, you've been identified as the guy who stabbed Henry. We just want to hear your side of the story."

No one could identify him. I was bluffing, but he didn't know that.

"I think maybe I need a lawyer," he said.

"Fine. If you want a lawyer, we're out of here," I said. "We're not interested in your side of the story. We're just going to book you for murder."

We got up and started for the door.

"Wait!", he said. (I knew he would.) He was shaking, deciding what to do. We stood there, expressionless.

"It was self-defense!"

"Look," I said. "Do you want a lawyer, or not?"

"No," he said. "I'll talk to you."

His story was that the victim attacked him with his gym bag. We had the bag. There was only clothing in it.

"Mike," I said, shaking my head. "You had all this time, and that's the best story you could come up with?"

We booked him into jail.

As I often say, we don't get the smart ones. If he'd stuck with his request for an attorney, we wouldn't have had enough to hold him.

At trial, his attorney moved to suppress his statement. His motion was denied, and Mike Adam pled guilty to murder.

Greg and I were on call in late December, 1998. A patrol officer called the office from the Carolyn Downs Medical Clinic in the Central Area of Seattle.

A young woman named Heidi Davis had come in to the clinic bleeding from her vagina. She was examined by a doctor who determined that she'd recently given birth. He asked her where the baby was. She didn't respond, so the police were called.

Davis had been brought to the clinic by her grandmother; she denied any knowledge that her granddaughter had even been pregnant.

Davis' grandmother gave the officers permission to search her house. Davis' aunt was at the house and let the officers in. They went to the basement area where Davis's room was. In a garbage can in a laundry room they found the body of a fully-developed baby boy, wrapped in a clear plastic bag which had been tied shut.

I arrived and went to the basement and looked in the can. The baby was curled in a fetal position, one hand in a fist by his face, perhaps put there as he desperately gasped for air, looking every bit like a sleeping newborn, except the purple color of his skin.

I've always been a hardened detective. Very little bothers me. I look at a mangled human body with all the passion of a mechanic examining a broken transmission. You can't do this job if you don't think that way. The exception is kids. I was in "work-mode" at that point, but later, after I got home, it got to me. I dealt with it, but I hated it. Kids are the ultimate helpless victims.

It pisses me off.

The Medical Examiner arrived at the scene. Dr. Dan Straathof was the pathologist along with the Investigator, Bill McClure.

Straathof told me he'd do the autopsy the next day.

Heidi Davis was eighteen-years-old. She'd been transferred to Providence Hospital, now called Swedish Cherry Hill Hospital, a few miles away. Mixsell and I went there to speak with her.

"We found the baby," I said.

"I only found out I was pregnant a week ago," she said. "I thought I was having cramps. I was on the toilet when the baby fell out. I cleaned his face and laid in bed with him. I woke up in the middle of the night, and he was dead."

The next day, she put the body in the plastic bag and tied it off dumping it in the trash like left over pizza. She went upstairs to watch Wheel of Fortune on TV.

She said that her aunt knew she had the baby and saw it.

We spoke to the aunt. She adamantly denied that she knew anything about a baby, or ever having seen him.

I placed Davis under arrest for murder. We had an officer guard her until she could be discharged and then booked into jail.

Richard Harruff assisted with the autopsy the next day. He was able to determine that the victim, known only as "Baby Boy Davis" had drawn breaths after birth, and had suffocated in the bag.

I was back in the office, when my phone rang. It was a girl who was a friend of Heidi Davis.

She wanted to talk. I went to meet her.

She was also eighteen, like Davis. They'd known each other from school. I could tell, she felt guilty about what she knew, and that she hadn't done anything before this happened.

"She told me she was pregnant," the girl said. "She didn't want the baby. She told me she was going to get rid of it.

"I begged her to let me have the baby! I told her I'd adopt it. She told me she wouldn't hurt the baby."

The friend was devastated. I felt sorry for her, but couldn't help but think to myself, if she'd just told someone, the baby would be alive today.

Kathy Goater was a prosecutor in the Special Assault Unit of the King County Prosecutor's office. Among other things, they prosecute child abuse cases. She and I discussed the case.

I respect Kathy a lot, but she wanted to have a philosophical discussion with me about the case. She hinted that this case was akin to abortion.

I didn't want to hear any of that bullshit. This was a premeditated murder. I thought it should be filed as a Murder in the First Degree.

"There's a professor at Princeton, Peter Singer," she said. "He thinks parents should be able to kill their child after birth if they decide they don't want it."

"Hitler probably had similar thoughts," I said. "What some sociopath at Princeton thinks has no bearing on the law."

Kathy is much more liberal than I am. Ultimately, she charged Davis with Murder 2, a charge usually levelled in a case where a murder is committed with no premeditation. This was planned in advance, and I believed should have been filed as Murder 1, a more serious crime.

Several weeks later, I was home on a day off. I had the news playing on a radio, when I heard a story about this case. It reported that Heidi Davis had pled guilty to Manslaughter in the Second Degree, which is the lowest level of criminal homicide in Washington State.

I went ape-shit.

Normally when the prosecutor is considering allowing a defendant to plead to a lower charge, they call the victim's family and the case detectives to get their input. Neither happened in this case.

Mark Larsen is the Chief Criminal Deputy at the prosecutor's office. He's a friend. We'd prosecuted murders together before. I called him at his office. It went to voice mail. I left him an expletive-ridden message. I asked him how the fuck let this had happened without my input.

A while later, I got a call from Scott O'Toole, another friend of mine in the prosecutor's office. He apologized. He was out of town when this happened. Jim Rogers, whom I didn't know at the time, but would later become a friend and a Superior Court Judge, had covered for him and didn't realize no one had spoken to me. Rogers was traveling in Europe.

I'd made quite a splash. A short time later, Rogers called me from Europe, falling all over himself apologizing. He said he didn't realize no one had spoken to me. I'd calmed down by that time, and told him I appreciated the call.

Davis was to be sentenced in a couple weeks by Judge Carol Schapira, with an agreed recommendation of three years in prison.

I knew very little about Judge Schapira, other than she had a reputation of going a little light on sentences for convicted criminals. I decided to write her a letter.

Judge Schapira,

I am one of the investigating detectives in the murder of Baby Boy Davis.

Soon, you will hold a sentencing hearing for Heidi Davis, who killed Baby Boy Davis.

This will not be like most sentencings.

There will be no victim impact statements; no tearful testimony from friends or family about how the death of Baby Boy Davis adversely effected their lives.

Baby Boy Davis was never cuddled. He was never loved. He wasn't even given a name.

There is no one to stand up for him.

Most murder victims do something to make their deaths at the hands of a murderer more likely, through choices that they made; at their lifestyle, or some other factor.

Baby Boy Davis played no part in his death save being conceived in the womb of a psychopath; someone who couldn't be bothered; who ignored friend's pleas not to go through with this. She opted to throw him away, like yesterday's trash. To slowly suffocate in a plastic bag in the bottom of a garbage can, just after the Christmas season.

Normally, when a plea-agreement is made, the prosecutor's office consults with the case detective. Because of a misunderstanding, that didn't happen in this case. Had it happened, I assure you, I would not have agreed to this plea.

I ask that you give Heidi Davis the highest sentence under the law for this heinous crime.

Detective Cloyd Steiger.

Doreen and I attended the sentencing a couple weeks later. No one there spoke for the victim. Judge Schapira invited me to speak. I addressed the court, reiterating what I said in the letter.

Judge Shapira said she was moved by my letter. Instead of three years, she sentenced Davis to over eight; the maximum sentence for Manslaughter 2.

Davis' public defender wasn't happy. He wasn't a bad guy, but I didn't give a shit. She still got about fifteen years less in prison than she should have.

In June of 1999, I was driving in Rainier Valley when a call came over the police radio. A hysterical man was calling. He'd found his mother and sister dead in the Mount Baker neighborhood. My ears perked up.

My instinct was to drive to the scene of a call like that, but we usually wait for patrol cars to respond, assess the scene and if

106

they want Homicide units to respond, they'll call. I slowly drove toward the address, and called my office on the phone to let them know what was going on.

About a minute after the call was dispatched, the first patrol cars arrived on the scene. Shortly thereafter, they said they needed Homicide. I arrived a couple minutes later.

I met with the first officers on the scene. They'd found three people dead inside the house. Two adult women and a female child. An infant was in a crib, unharmed. They took him from the house and he was being examined by medics, but appeared okay.

I went inside to look around.

The house was set up as a daycare, with kid's toys and paraphernalia everywhere, and cubby's where the kids could put their belongings, happy, colorful pictures adorning the walls in stark contrast to the horrific scene inside.

In a back bedroom, the body of a woman in her twenties sprawled across the bed, blood pooling on the comforter beneath her, a gunshot wound obvious in her head.

The body of an older woman lay at the foot of the bed, also dead from gunshot wounds, her arms wrapped around a little girl in a futile attempt to save her from the same fate.

All the victims were dressed in bedclothes, the attack seemingly coming during the night.

The woman on the bed was Artis Ingram, the mother of the dead little girl, Champagne Younger. The older woman was Ingram's mother, Patricia Whitfield.

As the day wore on, we learned more about this daycare. Whitfield and Ingram ran it.

Parents dropped their children there that morning without going in themselves. The kids watched television until it was time to go to school, across the street. The kids told their parents the victims had been "sleeping".

107

As the investigation proceeded, we learned that Patricia Whitfield had been in a dispute with her brother, Melvin Johnson, over the settlement of their parent's estate.

Guess who just became suspect #1? We went looking for Johnson.

We spoke to friends of Johnson.

Johnson showed up at their house unexpectedly in the middle of the night. They asked where he'd been. He made a slashing motion across his throat with his finger.

He was our guy.

He lived in a large house with a sweeping view of Lake Washington. We got a search warrant to search the house.

He didn't have a job. We wondered how he could afford a house like that. He wasn't home when we entered, but we found our answer on the kitchen table. The house was a Section 8 rental. He paid seventy-five dollars a month to live there. The state paid the rest.

I'll bet the neighbors were thrilled.

We found a handgun in the daylight basement. Johnson was a convicted felon and precluded from owning a firearm. It wasn't the murder weapon; it was a different caliber. But finding the gun gave us probable cause to arrest him for being a felon in possession of a firearm.

This wasn't my case. I was just helping out. Steve Kilburg and Kevin O'Keefe were the primary case detectives.

The prosecutor on the case was a friend, but she was very reluctant to charge with the evidence we had.

I suggested she charge him for the Felon in Possession. That would buy us time to build a case against him. That's what happened.

Johnson was convicted of the weapons charge and sentenced to five years in prison.

Once he got to prison, he did what all stupid people do. He told other inmates that he'd killed his sister, niece and grand-niece. There is no honor among thieves. They were lining up at the payphones to drop the dime on this guy.

The case was finally charged a few years after it was committed. Johnson was convicted of all three murders. Because of his greed, he'd not only killed his sister and niece, but an innocent child. He was sentenced to the rest of his life in prison.

11

September 8th, 1999 was a Wednesday. It was my son, Landon's 12th birthday. We had a birthday party scheduled for that weekend, but I rushed home from work to be with him and celebrate.

By 8:30 or so, he was in bed. At about 9:30, my phone rang. It was Ed Striedinger.

"We have a homicide in the 5300 block of 46th Avenue South."

Greg and I were next up for a murder, so instead of relaxing before heading to bed, I was out the door, in my car driving to the scene.

Striedinger and my old partner, John Nordlund were at the scene.

"Patrol officers got the victim's identification before he was transported to Harborview," Nordlund told me. He handed me the card. "He was pronounced DOA when he got there."

The ID was for Franklin Lee Brown. He was a 41-year-old male, the same age as me.

"There are some witnesses across the street," Striedinger said, pointing to a house. Greg and I walked over there.

We met with Gerald Joshua, William Rickmon and Ken Whitson.

"We've known Franklin for some time," Joshua said. "He's lived in the neighborhood, and does handyman work. He's kind of a drunk, but he's friendly and a harmless guy."

"Frank came to the front door about nine o'clock," Rickmon told us. "He asked where his hopper was."

A hopper is a devise used in drywalling.

"I told him it was next door. We keep a lot of tools there, because this house is under renovation and isn't secure.

"Frank went downstairs," he continued, "and got some other stuff. He was only in here about ten minutes, and then he left out the front door. I thought he was going next-door to get the hopper. I was in the bathroom and I heard arguing outside. I couldn't tell what was being said, but then I heard a bunch of sounds that I thought were firecrackers. I went to the window and looked out. I saw the police pulling up, and then I heard Frank was shot."

We went to another house across the street from the scene. We spoke to Scooter Van Lieu.

"I was in the house and heard arguing outside," Van Lieu told us. "I went to the kitchen window and looked out. I saw Frank. I only met Frank a couple weeks ago. He was arguing with a guy I didn't recognize. He looked like a black guy. I couldn't hear what they were saying, but it was pretty heated.

"I saw another black guy standing south of Frank and the other guy. It looked like that guy was just watching the argument. He didn't get involved.

"I went out the kitchen door and came around the north side of my house. I tried to stay out of sight.

"I heard 'nigger this', and 'nigger that.' I think it was the black guy calling Frank a nigger.

"Then I saw the black guy pull a gun from the front of his waistband. He said, 'You're gonna die, nigger,' and then he pointed the gun at Frank and fired. Frank turned his back and the guy fired a bunch of shots at his back. After that, he and the other black guy who'd been watching ran south on 46th Avenue."

"What did the shooter look like?" I asked.

"Like I said, I think he was black. He was between twenty and twenty-five. He had long hair down to his shoulders, and his head was shaved on the sides. I think he may have been wearing Geri-curl, because his hair looked wet."

Michael Gray was with Van Lieu. We interviewed him as well.

"The other black guy that was with the shooter was younger, probably a teenager, with short black hair. He had a blue and gold football jersey on. I think it was number eighty. It looked like it could have been a Rams jersey.

"I saw that guy get out of a car before the shooting," he said. "It was a white, early 90's Buick Skylark-type car. There was a different guy driving, and a female in the front seat."

As we stood at the scene while it was processed, I glanced up at the house this happened in front of. The curtains were pulled back slightly. A young boy, about thirteen years-old peered out at us.

The next morning, I attended Brown's autopsy. He'd been shot one time in the side of the head. There were four perpendicular entrance and exit wounds that entered his chest and exited his back. That led us to believe that after the first shot, which immediately dropped Brown, the four coupe de grace shots had been pumped into him as he lay on the ground, his lifeblood streaming from him.

After the autopsy, Mixsell and I, along with prosecutor James Konat, returned to the scene.

Konat was one of the best prosecutors I'd ever worked with. He commanded a courtroom. His style was animated and entertaining. If your family member, God forbid, was ever murdered, Konat was the one you would want to prosecute the case. He also liked the nitty-gritty of homicide investigation. He wanted to be there when the doors were kicked in, and the chase was on. I think he secretly wanted to be a Homicide Detective instead of a prosecutor.

We went to the spot where Franklin Brown died. We brought shovels and other tools. We peeled back the layer of sod from the planting strip, then slowly dug down until we found them. Four spent bullets, in nearly pristine condition. They were fired directly into the ground; proof that after Franklin Brown was already mortally wounded, the shooter stood over him and fired four more rounds into him.

As we gloated over our find, I looked up at the house we were in front of again. I saw the living room curtain of this split-entry house pulled back ever so slightly again.

I walked up to the house and knocked on the door. A boy in his early-teens answered.

"You saw what happened, didn't you?" I asked.

"Yes."

"What did you see?"

He told me that he'd heard loud voices in front of his house the night before. He snuck around the side of the house and beside a car parked in his driveway. He recognized Brown. He heard a guy he didn't know say, "Are you calling me a nigger?"

Brown said, "I'm not calling you anything."

The other guy said, "Nobody calls me nigger!" pulled out a gun. He held it up to Brown's head.

Brown repeated, "I didn't call you anything."

The guy shot Brown, who dropped to the ground immediately. The guy then stood over Brown and pumped several more rounds into him.

"Do you know the shooter?" I asked.

"No," he said. "But I know the younger black guy that was with him. He lives just around the corner."

I put the kid in my car. I drove around the corner.

"Just point to his house when we pass it." I said.

As we passed a house, he pointed to it.

"He lives there."

I drove back around the block and dropped him at his house.

We went back and knocked on the door. Ronald Banks answered the door. We took him downtown to the Homicide office.

I put him in an interview room. I asked him about the shooting. He denied knowing anything about the shooting.

On TV shows, when the detective is interviewing a suspect, there's often a lot of yelling and pounding on the table. In real life, that almost never happens in a suspect interview. The interview can be intense, but in a different way.

This guy wasn't the suspect.

The kind of interview I just described is really for guys just like this. Witnesses who don't want to tell what they know.

The interview with Banks was rather animated. He continued to deny knowledge of the shooting, until I used my charming ways to get him to cooperate.

Finally, he relented.

"The guy goes by 'D' or 'Gameboy'. I think his real name is Devon."

"How do you know him?" I asked.

"Last summer, people used to be in the alley behind my house. That's where I met him.

"I think he just got out."

"Just got out of what?" I asked.

"Out of jail, or juvenile, or something," he said.

"So you just started hanging out with him?"

"Yes."

"How often do you hang out with him?"

"About every two weeks or so."

"Is he a gang-banger?" I asked.

"Yes."

"What gang does he claim?"

"I don't know," he said. "He's a Crip, but I don't know what kind."

"So let's talk about yesterday," I said. "What were you doing?"

"I was walking from Chuck's, (grocery store). I had some chicken and I was walking by a friend's house and D was sitting outside."

"Why don't you describe Devon."

"I don't know what race he is," he said. "He could be Mexican or Samoan."

"How tall is he?"

"He's about six-two."

"How much do you think he weighs?"

"A bill-fifty."

"How does he wear his hair?"

"Usually in a ponytail."

"Tell me what happened when you saw him," I said.

"I told him I was going to Jason's house."

"Jason who?"

"Jason Whiten."

"Where does Jason live?"

"47th and Nelson."

"So what happened next?"

"I went to Jason's house, and about eight or eight-thirty, Devon knocked on Jason's door. I answered the door, and he had a forty (large beer) in his hand. He said, 'What's up?' He came in.

"We watched TV for a while, but nothing was on, so we decided to go to Chuck's."

"What were you going to do at Chuck's?" I asked.

"We were going to grab some more forties."

"Devon is old enough to buy beer for you?"

"Yeah."

"Then what happened?"

"We was just walking, and a car pulled up. A lady was in it. She wanted to buy some drugs."

"What kind of car was it?"

"A dark blue Dodge Dynasty."

"Why would she think you were selling drugs?" I asked.

"Cause we was walking down the street."

"Does that happen a lot in your neighborhood?"

"Yeah."

"What happened next?"

"He was a house or two ahead of me, and all of the sudden, he's running through Franklin's pockets."

"So you knew Franklin?"

"Yeah. He cuts my yard."

"Did you get along with him?"

"Yeah. We talked every day."

"Did Devon say anything to Franklin about what he was looking for?"

"He asked Franklin if he had any money."

"Did you think he was going to jack him?" I asked.

"I didn't know. At the time, I didn't even know he had a gun."

"What did you do?"

"Me and Jason just kept walking past him, walking slowly. After we got past him, I kept telling Devon, 'Come on,'.

"Did he listen to you?"

"No, he didn't hear one word I said. Him and Franklin was arguing, and he was callin' Franklin a nigger."

"Is Franklin black?"

"No. He's white, I think."

"What happened next?"

"Franklin said he wasn't a nigger, and Devon said, 'Well I'm a nigger,' and then he pulled the gun out of his back pocket.

"I'm up the block then, and I'm yelling, 'Come on! Come on!' but he still ain't hearing me. He put the forty down before he pulled the gun, then he picks it up, so I think he's coming and I think Franklin said something to him, and he puts the forty down again and pulls the gun out again.

"I turn my back to walk away and I hear two gunshots, and I turns around I see a spark and I just run and as I'm running down the street, I hear like four more shots."

Next, we picked up Jason Whiten. Mixsell interviewed him. He told a story consistent with Banks.

We ran Devon Adams in the computer systems. His mother lived in Magnolia, an upper-middle class neighborhood in Seattle, and he had a girlfriend who lived in West Seattle. We got search warrants and went to both, but he wasn't there.

117

The next day, we got a call from Mike Danko, a local defense attorney.

"I have Devon Adams with me. I'm going to bring him to your office, so he can turn himself in. He's exercising his right to remain silent, and will not make a statement."

Danko arrived a short time later with Adams. We processed him and booked him into jail.

A couple days later, he was charged with Murder 1.

Several months later we went to trial. We were in Carol Shapira's courtroom, the same judge who'd handled the Heidi Davis infanticide case.

I was on the stand. During a break, Konat spoke to me.

"The defense is going to say you browbeat Ronald Banks into identifying the shooter," he said.

"Really?" I replied. "Why don't you ask me about it on the stand."

"What are you going to say?" he asked.

"Just ask me." I said.

Most prosecutors would insist that I tell them what I'm going to say. Konat and I are friends. We trust each other impeccably; we're both fly-by-the-seat-of-your-pants kind of guys.

"Okay," he said.

The break ended, and I was back on the stand. Konat resumed questioning me.

"Detective Steiger, when you first met Mr. Banks, was he cooperative with you?"

"No, he wasn't." I said.

"Was he willing to tell you what he knew about this case?"

"No, he wasn't."

"Well, did you say or do anything to get him to cooperate?"

"I told Ronald," I said, "If you tell me the truth, we can be friends for life. But if you lie to me even once, I'm going to fuck you like a big-dog."

The courtroom erupted with laughter, including the jury. The wind was taken from the defenses sails.

When I tell that story, people inevitably ask me, "Didn't you get in trouble for saying that?"

My answer is always, "I could have gotten in trouble for not saying that; it was the truth."

Later, I was being cross-examined by the defense. With that angle taken away, the defense attorney attacked me on several other fronts. We were engaged in back and forth wrangling, practically gnarling at each other.

As is often the case, the courtroom was full of high school students there on a field trip to observe the trial.

When my testimony was complete, the case was adjourned for the lunch break.

I spoke to Konat for a few moments before leaving the courtroom. When I did, I saw the defense attorney in the hallway, surrounded by the high school students who had been in the courtroom moments before.

As I passed, I reached in and shook his hand.

"Thanks, Mike," I said to him.

"Sure thing, Cloyd. See you next time."

The kids stood dumbfounded by what they saw. A moment ago, we'd been at each other's throats in the courtroom. Now we acted as though we were friends.

The truth is, we were friends. What happened in the courtroom was just business. It's not personal. I liken it to the old cartoons, where the sheepdog and coyote show up in the morning and punch in.

"Morning Sam."

"Morning Ralph".

Then they spend the day trying to kill each other.

Then at the end of the day, they punch out.

"See you tomorrow, Sam."

"Goodnight, Ralph."

About a year and a half later, I was in Denver with Mike Ciesynski on a case. We were returning to the airport to turn in our rental car and fly back to Seattle, when we heard that a 6.8 magnitude earthquake had struck at home. All flights to Seattle were cancelled. We were stuck in Denver.

We got a hotel near the airport.

The next day, we were back at the airport, trying to get a flight to Seattle. After about twelve hours, we boarded a plane for home.

As we boarded, I was walking through first class. A passenger called to me.

"Hey, you! Come here!"

As I approached he said, "Do you remember me?"

I had no idea who this guy was. I lied.

"You look familiar."

"I was on that jury, when you said you were going to fuck that guy like a big dog! That was great!"

12

I was in the office on a quiet Thursday morning in early November, 1999. I sipped coffee at my desk while I updated a report of a homicide I was investigating, when the peaceful, routine day went out the window.

The main phone line in the office rang. A moment later, one of the sergeants bellowed out.

"We've got a shooting at the Northlake Shipyard, 1441 North Northlake Way. Multiple victims are down."

I jumped in a car and headed that way, just across the Fremont Bridge on the north side of Lake Union. It was only a couple blocks from the Harbor Station, were all the police boats work from.

Four people had been shot. One was dead at the scene and others had been transported to Harborview. A second victim died shortly after arrival at the hospital. The shooter was gone.

The scene was chaotic; medics treated the wounded, patrol and SWAT officers, with their guns drawn, searched the area for the shooter, a large crowd of onlookers peering in. News cameras were everywhere.

According to witnesses, a man dressed in military fatigues entered the business armed with a semiautomatic handgun, and shot everyone he saw.

The interior of the business was equally chaotic. Blood-covered floors, chairs overturned, the body of the one victim pronounced dead at the scene, and medical debris left by medics desperately trying to save the lives of other victims.

Mike Ciesynski and Dick Gagnon were the primary detectives, but early on, everyone worked on the case.

Pandemonium raged around us. Department commanders, including the Chief of Police were outside, patrol and SWAT resources scrambled around, but our job was to bring things under control. Sometimes commanders with no investigation experience don't get that; running amok can only hurt the investigation. We have to slow everything down; do the investigation in a slow and meticulous manner.

One victim had seen the shooter, and was alert enough to work with a forensic artist to develop a sketch. We sent Betty Kincaid to Harborview to work with him. Once she developed a sketch, we released it to the media.

Mike Ciesynski came to me.

"I got a tip from a guy doing an L&I (Labor and Industries) investigation on a guy. He said the guy looks just like the composite sketch we put out. He's been recording this guy doing all kinds of physical work, and he's supposed to be disabled. They're going to deny his disability and he knew it.

"The investigator told me the guy claimed to have been injured while he worked at Northlake Shipyard. His name is Keven Cruz."

I gathered information about Cruz.

He lived with his mother, an airline employee. I checked him for warrants. He had none. When I ran is driver's license status, I found something very interesting.

"He renewed his license today," I told Ciesynski. "But his license wasn't expired and didn't need to be renewed."

I ordered his new driver's license photo from the Department of Licensing, as well as a copy of the photo from his old license.

His old photo showed him with shoulder-length black hair, just like the depiction of the shooter in the composite sketch. The new photo showed him with short hair.

What a coincidence.

I put a photomontage together including Cruz's photo with five other males of reasonably similar appearance. That evening, I went to Harborview to meet with a surviving victim.

The victim I met didn't know Cruz. He'd been at the shipyard that day for a meeting with the owner, and was in the wrong place at the wrong time.

I showed him the montage. He looked at all the photos carefully. He picked out a photo of Cruz, along with another photo that I'd chosen at random for the montage.

"It could be either of these guys," he said.

That's what we refer to as an equivocal pick. He didn't confidently choose the photo of Cruz, but neither did he eliminate the photo. A small twig on the pile, but not enough to act on.

The case went on for a few weeks. Cruz was still the primary suspect.

The foliage was falling off leaves in the area for the winter. A man walked past the Northlake Shipyard, and near a bushy area just up the street. The bush had been full of leaves on the day of the shooting, but they had fallen off since. When he looked over at the bushes on that day, he saw a gym bag. He opened it up. There was a gun inside; a 9mm semiautomatic pistol; the same type of weapon used in the shooting. He called the police.

There were other things in the bag too. Things associated with Kevin Cruz's mother and the airline where she worked.

We served a search warrant on Cruz's house.

In Cruz's bedroom, under his bed, we found an unfired 9mm cartridge.

123

The gun found in the bag was identified ballistically as the weapon used to commit the murders. Moreover, the live 9mm cartridge found under Kevin Cruz's bed was also tied to the gun. It had been cycled through the weapon, leaving its characteristic marks on the round.

Put a fork in it; it's done.

Cruz was charged with Aggravated Murder; the only crime in Washington State that carries with it the possibility of the death penalty.

Cruz was represented at trial by two attorneys. Tony Savage was an old-school defense attorney. He was respected by the police and prosecutors as a professional attorney who played no games.

His co-counsel, not so much. He was a true-believer, who took his adversarial relationship with the police and prosecutor personally. Most attorney's I've dealt with vigorously defend their clients, but in the end, it's only business.

During my testimony in the case, I was cross-examined by the co-counsel. He harped about me saying that Cruz had gotten a new driver's license the day after the shooting when he didn't need to.

"Why do you think that's important?" he asked.

"Are you asking me my opinion as to why that happened?" I asked.

"Yes," he replied.

"We'd just released to the public a sketch of the shooter with long hair that looked a lot like Kevin Cruz," I said. "I think he was trying to change his appearance so he didn't look like the sketch, and have identification that also didn't look like the sketch."

Stupid question.

Cruz put forth an insanity defense. He was convicted on all counts, but the jury could not agree unanimously that he should be sentenced to death. He was given life in prison without the possibility of parole.

13

Sometimes working these cases, names and faces come up more than once. Today's witness is tomorrow's suspect or victim. It happens all the time.

Early on Easter morning, 1995, I had been called along with other detectives to a murder scene in Yesler Terrace.

The Terrace is a housing project on First Hill, adjacent to Harborview Medical Center, overlooking downtown Seattle. It is made up of several buildings, originally built as housing for Boeing employees, particularly during World War II. Several "Rosie the Riveter" lived there with their families during the war effort.

After the war, they were taken over by the Housing Authority as subsidized housing. They became the projects.

This scene was an apparent domestic violence murder, though in this case, the woman killed the man, the opposite of what is usually the case.

Geraldine Hendrickson had stabbed her live-in boyfriend in the heart with a knife while he slept. He was transported a couple blocks to Harborview. He wasn't dead yet, but wasn't expected to survive.

We were at the scene a short time when we got the call from an officer at the hospital telling us that he'd been pronounced dead.

A short while later, we received another call. The reports of his death had been greatly exaggerated.

Still later, another call. He was dead.

"I know it's Easter and all," I said, "but is he dead or not?"

They assured us that he's not only clearly dead, he's clearly quite sincerely dead.

There was a Valentine's Day card on the refrigerator. It was from the victim to Geraldine. "I just love the shit out of you," was written inside.

How romantic.

This wasn't my case. Dick Gagnon was the primary detective, so my involvement ended after the first night.

At trial, Geraldine put forth a battered-women's defense. The jury convicted her of manslaughter.

In May of 1998, Greg Mixsell was working on a murder that happened in a Belltown apartment. Belltown is the north section of downtown Seattle, south of the Seattle Center, where the Space Needle is located.

A woman had been found in the common bathroom of a urine-soaked apartment building there. I hadn't been to the scene of this murder, but Greg asked me to help him with the case.

Some people in the building had a party. The victim was there. People saw her leave the apartment with a man. They found her unconscious in the bathroom. She was taken to Harborview by medics, but was pronounced dead.

The victim was Geraldine Hendrickson.

Karma's a bitch. If she'd been convicted of murder like she should have, she'd likely have been sentenced to more than twenty-years in prison and would still be alive.

The autopsy showed that she'd died of a crushed trachea. The guy who left the party with her was identified as Robert Wentz. We put the dogs out to find Wentz.

A couple days later, Wentz was picked up and brought to the Homicide office. We had him in the interview room.

"We were at the party, and she was going to have sex with me!" he said. "We went to the bathroom, and when we got in, she pulled a knife on me! She tried to stab me!" He held up his hand. There was a healing stab wound in the middle of his palm.

"I pushed her away and ran! I didn't even know she died!"

She'd apparently hit her throat on the edge of a claw-foot tub that was in the bathroom.

Mixsell and I left the interview room to talk about it.

"We do know she has a history of stabbing men," I told Greg. "And with the stab wound on his hand, I think he has a reasonable self-defense claim."

We let Wentz go. The prosecutor declined to prosecute.

In April of 2000, I was in court testifying in a murder trial. My cell phone was vibrating continually while I was on the stand. It was the end of the day, and soon I was off the stand. I called my office.

An elderly woman had been found murdered in her apartment at 500 Wall Street in Belltown. I was next-up for a murder, so I left court and went to the scene.

The apartment overlooked the Monorail tracks which transports people back and forth from Westlake Center downtown to the Seattle Center, the site of the 1962 World's Fair, for which the monorail was built.

The building was prime real estate. At the time it was a very nice senior apartment building, but later transitioned into expensive downtown condos.

The victim was Esther Vinikow, 86 years old, a retired baker, still vibrant and active despite her age.

I walked past the uniformed officers cordoning off the hallway outside her apartment, ducked under the yellow tape and entered the apartment. Esther laid on the floor in the bedroom, naked from the waist down, with only a bra on, a large butcher knife in her throat, stuck in the floor below her. It seemed apparent she'd been sexually assaulted. It was every elderly woman's worst nightmare.

The building was a lock-out, requiring a key to enter the front door, with surveillance cameras above the door. We asked about recordings from the door; there were none.

While the apartment was being processed, I stood in the bedroom, over her body, taking in the scene.

"Who did this to you, Esther?" I muttered under my breath.

The knife in the woman's throat was a typical butcher knife found in any kitchen knife set. There was also a black folding-blade knife recovered at the scene, as well as white Eddie Bauer jeans.

My eyes slowly scanned the scene. I could tell the apartment was normally well-kept, with everything neat and in its place. Someone had trashed the place during this crime, rifling through doors and throwing things everywhere.

There was an open box of checks on the floor. After it was photographed, I went through the box. Just as I suspected, there was a pad of checks missing.

The account was with Washington Mutual Bank.

I drove to the downtown branch of Washington Mutual and met with the manager.

I gave him the missing check numbers on the account.

"I want you to flag these checks on this account. If someone tries to pass a check from this group, I don't want you to deny the check, I just want the person handing the transaction to stall and call the police."

My partner at the time was Donna O'Neal.

I went to the autopsy the next morning. Dr. Paul Gosink conducted the autopsy.

He determined that the stabbing through the throat by the butcher knife had been done post-mortem. It appeared Esther had been killed by suffocation.

He also found vaginal tearing; Esther had been raped.

Later, I got a call from a patrol officer. He was at the downtown Washington Mutual branch. A woman had tried to cash one of the missing checks. He had her in custody.

"Bring her to my office," I told him.

Awhile later, the patrol officers arrived with a young woman in tow named Margie Bauelos. We put her into an interview room.

I let her stew for a bit, then O'Neal and I went in.

"Do you know Esther Vinikow?" I asked.

"Yeah, I did some work for her. That's why she wrote me the check," she said.

I laid down an in-life photo of Esther.

"Yeah, that's Esther," she said.

"Maybe she looked more like this when you last saw her," I said, laying down a photo of Esther from the murder scene.

When she saw the photo, Bauelos shrieked and put her hands over her face, tears welling in her eyes.

"A woman named Yollie told me he'd give me a hundred dollars to cash the check. I don't know anything about a murder! She was waiting for me outside the bank! I think she got the check from her boyfriend. He was outside too."

"Who is he?" I pressed.

"He's a Native guy. I don't know his name. I've seen him around Belltown."

We put Bauelos in a car and headed to Belltown. Driving up and down the streets, we hoped she'd see the guy hanging out on a corner somewhere.

By that time, Bauelos was being cooperative. She was chatting away, telling us various places she'd seen him before. We drove to each of those spots, but he wasn't there.

As I drove southbound on 5th Avenue, beneath the monorail tracks she said, "He told me he'd killed a girl in a bathroom in Belltown, but he didn't get charged."

I stopped the car in the middle of the street and turned to face her in the back seat.

"He told you what?"

She repeated what she'd said.

I raced back to the office. I put her back in the interview room, and tracked down the Geraldine Hendrickson case file. Once I found it, I burst into the room. I opened the file to the picture of Robert Lee Wentz.

"That's him!" she said, pointing to the photo.

I put a bulletin out state-wide. There was probable cause to arrest Robert Wentz for the murder of Esther Vinikow.

We spent the next three days trying to find him.

We ran "Yollie" in a database of persons who had been booked into the King County jail. A number of hits showed women with the name Yolanda. The first one on the list was Yolanda Lopez; it listed her AKA as Yollie.

We showed Bauelos the photo of Lopez. She identified her as the Yollie she knew from the street, who had given her the check.

Detective Gene Ramirez told us he knew Yolanda Lopez from a previous case. The next day, Ramirez brought Lopez into the Homicide office. We put her in an interview room.

Donna and I interviewed her.

She told us she is Robert Wentz' girlfriend.

"I met Robert on Pike Avenue,(sic) between first and second. He had a check to cash and jewelry he wanted to pawn. I asked him where they came from, and he told me he got them in a 'lick'."

She explained that a "lick" meant a robbery.

"He told me he'd fucked up real bad. He said he stabbed a woman in the neck. I thought he was on drug rantings."

Wentz told Lopez that the woman told him her daughter was away on vacation. She told him she had jewelry worth money.

"He told me he got the butcher knife from the woman's kitchen."

She said that they went to pawn shops to pawn the jewelry, using friends from the street who had ID. Wentz had silverware that he traded for drugs on the street.

We asked Lopez if Wentz carried a knife. She said he had a folding knife with a black handle. We showed her a photo of the one recovered at the scene. She said it looks like his knife. We also showed her a photo of the white jeans recovered at the scene. She said they were her jeans. She explained that she and Wentz share clothes. She knew they were her jeans because of a crease near the bottom. She explained that when she wears the jeans, she has to fold them up, because they're too long for her.

"I was at my parents' house later that night. My mom had been out playing bingo and got home just before the eleven o'clock news."

Her mother turned on the news.

"There was a story about the woman being murdered in her apartment.

"That's when it hit me.

"I went out to meet Robert near Franklin High School. I asked him to tell me what really happened.

"He told me it was best if I didn't know."

After our interview with Lopez, Gene Ramirez took her to jail. While she was being booked, she remembered that Wentz had given her a piece of jewelry. She handed it over to Ramirez.

Later that evening we got a call from Issaquah Police. Issaquah is a suburb of Seattle, nestled against the western slopes of the Cascade Mountains, twenty miles east of the city. They had Wentz in custody. He'd been riding buses from Seattle to Issaquah and back.

Donna O'Neal and Sergeant Cindy Tallman went to Issaquah to pick him up.

When they returned to the office with him, we put Wentz in an interview room. O'Neal and I went in.

We started the interview at about 8:45 PM. It was audio recorded.

Wentz stared at the floor, brooding and silent.

He told us that before murder, he'd been at the Seattle Center.

"What were you doing at the Seattle Center?" I asked.

"Drinking," he said, his answers terse.

He said he was there with a few other people, just getting drunk, when he got into a fight with one of them.

"How much had you had to drink, do you think?" I asked.

"Between there and downtown," he answered, "quite a bit."

He was doing what a lot of suspect's do in interviews; trying to answer yes and no, sometimes merely nodding his head, causing me to insist he answer audibly so the recorder could pick him up.

When left the Seattle Center, he was intending to go downtown.

"What were you going to do downtown?" I asked.

"Drink," he said.

"How much money did you have when you left the Center?" I asked.

"Maybe a dollar."

"Not enough to drink."

"No."

"What do you normally do when you don't have money to drink?" I asked.

"Normally pan-handle, or I'll burn somebody."

"What do you mean by 'burn somebody'?" I asked.

"Sell them bunk." (Fake drugs).

"Do you ever rob people?"

"If they give me money for drugs or something, I'll just take it."

"Is that what you were going to do that day?" I asked.

"Uh huh.

"And I seen a lady walking with her purse."

"What did she look like, Robert?"

"I don't even know what she was wearing."

"What would you use to describe her?" O'Neal asked.

"How old was she, for example?" I added.

"She was old."

"Was she a white lady, a black lady, Asian lady?" I asked.

"She was white."

He said he saw she had a purse in a shopping bag.

"Where was she carrying it?" I asked.

"In her hand," he said.

"In her hand?" O'Neal repeated. "What were you thinking?"

"That I could just run up and grab it.," he said.

"How come you didn't?" she asked.

"Too many people."

"So what did you do instead?"

"Sat there and followed her, and I was looking for the right time."

"How far back from her where you?" she asked.

"About fifty feet," he said.

"What did you do when she went in the apartment building?"

"I sat there and followed her."

"How did you get in the front door?" I asked.

"I…'cause I remember I grabbed it."

"When you followed her in, where did she go," O'Neal asked.

"To the elevator."

"Did she get on the elevator?"

"Yes."

"And did you get on the elevator?"

"Yes."

"What floor did you go to?"

"The fourth floor."

This is corroborative information tending to show that he wasn't just making a false confession. He knew what floor her apartment was on.

"What happened when you got to the fourth floor?" O'Neal asked.

"She stepped out, and I stepped out behind her."

"What way did she turn when she got off?"

"To the right," he said.

"and then she went and turned left," he continued.

Another corroborative statement.

"What did you do?"

"I followed her."

"Where did you end up?"

"Came to the end of the hallway."

"What was at the end of the hallway?"

"Two doors. Two apartments."

"Which one did she go to?

"The one on the right."

More corroboration.

"What did you do?"

"Went to the left one."

"What did you do that for?" Donna asked.

"So she wouldn't know I was going to take her purse."

"What happened then?"

"Turned around, and she was already in the door."

"What did you do?"

"Tried to grab the (purse)."

"What happened?"

"She slammed the door on my arm."

"How did that make you feel?"

"I got mad."

"What happened when you got mad?"

"Pushed the door open."

"What happened to the woman when you pushed the door open?"

"She fell down."

"What did you do then?"

"I picked her up."

"What did you do then?"

"I went and sat on the couch."

"What did she say to you?"

"She said, 'Don't hurt me.'"

"How many times did she say that?"

"Three or four times.

"I asked her for some money. She told me she only had five or six bucks."

He said he took the money out of her purse. He described searching the apartment for more valuables, adding more corroborative details as he did.

He was in the bedroom when he heard Esther try to leave the apartment.

"How did you know she was trying to get out."

"I heard her messing with the door.."

"How did that make you feel?"

"I was just shocked that she would do that."

"When she was trying to get out the door, what did you do? O'Neal continued.

"I kicked the door."

"What happened when you kicked the door?"

"She cut her hand. She showed it to me."

"What did she say?"

"She said, 'Oh, my hand'."

"What happened after that?"

"I told her I was sorry about her hand."

"What happened next?"

"I took her to the bedroom, because sometimes old people hide money in the bedroom. I asked her for more money. She said she didn't have any more."

"What did you do then, Robert?

"I raped her," he said, his voice barely about a whisper.

He described her getting on the floor and he pulling her pants off.

"What did she say to you?"

"She said, 'be careful'."

"After that point, what happened? I asked.

"She pulled my hair."

"What did you do?"

"I told her to quit."

"Did she quit?"

"No."

"How did that make you feel?"

"Mad."

"Do you know which hand she was using? Her right or her left hand?"

"Both."

"What did you do when she wouldn't stop pulling your hair, Robert?" O'Neal asked.

"Tried to make her let go."

"And how did you do that?"

"Used a pillow."

"Okay, so you got the pillow. Then what happened?" I asked.

"I just put the pillow over her face."

"Why did you put the pillow over her face?" Donna asked.

He described holding the pillow over her face, forcing it with one hand, while she struggled. Eventually, she stopped moving.

He got up and went to the hutch, jimmying the drawer open with his black-handled folding-blade knife.

"What happened to the knife?" I asked.

"I don't know."

"What else happened when you were in the kitchen?"

"I grabbed another one."

"Another what?"

"Knife."

"After you got the knife, what did you do?" I asked. "I went back in the bedroom."

"Okay, what did you do in the bedroom?"

"I cut her in the throat."

"What were you thinking, or how did you feel when you were doing that?"

"Mad."

He described standing over her body, knife in hand, muttering, "I told her I was sorry…I said, 'why did you have to…'" his voice trailed off.

"What did you think was going to happen when you stabbed her?"

"She was already dead."

He'd stabbed her eight times in the head and neck area.

"Why were you mad?"

"Because I was in trouble now. I told her I was mad at her for dying."

He described taking one pack of checks, some jewelry and silverware and leaving.

We booked Wentz into jail. He was charged with Aggravated Murder, which carries the possibility of the death penalty.

Wentz ultimately pled guilty to Aggravated Murder after the state agreed not to seek the death penalty against him. He was sentenced to life in prison without the possibility of parole

14

Donna O'Neal and I were in the office on a Saturday night in September of 2000, when we were called to a homicide scene in West Seattle.

A white male had been found dead in an alley. He'd been shot several times in the body and head. A known gang-banger, his body was covered with tattoos.

The case detectives were John Boatman and Gene Ramirez. It was a relatively "routine" murder.

The next night, Sunday, O'Neal and I were in the office again. Like most Sundays it was a very quiet night. At about nine PM, I told Donna to go home; I'd cover the office for the rest of the evening.

She left.

About an hour later, the main phone line into Homicide rang. There'd been a shooting on 4th Avenue South, near the Kingdome. There was one dead at the scene and several others wounded. I called O'Neal back, and then called several other detectives in to help.

The location of the shooting was only a few blocks from headquarters, so I soon arrived at the still-dynamic scene. Medic units were on the scene treating the wounded. The patrol sergeant told me what he knew.

"There was a family in a car stopped at the light. A guy walked up to the car and just started shooting. A guy in the back seat was killed; three others were wounded. One girl in the car wasn't hit."

It was a Hispanic family, and they were going to a semi-regular Mexican dance near the Kingdome.

Because of the murder of the gang-banger in the alley the night before, O'Neal and I were next up. This murder was ours.

The next day, I submitted the spent shell casings we had recovered at the scene to the crime lab. They called me a day later.

"The casings from your shooting are from the same gun as the shooting in West Seattle the night before."

We met with Boatman and Ramirez, and joined our investigations.

I had one of my surviving victims meet with Betty Kincaid, my favorite Forensic Artist. Ramirez gave me shit about it.

"Those things are a waste of time," he said. "They never look like the real guy."

"Apparently you've been using the wrong artist," I said. "I've had really good luck with Betty."

Betty drew the sketch. It looked pretty good; like a real person. If someone saw the suspect, they'd recognize him from the sketch.

A few days later a tip was phoned into the office. The shooter in both our cases was a member of MS-13, a notorious gang from Central America and Mexico. The caller told us the group was staying at a house in Renton, a suburb just south of Seattle.

We went to Renton to scope out the house. There was a condominium complex under construction right across the street. We spoke with the construction superintendent, and asked if we could set up surveillance in a unit across from the banger's house. He agreed.

There was no window installed yet in the unfinished condo we'd be using; we had a mirrored pane installed, so we could see out, but no one could see in.

We set up a video recorder inside, and took turns watching the house, seven days a week. Ramirez was watching one day when he saw a Hispanic male walking down the street in front of the house with a girl. The guy could have posed for the sketch Betty had produced. Ramirez recorded the guy and girl walking down the sidewalk.

We now had video of a possible suspect, but didn't have a photo or name to make a montage to show witnesses.

We contacted the Drama teacher at Cleveland High School in South Seattle. We told him we'd like to find groups of people who look reasonably like the guy we filmed. We'd then tape them walking down the sidewalk with girls and make a video montage. He agreed to help.

We went to the school and picked out five guys that looked reasonably like our guy. We then found a street that was similar to the street Ramirez had taped them walking on. We filmed five other pairs of young men and women walking down the street, chatting as the two we saw were doing.

We created a video montage of the students we recorded, along with the guy we thought was our shooter. We showed it to witnesses in the two murders we were investigating.

Each of the witnesses we showed the video montage to identified the video of the guy Ramirez had seen as the person they saw at each of the two shootings. That gave us probable cause to raid the house in Renton.

I wrote an Affidavit for Search Warrant for the house. A judge signed the warrant.

We decided to have SWAT make entry at the house in the early morning hours and take everyone inside into custody.

We met at four AM. We had a helicopter in the air over the house. SWAT went in at about five o'clock.

We brought everyone in the house to the Homicide office. The guy in the video wasn't there.

Through questioning the other people in custody, we learned that the guy we were looking for was in Immigration custody. His name was Emmanuel Grande-Martinez.

We contacted the INS. They released Grande-Martinez to us. We had him transported to the Homicide office.

I questioned him in an interrogation room.

"I know you shot the guy in West Seattle, and the people in the car downtown," I said.

"No officer. I did not shoot anybody!" he insisted in a heavy Hispanic accent.

It went on like that for a couple hours.

I stepped out of the interrogation room for a moment. There was a metal detector lying on a table just outside. I went back in.

"Are you willing to take a polygraph?"

"I don't know what that is," he said.

"It's a lie-detector."

"Oh...Okay."

I went back out and retrieved the metal detector. I had him step out of the room. I put the metal detector on his shirt, over a metallic button.

"Did you shoot the guy in West Seattle?"

"No."

I pushed the trigger on the metal detector. It let out a squeal.

"Did you shoot the people in the car?"

"No."

Once again, it let out a squeal.

"Oh, man!" he said.

Ila Birkland was a long-time secretary in Homicide. Her desk was just a few feet from where I was conducting the "polygraph."

I thought she would shit herself trying not to laugh.

Grande-Martinez pled guilty to the murders and shootings. He was sentenced to more than fifty-years in prison.

Elmer Cisneros was the leader of the local group. He'd ordered at least the murder of the guy in West Seattle. He was convicted and sent to prison as well.

In the summer of 2001, Mike Ciesynski and I were partners. We were called one day to the scene of a dead body found on the side of the road in a wooded area, up the hill from Harbor Avenue SW in West Seattle.

We arrived at the scene on a winding wooded road. Harbor Avenue is across Elliott Bay from downtown. It has million-dollar views of the bay and the downtown skyline on the other side. It's definitely not the ghetto.

The decedent, a Hispanic man in his twenties, had been shot once in the head. The incoming 911 call was anonymous. It came from a payphone at a Safeway store at the top of the hill.

In the days following the discovery, we identified the victim. We spoke to some of his friends, none of which claimed to know what had happened or why. Finally, one day, I got an anonymous call. The caller said that he saw an acquaintance of the victim at a self-service car wash at 3 AM on the morning the victim was found, washing his car.

I told Mike what the caller told me.

"That's not necessarily suspicious," he said.

145

"He was spraying water into the inside of the car."

"Oh."

The man the caller was telling me about worked at a fish processing plant in Ballard near Fisherman's Terminal, where all the Alaska commercial fishing boats are based, including several featured on "Deadliest Catch" on TV. Mike and I drove there to talk to this guy.

We met with a supervisor.

"We need to speak with Jose," I told him.

A few minutes later, Jose came to the office where we waited.

"What do you know about Fernando's death?" I asked.

"Nothing." Jose replied.

"Do you have a car here?"

"Yes. It's in the parking lot.

"Can we see it?"

Jose walked us out to the lot where his car was parked.

"Can we look inside?" I asked.

He opened the driver's door. It was a four-door. I opened the back seat door; I didn't see anything.

I went to the passenger side, and opened the back door there. In the area between the door and the back seat, was a piece of a human brain. I looked at it, and then at Jose's ashen face.

"Luuucccccy!" I said. "You got some 'splainin' to do!"

On a sunny afternoon the following August, I made a command decision. It was such a nice day I was not going to work late. I was going home.

I was in shorts and a tank top in my back yard relaxing in a lawn chair when my phone rang. Ed Striedinger, my academy classmate, now a sergeant in Homicide, was calling.

"Are you available?" he asked.

"I'm always available."

"We've got a situation in Rainier Beach. There are two dead at the scene and a third who may die. Two of them are kids. When the officers arrived, the suspect was still there. They got in a shooting with him. He's dead at the scene too."

So much for relaxing on a nice summer afternoon at home.

"I'm on my way," I said.

I changed and was out the door.

There was pandemonium when I arrived, hordes of people outside the yellow tape, news cameras everywhere, helicopters in the air. The Chief of Police stood before a throng of reporters and cameras, the gloom on his face in contrast to the beautiful summer late afternoon.

I walked up to Striedinger.

"The suspect is a twenty-year old male named Devon Jackson. He lived in the house. He was apparently shurmed," (shurm is marijuana soaked in either formaldehyde or PCP—people under the influence of shurm are often violent and unpredictable). "He had a gun. He shot and killed a nineteen-year-old relative in the house, then he beat a twenty-month-old to death, and stabbed a six-year-old girl several times. She was taken to Harborview in critical condition.

"He came out of the house, gun in hand when patrol arrived. Several officers fired. He's dead outside."

147

I walked up to the house, entering an eerily quiet place that moments before had been overwhelmed with violence, the smell of blood mixed with cordite hung in the air.

A nineteen-year-old man was sprawled across the couch; his life blood leaked everywhere, the clouded, endless stare of death on his face.

Another room was to the left. The lifeless body of what only shortly before had been a beautiful twenty-month-old boy lay on the floor, covered in blood.

"Jesus Christ," I mumbled to myself, allowing only that one moment of human empathy before switching back into "work mode" and doing my job.

The bathtub in the next room was blood-soaked, apparently from the six-year-old who had been rushed to the hospital. From the volume of blood in the tub I didn't hold out a lot of hope for her survival.

I was there for several hours. The scene was processed, the bodies removed by the Medical Examiner, and our actions recorded. Then we were done. It was anti-climactic; the suspect was dead, there would be no arrest or prosecution.

That Friday, I sat on the couch in my family room, watching a movie with my three boys. A family movie; no violence.

I hugged them close as we watched; grateful they didn't have to live in the world that I worked in.

15

Sometimes people are too stupid for their own good. I see it all the time. The ignorance is numbing.

On a Saturday afternoon in mid-August, 2001, Mike Ciesynski and I were called to an address in South Seattle. A woman was in her home. A young man was visiting. Her estranged boyfriend, against whom she had a restraining order, showed up at the house. He barged in, punching the male visitor, then assaulted the woman.

The visitor went out to his car parked in front of the house and retrieved a gun, and then returned to the house. He fired one shot from across the room, striking the estranged boyfriend in the head and killing him, and then fled.

We interviewed the woman. She'd recently met this young man who may have saved her life. His name was Antoine Surge, but he went by the sobriquet "Li'l Nut."

Since Li'l Nut fled the scene, he wasn't available for an interview. We ran his name in the computer systems. He was a known gang-banger and a convicted felon. We set the dogs out to find Li'l Nut.

By the next day, "Nut" was in custody. We had him brought to the Homicide office. Before we interviewed him, Mike and I discussed the case.

"He's a convicted felon, so we have to do him for the Felon in Possession of a Firearm charge," I said, "but I think he has a valid 'Defense of Others' claim for the shooting."

Mike agreed.

We went into the interview room ready to lob more softballs than at a company picnic. He just needed to say the right words and there'd be no murder charge.

149

"So Nut," I said. "Tell us what happened."

"I was visitin' this female," he said. "Dude shows up and slapped me. I run to my car and gets my gun. When I gets back, he's slappin' the female. I shot him from across the room and nailed him."

He almost gloated about shooting from across the room and hitting the guy, which no doubt had been a lucky shot.

"So you thought he was going to hurt the girl and you defended her, right?" I asked, almost nodding myself to guide him through the question.

"What?" he said.

"You tried to protect the girl from this guy."

"No, man. That motherfucker bitch-slapped me. No one do that. I kill the motherfucker!"

Mike and I looked at each other. What a moron, I thought.

He got twenty-five years for murder and another five for the Felon in Possession.

Genius.

I was off duty on an afternoon in September of that year. My youngest son, Dylan, was entering the third grade at an elementary school two blocks from my house. Doreen and I were at an open house at the school.

My work cell phone rang. I recognized the number as the Seattle 911 center. I answered.

"Cloyd, it's Jay."

Jay Nicholson retired as a Robbery Detective for SPD. He took a civilian job in the 911 center after retirement. We were good friends.

"Hey, buddy. What's up?"

"Do you have a sister that lives in Puyallup?" he asked.

My oldest sister, Vicky.

"Yeah, why?"

"We got a call from the Pierce County Sheriff. They're at your sister's house. It's not good, Cloyd."

As soon as he said that I knew: Vicky was dead.

"A neighbor told them her brother was a Seattle detective, so they called us. I'm really sorry, Cloyd."

"Thanks, Jay. I'm not really surprised by this call. I'm glad it was you who called me."

"Let me know if there's anything I can do for you," he said.

Doreen was speaking to a neighbor of ours. I walked up to her.

"Do you have to go to work?" she asked.

I whispered into her ear that my sister was dead.

"What?" she said.

We took Dylan home and left him with my other two boys, and then Doreen and I drove to Puyallup.

Vicky was eight years older than me; she was going to turn fifty-one in a month.

We had different mothers, but our dad had custody of her when we were growing up, and she considered my mother her mother as well. Vicky's biological mother, Mildred, was a serious alcoholic. I had no idea until a few years before, that Vicky was as well.

I'd been working as a detective in Sex Crimes a few years earlier, when I got a call from my mother.

"Vicky's in the hospital in Tacoma. You'd better get down here; she's probably not going to survive."

Doreen and I rushed down there. She was in Intensive Care; her liver was failing.

She'd contracted hepatitis B as an eighteen-year-old. I was ten at the time, and didn't really understand what was happening. She was hospitalized for a long time; her liver had been seriously damaged. I thought this was about that, and partially, it was. Her liver was failing, but it was because she was a closet alcoholic. I don't think I'd ever seen her take a drink, not that we'd spent a lot of time together over the last few years, except holidays and family occasions.

She recovered from that episode. I spoke with her in the hospital. She whined, almost child-like.

"You can't do this," I said. "You may as well borrow my gun and blow your brains out, because the results will be the same."

She cried like a baby.

"I'll stop drinking," she said.

I knew she wouldn't.

When Doreen and I arrived at her house in Puyallup, a sheriff's deputy sat outside in his patrol car. He told me that neighbors found her. Medics had responded, but pronounced her dead.

We entered her apartment. Empty liquor bottles everywhere, she laid on her back in the middle of the floor, that familiar empty clouded stare on her face. I knelt down by her body started an examination, pulling back her eyelids and lips, looking for evidence of petechial hemorrhage, a sign of strangulation, but finding none.

I lifted her head to look at her neck for any sign of strangulation there. I checked her ears for blood, palpated her head for any irregularities.

"Oh, my God." I heard Doreen mutter behind me, not used to death like I am, as I continued my examination, rolling her over and examining her back, finally satisfied that this wasn't anything other than what it appeared to be.

Vicky had divorced her husband of more than twenty years a few years before. She had a boyfriend, whom I'd met; I thought he was a little sketchy. I wanted to be sure he didn't do this.

I called a funeral home and waited until they arrived to remove her body.

Vicky had a son, my nephew, Larry. He was married with children of his own. I drove to his house. By the time I got there, it was after nine in the evening. When Larry opened the door, he was surprised to see me.

"Larry, your mom's dead," I told him, and then explained what had happened. He was shocked, but not too surprised. I talked to him for about twenty minutes, then I gave him a hug and left.

Now I needed to tell my parents.

There's nothing worse that can happen to a parent, than to lose a child. I know that from speaking to scores of parents to whom it had happened.

My mother recently had surgery, and was still in the hospital. My dad had just gotten home from there when I arrived.

I told him Vicky was dead. His shoulders slumped.

"I always knew she'd go before me," he said.

"Do you want me to tell mom?" I asked.

"No, I'll tell her."

Vicky wouldn't be the only sister I would lose.

16

My office phone rang in July of 2003.

"You have a collect call from an inmate at the King County Jail..."

I waited as the recording outlined my options for the call. Finally, it prompted me to press one to accept the call. I pressed one.

Only good things can come to a detective receiving a call from jail or prison. Either a suspect is calling and wants to talk about his or her case, or another inmate is snitching off a suspect.

The city can pay for the call.

This time, the call was from an informant I'd used many times before. To protect his identity, I'll call him Paul. (To other detectives I worked with, he was affectionately known as "Huggy Bear", the informant character from Starsky and Hutch.)

Today, Paul was in a snit.

"There's a guy in here," he whispered into the phone, "who's trying to hire me to kill his whole family."

Paul is a prolific snitch. Though he's snitched off many murders for me, he's never asked for anything in return. He has an extensive criminal history, but doesn't like murderers. His girlfriend was raped and murdered a few years ago.

Actually, he only asked one thing from me. He asked that I call his mother and tell her he was doing something good.

I did.

"Who is this guy?" I asked him.

"His name's Bill Jensen. He's on the 11th floor of the jail with me," he said.

"I'll check him out," I said, and hung up.

I pulled up the King County Jail booking system on my computer. Sure enough, there was a William Jensen booked in the jail and housed on the 11th floor on a domestic violence charge.

There was a flag beneath his name.

"Retired King County Sheriff."

Oh, shit, I thought.

I went through the tunnel that connects Seattle Police headquarters with the downtown jail, checked Paul out and brought him to my office.

Paul was agitated.

"Cloyd, this guy is serious," he said. "He hired me the last time I was in jail. He told me he'd give me one hundred and fifty thousand dollars to kill his wife, sister-in-law, and his daughter."

"Wait a minute, what? He hired you the last time you were in jail? When was that?"

"It was a couple weeks ago. He gave me detailed instructions and descriptions of his wife and sister-in-law, the cars they drove and where the house was. After I got out, I met Jensen's sister. She gave me a couple thousand dollars advance."

Here's the thing about Paul as an informant. When he's in custody, he's the best. People tell him about the murders they committed, in intimate detail. He looks and acts like some Mafioso killer; a tough guy. When he's sober, he's actually a pretty nice guy. He tries really hard to do good.

He's always housed in isolation because he gets in fights in general population, so the conversations are through cracks in the door, or at the cell window. He takes copious notes about the conversations. When he thinks he has enough, he calls me.

But when Paul is out, I never hear from him. He goes on a binge, mostly drinking, and is unreliable. Every time he's in, he

155

swears to me that he's not going to drink when he gets out. He's going straight. He'll call me. He fails every time.

"What happened to the money she gave you?" I asked.

"I drank it up," he admitted.

Though he puts forth this persona of a street tough, he's like a puppy dog with me, wanting approval.

"Holy shit, Paul! When you didn't kill his family, he might have hired someone else to do it!"

"I told him I have a girlfriend named Lisa," Paul said. "She's a black girl. I told him Lisa might come to visit him to get more information."

Paul gave me the paper he'd written all the information on about Jensen's family. His wife's name was Sue. He had a nineteen-year-old daughter and a fourteen-year-old son.

I took Paul back to jail.

Since I didn't know if Jensen had hired someone else to kill the victims, I thought they could be in immediate danger.

I drove to their Eastside home. By that time, it was almost nine-thirty at night. I called Sue Jensen's phone.

"Mrs. Jensen, my name is Cloyd Steiger. I'm a Homicide Detective with the Seattle Police Department. I'm on my way to speak with you. I'm calling so you won't be alarmed when I show up at your door."

"Okay," she said, a leery tone to her voice.

When I arrived, I knocked on her front door. She looked out an upstairs window.

"Do you have a badge I can see?" she asked.

"Of course," I said, showing it to her.

She opened the door, still leery, but invited me in.

"I don't know how to tell you this," I said, "but your husband is trying to hire someone to kill you and your sister. You need to get out of here and go somewhere. Not to your sister's house; she has to leave too. You need to go where no one could find you. Don't tell anyone where you are going."

Her face blanched.

"I knew it!" she said. "Where should we go?"

"I don't know, a hotel or something. I want you out of here tonight until I determine you're safe. It may take a couple days. Remember, don't tell anyone where you're going, so it doesn't get back to your husband."

She gathered her kids and things to leave.

Once I assured she and her sister were safe, I could breathe easier. Now I had time to work this.

The next day, I called Marilyn Brenneman in the Prosecutor's Office. She worked in the Special Investigations Section. Among the crimes they work on are official corruption cases. They also handled wire authorizations, which I thought I'd probably need for this case.

I told her what I had.

"I'll be right over," she said.

When she arrived at my office, she had a second prosecutor with her. It was Cheryl Snow, the head of the office's Domestic Violence Section. She was very familiar with Bill Jensen.

I didn't know Cheryl at the time, but she later worked in the Homicide Section of the prosecutor's office and we worked many murders together.

I'd audio and video recorded Paul as he told me about the case. I played the video for Brenneman and Snow.

"I think we need to move on this," Marilyn said.

I agreed.

I suggested we send an undercover detective to the jail with a wire to see if Jensen was serious.

Paul told Jensen that his girlfriend, Lisa might visit him in the jail. I needed to find a black female who could pose as Lisa to send in.

I immediately thought of Sharon Stevens.

Sharon was a detective in Sex Crimes, one floor down from Homicide. A very competent detective, I knew she could play the part of Lisa.

I went downstairs to see Sharon. I told her what I had.

"Do you want to have some fun and play Lisa?" I asked.

"Absolutely," she said.

While I went back to the jail to get Paul, Sharon came to my office.

I put Paul back in an interview room. I gave him a pen and paper.

"I want you to write a letter introducing Lisa to him, so he'll know she's with you and the plan is still on if he wants."

I brought Stevens in the room and introduced her to Paul.

"She'll be really good," Paul said after meeting Stevens.

Paul wrote this in his letter:

*Bill, I'm in jail for DOC, (*Department of Corrections*), for not reporting on time. As I've been to lousy getting everything set up.*

-This is Lisa, My Partner that I told you all about. I also brought my Brother For back up and He will be taking out the Party's!! He wants you to release him the Oxy scrips For his work and we will contact sis for incentive.

The job is all set as we planned I have the van & car and a Apt. in Kirkland to take care of the pick up and Follow up Accident."

And if all goes as planned you be out by the 1st so be ready to Transfer you Bond. You and I will take car of the Final $150,000 pluss Bonus just you and I,

My Brother as I told you will take care of our end you just keep taking care of yous and I'll see you in a couple wks I may only get 20 days and I'm doing this—this way so my word to you on my part is taken care of, My Brother and Lisa Don't play, so Work it.

Flying King

Flying King was a code word Paul had worked out with Jensen so Jensen would know any communication he had with Paul was legitimate.

Sharon Stevens changed into street clothes. She took the letter and walked across the street to the King County Jail.

There's a conference room in the southwest corner of the 7th floor of Seattle Police Headquarters where the Homicide offices are. It has floor to ceiling glass on the south and west sides, offering great views of Elliott Bay and Pioneer Square. It also looks directly down on the downtown King County Jail.

I sat in the room by myself, watching as Sharon crossed James Street and entered the front door of the jail.

I stayed there, looking out the window for just over a half hour before Sharon came back out. I could tell by her gait; things had gone well. She almost ran to the front door of headquarters.

When she came into the Homicide office, she was giddy.

159

"I held the letter up to the glass for Jensen to read. After he was done, I tore it up and put it in the envelope."

They had spoken through telephone receivers, thick glass separating them.

"He told me it was a go. He said it has to be done by August first."

We had one week.

The next day, Marilyn Brenneman and I got together. Our plan was to send Stevens back in, this time wearing a wire to record her conversation with Jensen. We'd need a court order to do that. We drafted the affidavit for the order. Later, we presented the affidavit to a judge, who authorized the wire.

The Criminal Intelligence Section is also housed on the seventh floor at headquarters. They have surreptitious recording equipment, so I needed their help.

Detective Dale Nixdorf was assigned to assist me.

There were logistical problems. The call would have to occur in the visiting area of the jail. Stevens and Jensen would be on opposite sides of the glass and the conversation would take place over telephone receivers. The Intelligence Section didn't have the right equipment to do the recording.

Nixdorf called someone he knew at the DEA. They had equipment that would work. They sent an agent over to help.

We needed to make sure no one else was in the visiting area when this happened. We didn't want to pick up other people's conversations. We talked to the jail and arranged it so no one else would be in the room during their conversation.

I went back to the jail to get Paul.

"I want you to write another note," I told hm. This time I want you to ask for more front money and address the issue of the three victims, and the price he'll pay."

This is what Paul wrote:

160

Bill,

I'm a bit disappointed that you don't have the work $ As I' About Short of Funds to run this OP, and them have to Finish the Job without me giving them some Relax Funds S if you can come up with some!! Tell Lisa How when and on one. Also Asure her about the $150,000 on the 3 so she can tell my Brother you are as real As I say!! We are ready to move except as I've stated already! So work it out!!

Get This Done. And we will see each other in a wk or 2 Also Lisa had a Portland Dr. Lic So if you need to talk again soon she can come and see you with that ID one tie as an out of state visitor. Get this done and let's do this.

Sincerely,

Flying King

In the margins of the note, Paul wrote:

Be straight with Lisa she my people's.

Also the Bonus must be in the work!!!

Like with the first note, I made a photocopy and then folded the original, placing it in an envelope.

Nixdorf and the DEA agent went to the jail to set up the recording device. Once it was ready, they called me to let me know. They sat in a nearby control room where they could monitor the conversation.

I sent Sharon back over to the jail. I then assumed my spot in the conference room, alone. Again, I watched her cross the street and enter the jail.

She was gone much longer this time. As I sat there waiting, I didn't know if that was good or bad. When she finally exited the building, she had the same fast-paced gait as before. I felt better.

She burst into the Homicide office.

"Holy shit, that asshole wants us to kill his fourteen-year-old son too!

"It's about money," (it almost always is), "I asked him if his wife, daughter and sister-in-law are dead, won't his son inherit the money? He thought about it and told me to just 'clean house'. I said, 'Your son too?' He said, 'Yes'."

Jensen had given specifics about those he wanted killed; he gave descriptions of their cars and gave other identifying information.

He'd agreed to pay more money when he added his son to the list of those to be killed.

That night, Detective Al Cruise and I walked over to the jail. We went to the eleventh floor where Jensen was housed.

When he was brought into the room, I introduced Al and myself, telling him we were with Seattle Police Homicide.

I'm sure he was giddy inside, expecting me to tell him his whole family had been killed.

I had a buzz-kill for him.

"Bill, you're under arrest for Solicitation to Commit Murder."

His face blanched.

I advised him of his rights. He said he understood.

"Are you going to deny this?" I asked.

He just stared at me and said nothing.

"Do you have any questions?" I asked.

"No."

"Then go back to your cell, you fucking piece of shit." I said.

He walked away, wide-eyed.

Several months later, we went to court. The trial was held in the courtroom of Judge Richard Jones, half-brother of musician Quincy Jones. Jensen was represented by Jim Conroy. Conroy is a competent attorney. We'd gone toe to toe many times, but outside the courtroom, we got along just fine.

The night before Paul was set to testify, he hadn't contacted the prosecutor and he wasn't in custody. That was a problem. Like I said earlier, Paul is very unreliable when he's not in jail.

Sometimes working as a homicide detective is being a babysitter; especially when you're getting ready for trial. I hated that part of the job.

That night, I drove around all the areas I knew Paul to hang around when he wasn't in jail. I finally found him, drunk on his ass, like he always is when he's not in custody.

The thing about Paul: He's not just a drunk; he's a mean and obnoxious drunk. When he's in custody and sobers up, he's not a bad guy.

"Paul, what are you doing?" I said to him.

"Fuck you man!" he yelled at me.

I got right up in his face.

"Get in my car. Now!"

He stared at me for a moment, then walked over and got in my car.

Paul's liver is so bad, even if he doesn't drink another drop, it takes a couple days to sober up.

I drove him to a motel out by the airport, away from the city and his friends. I got him a room.

"I'm coming here to get you at eight in the morning. You'd better be up and ready."

"I'm sorry, Cloyd," he said.

163

Oh, God. Now he's going to whine like a baby. I think I prefer him as an asshole.

The next morning at eight, I was at his door. I knocked. There was no answer. I was getting pissed. Just as I was turning to walk to my car and figure out what to do next, the door opened.

"Sorry, man. I was in the can."

He was better than the night before, but still drunk. I got him a coffee and something to eat on the road, and then drove straight to the courthouse.

When we entered the area where the trial would be held, news cameras lined the hallway. This case got a lot of local attention because Jensen had been a cop.

When Paul saw the cameras, he perked up. He was a big deal.

Though he was still drunk, when he took the stand he did a good job. He answered all the questions he was asked and didn't embellish anything.

He held his own during withering cross-examination by Jim Conroy.

"Isn't it true, you were in a gang?" Conroy asked.

"Yes. I was in the Latin Kings. Three of us led the gang. Three kings like a deck of cards."

"Doesn't a deck of cards have four kings?" Conroy asked.

"We never played with a full deck."

Zing.

Later, it was my turn on the stand.

I love testifying in big cases like this. I'm never nervous; it's second nature to me. I enjoy verbal sparring with the defense.

During cross examination, Conroy asked me about my relationship with Paul.

"Detective Steiger, are you aware of (Paul's) criminal history?"

"Yes I am."

"Would you agree, it's an extensive history?"

"Yes, I would agree, it's an extensive history."

"And yet when he comes to you with matters like this, you listen to him?"

"You know, Mr. Conroy," I said. "I went to the Boy Scouts, but they don't seem to know anything about crime. If you want to know about crime, you have to go to a crook."

Later, Conroy asked me about when I arrested Jensen.

"Did you call my client a piece of shit when you visited him in jail?"

"Yes I did." I said.

On re-direct, Marilyn asked me about that.

"Detective Steiger, why did you call Mr. Jensen a piece of shit?"

"Because I knew what would happen," I answered. "The news reports wouldn't say that a man tried to have his whole family killed. They'd all say that a former cop tried to have his whole family killed. It would reflect badly on all the good cops that work hard and do a good job every day. I take pride in my profession and I'm tired of people who diminish that."

"That opinion you expressed that night," she asked. "Do you still hold that opinion today?"

"Yes I do." I answered.

There were several reporters in the hallway outside the courtroom watching the proceedings on a monitor. When I left the courtroom and stepped into the hall, they stood on their feet, applauding.

Jensen was convicted. He was sentenced to sixty years in prison. He was in poor health. It was a life sentence.

17

Seafair is an annual event in Seattle. It lasts a couple weeks at the end of July and the beginning of August.

It's a time of festivals and parades in different neighborhoods in the city, including the Torchlight Parade downtown attended by a couple hundred thousand people, and culminates with hydroplane races on Lake Washington that feature an airshow, the stars of which are the Navy's Blue Angels. There are usually well over a hundred thousand spectators for that as well.

I was home on race day, 2003. I've worked a lot of Seafair events in my career. With the huge crowds and their corresponding problems, the last place you'd find me in my free time was anywhere near a Seafair event.

My phone rang in the early afternoon. A woman's body had been found off of 54th Avenue South, near the race course.

I was going down there after all.

My partner Mike Ciesynski was out of town, so I'd be flying solo on this one.

I arrived at the scene, ensconced in the ubiquitous yellow tape, patrol cars blocking off each end of the boulevard surrounding where the body had been found.

There were a lot of news cameras. The victim had been found near an area where hundreds of thousands of people, mostly families, were gathering for a day of fun.

I approached the patrol sergeant at the scene.

"People were walking to the races. One of them glanced down and saw her. They thought it was a mannequin at first, but when they looked closer, they saw that it was a real body."

167

I stood on the edge of the road and looked over the side. The nude body of a female victim lay in a fetal position, blood visible by her mouth and nose. It was purge, common in dead bodies, it isn't a result of an injury or assault

When a person dies, the fluid in the body is pulled by gravity to the lowest point. After a while, it settles there and becomes fixed. That part of the body is discolored, usually a purplish color. It's called post-mortem lividity, or livor mortis. This woman was lying face down, but there was lividity on her back. She'd been dumped here a substantial time after death, having originally laid on her back in the hours just after death.

Stuck to her back was a small piece of green plastic. It looked like a remnant of a lawn and garden trash bag.

Other detectives were there photographing and processing the scene.

Dr. Richard Harruff arrived along with his Medical Examiner Investigator, Jim Sosik. We never touch a body before the ME gets there. Now we could pull her out and look more closely at her.

We placed a white sheet on the ground next to her and rolled her onto it. We grabbed the sheet at both ends and brought her up to the street.

Once we had her on the street and opened the sheet, we saw that something was written across her abdomen, probably with a Sharpie.

It said, "Nigger Bitch".

Harruff examined her at the scene. It looked like manual strangulation, (meaning done with hands, as opposed to ligature strangulation done with a rope or cord; that leaves a distinctive furrow on the neck which is obvious and easily identifiable) but he couldn't be sure until the autopsy. They took her to the Medical Examiner's office.

The first order of business was to identify her. We had no idea who she was.

I would have to wait until Monday to have her prints rolled and checked in AFIS, (the Automated Fingerprint Identification System).

Monday morning, I went directly to the Medical Examiner's office to attend the autopsy. The cause of death was confirmed: it was manual strangulation.

Her fingerprints were rolled and entered into AFIS. We got a hit. Our victim was Julie Sterling. She had a record as a drug user and sometime prostitute.

Because this had been a prominent story on the local news, the phones in the Homicide office were constantly ringing with people having information they thought was important. Most of it wasn't.

Gene Ramirez answered a call. A woman wanted to remain anonymous. She said that a friend of hers had been at a party when a relative told people that he'd seen a body in a garbage bag in the home of someone known as "Peanut". The caller said she thought Peanut's real name was Charles Jackson, but she wasn't sure. She said he lives near Genesee Park in Rainier Valley.

When Ramirez tried to press her for more information, she hung up. Fortunately for us, we have caller ID and Ramirez had her phone number.

When he told me about the call, my ears perked up. No one knew about the garbage bag remnant that had been on the body. That the caller had mentioned it made this a high priority lead.

I tracked down the caller, showing up at her door. She wasn't thrilled to see me, but was cooperative enough.

She hadn't heard this comment herself, but heard it from a friend that lived in Tacoma.

I was in my office, looking up information about that friend when she called me.

"I heard you want to talk to me," she said.

"Yes I do."

"I'm at work until 4:30, but then I can talk to you."

She gave me the address where she worked in Tacoma. I told her I'd pick her up.

I met her at her job, and drove her to downtown Seattle.

"We had a family barbecue on race day," she said. "My uncle Donnie was there. He was telling everybody that he'd been at Peanut's house a couple days earlier and Peanut told him he had a woman's body in a garbage bag. Donnie didn't believe him, but then he saw the garbage bag and he could see a foot in it.

"I know Peanut. We grew up in the same neighborhood off 46th. His real name is Charles Jackson."

We drove to Genesee Park, and she pointed out Jackson's house, and then we returned to my office.

I pulled up a photo of Charles Lorenzo Jackson who had used the address of the house she pointed out.

"That's Peanut," she said.

She told me her uncle was Donnie Phillips, and that he lived in the Renton Highlands, southeast of Seattle.

I ran Phillips' name too, and showed her a photo. She confirmed he was her uncle.

Phillips had an outstanding misdemeanor warrant for his arrest.

How convenient.

I drove her home to Tacoma.

Myself and five other detectives drove to the Renton Highlands to meet Donnie Phillips.

I knocked on the door. Phillips answered.

I reached across the doorway and pulled him out.

"Donnie, you're under arrest."

I put the cuffs on him.

We walked him to our car and put him in the back seat.

"What's this about?" he asked.

"Hmm, let's see," I said. "Six Seattle detectives show up at your house to pick your ass up without a word. Donald, I'm guessing you can figure this out."

His eyes widened, and he visibly shook.

"Look man. I don't know nothing about how she got killed. He just asked me to come help him get rid of the body."

"We'll talk when we get downtown."

We rode the rest of the way in silence.

At headquarters, I put him in an interview room. He was busting at the seams to talk to me. I let him sweat awhile. Finally, I walked in and sat down.

"You have one chance to talk to me. If you lie even once, you're done."

"Man, I've known Peanut all my life," he said. "He lives at that house with his mother. She lives upstairs, and he lives in the basement.

"He called me on Saturday and asked me to come over. When I gets there, he walks me to an area in the basement. There's a big plastic tub there. There was a big green garbage bag inside the tub. He opens it, and I can see a body. It smelled bad. He wanted me to help him dump the body. I didn't want nothin' to do with it. He said, 'I can't do it alone', so I helped him. We loaded it up in his car and drove to the spot and dumped it.

"I ain't seen Peanut since."

"Is Peanut at his house all the time?" I asked.

"Either there, or at his girlfriend's house."

We loaded Donnie up in the car. We drove past the house his niece had pointed out.

"That's Peanut's house right there," he said.

He then led us to another Rainier Valley address.

"His girlfriend live right there. If he ain't at home, he be there."

We took Phillips back downtown and booked him for his warrant.

I wrote a search warrant for both addresses.

We showed up at Jackson's house. By then, it was after two o'clock in the morning. We knocked on the door. Jackson's mother answered, bleary-eyed. We entered and went to the basement; Jackson wasn't there.

We told her she'd have to vacate the house; we'd be searching it. We left patrol officers to sit on the house while we went to the girlfriend's house. It was three o'clock in the morning.

We knocked on the door and announced that we had a warrant. When no one answered, I used my size 12 universal key, (my foot) to open the door. We rushed to the bedroom; Jackson was in bed with his girlfriend. I stuck my gun in his nose.

"Don't even move Charles," I said. "You're under arrest."

We took Jackson downtown to the Homicide office. I placed him in Interview Room #1, the same one Donnie Jackson had given him up in hours earlier.

Before I went in to talk to him, I got a call from detectives at his house.

"This place is creepy. It reminds me of the movie Seven. There are bottles and jars all over, half filled with piss. It really stinks down here."

Gene Ramirez and I went in for the interview.

Jackson sat in a chair. He was agitated, rocking back and forth.

"I'm not going back to prison," he said. "You're going to have to shoot me."

"We're not going to shoot you, Charles," I said. In the back of my mind, I wasn't so sure.

We had an officer just outside the door with a Taser in case we needed it.

After talking to him for several minutes about unrelated things, I steered the conversation to the victim.

"She ripped me off before. I saw her in a bar off of Rainier Avenue, and brought her back to my place. I bought some beer on the way.

"When we got to my house, she picked up a can. I think she thought it was one of the beers, but it was a can of piss. She started drinking from it. There was a lid from a little liquor bottle, like the airlines use, and a piece of a plastic garbage bag in it. She swallowed that and started choking.

"I tried to save her, but I couldn't."

I stared at him a moment, not saying anything.

Finally, I said "So why didn't you call 911?"

"I didn't think anyone would believe me," he said.

"You know what?" I said. "I think you're right. No one would have believed you. Do you know why? Because that's the most ridiculous fucking story I've ever heard. You had all this time, and that's the best you could come up with?

"Tell me," I continued. "At what point do you think she realized that what she was gulping down wasn't that cold beer she thought, but days old piss? Do you think it was after three or four gulps? Enough that a bottle cap and plastic came out and became lodged in her throat?"

Of course, the autopsy showed hemorrhage on the outside of her trachea, which wouldn't happen if she choked on something.

Ramirez got up and left the room. He returned a moment later with a can of orange soda and an airline bottle of vodka, (that he was conveniently able to find in the office), as well as a plastic garbage bag. He laid them on the table.

"How big a piece of garbage bag was it?" he asked.

"A little piece," Jackson answered.

Ramirez tore a corner of the bag.

"This big?"

"About that." Jackson said.

Ramirez unscrewed the vodka bottle and wrapped the lid in the plastic. Then he opened the can of soda and shoved the cap and plastic inside.

He picked up the can and took a swig. The lid and plastic didn't come out.

"She took a bigger drink than that," Jackson said.

Ramirez took an even bigger drink. Still nothing came out.

"You're not going to tell me she drank more piss than that without realizing it wasn't beer." I said.

Jackson shrugged.

Ramirez chugged down the rest of the can of soda, and then slammed the can on the table. The plastic and lid didn't come out.

"I think your story's bullshit," he said.

Like often happens in interrogations, when the first story doesn't work out, the suspect completely changes the story and expects us to buy it.

"Okay," Jackson said. "We were having sex and her throat was against the dresser. I didn't even know she was dead."

Really?

174

"So tell me about the writing on her body," I said.

He looked down at the floor and mumbled.

"I don't know nothin' about no writing on her body."

I showed him a photo of her body with the "Nigger Bitch" writing.

"Oh, yeah. I did that to throw people off."

"If you didn't murder her, why would you have to throw anyone off?" I asked.

He rocked in his chair again.

"I ain't goin' back to prison," he said.

Actually, Charles, you are.

Fearing he may try to grab one of our guns, we ended the interview and left the room.

About twenty hours after I'd gotten to work that day, we booked Charles into jail for the murder of Julie Sterling.

The next day, I submitted evidence to the crime lab, including fingernail clippings taken from Sterling at her autopsy. It was likely she'd scratched him as he was strangling her.

A few weeks later, I received lab results.

The lab had found Jackson's DNA on her fingernails. They quantified it by saying the chances of randomly finding a matching DNA sample from the public at large is one in fifty-four quintillion.

This is what fifty-four quintillion looks like written out: 54,000,000,000,000,000,000.

That's a big-assed number.

The jury didn't believe his bullshit story either. Jackson was convicted at trial.

18

In October of 2004, I was in South Seattle in the late afternoon when I heard a report of a shooting over the police frequency that covers the Southwest Precinct. The shooting was near 8th Avenue South and Cloverdale Street, in South Park.

I phoned the office to let them know about the call. Soon after, I heard the patrol units at the scene calling for Homicide to respond. I drove to the scene.

A medic unit was on the scene when I arrived. A young Hispanic male was being treated in the back. He had been shot in the head and was not expected to survive.

I called Russ Weklych and Al Cruise who were next-up for a murder. I let them know, they probably had their case.

I stayed and helped at the scene. As expected, the 20-year-old victim died at Harborview.

I wasn't primary, so my involvement, at least at that point, ended.

Cruise and Weklych worked the case and developed leads.

A week later, I was getting ready for work in the morning. As usual, I had the local news on the television. I often see things on the news that effect my morning once I get to work.

There was a story about a guy who'd shot at two federal agents in Federal Way. It's across town from where I live, but I'm very familiar with the area.

When I got to work, there was a buzz in the office. The person who shot at the federal agents was a guy Cruise and Weklych had identified as a possible suspect in their murder.

"Are you available to help with this case?" Cruise asked me.

"Absolutely," I said.

176

"We're going to a meeting at the Federal Way police station this afternoon. Why don't you meet us there?" he said.

The Federal Way Police Department has about a hundred officers, in a city with a population of about a hundred thousand.

One of my pet peeves with these small to medium sized agencies is when they get a high-profile crime like this, commanders, who probably have never personally investigated a major case, take over. The results are often predictable: This was no exception.

We attended the meeting run by commanders. The detectives said nothing. At the end, they discussed setting up another meeting.

Give me a break. We don't need no stinking meeting, man. We left to go find the bad guy.

We drove to Renton, a suburb south of Seattle. The shooter's family lived there. We spoke to his mother and sister.

"We haven't seen him in a few weeks," the sister told me.

"Really?" I asked.

"Really," she said.

"Are you Catholic?" I asked.

"Yes," she answered feebly.

"Do you have a rosary?"

"Yes," she said.

"Go get it."

She went to a back room, returning a moment later, rosary in hand.

"Repeat after me," I said. "Holy Mary, mother of God."

"Holy Mary, mother of God," she repeated.

"I swear upon my eternal damnation; I'm not lying to this detective."

Her eyes welled with tears as she stared at me. She didn't say anything for several seconds.

I just stared at her.

"He was here yesterday," she finally whispered.

We were able to identify the guy who'd been with our shooter when he shot at the federal agents. We, along with FBI and ICE agents, set up a stakeout on his Federal Way apartment.

He came home at 10:30 that night. We let him get inside the apartment, and then hit it. When I walked in, he was yelling something in Spanish. One of the ICE agents with us spoke Spanish.

"What's he saying?" I asked the agent.

"He's saying he wants a lawyer," the agent told me. "What should I tell him?"

"Tell him, 'Fuck your lawyer'."

"Really?" the agent asked.

"Really." I said. There is nothing in the Constitution or case law that says a witness to a crime has a right to a lawyer. This guy didn't shoot at the agents, and he wasn't a suspect in our murder.

As we walked the guy out to our car, we passed the FBI supervisor. He had a cellphone to his ear.

"I'm on the phone with the US Attorney," he said. "He says we can't talk to him."

"Goddamn, that's good!" I said.

"What?" he asked.

"It's a really good thing that I don't work for the US Attorney."

I put him in our car and we drove away.

We took him to the Federal Way police station. Gene Ramirez speaks fluent Spanish. We had him drive out to interview the guy.

It'd been a long day and I was dog-tired. I was only a couple minutes from my house, and was hoping I'd soon be able to just go home.

While Ramirez interviewed the guy, Russ Weklych and I went to the apartment where the shooter had been staying when he shot at the federal guys. It'd already been searched by Federal Way police, but they didn't find anything.

Ramirez called from the police station.

"The gun is in the bedroom closet, under some clothes."

We went to the bedroom and lifted a pile of clothing from the closet floor; there it was.

The witness also told Ramirez that the shooter was staying in Everett.

Shit. I'd really hoped to be able to just go the two miles to my house. Instead, I was driving fifty miles north to Everett.

The address actually ended up being in unincorporated Snohomish County.

During Ramirez' interview with this guy, he actually implicated himself in a murder that had happened in Snohomish County a couple weeks earlier that we didn't even know about. We called the detectives working that case and had them meet us at the apartment where our guy was supposed to be staying.

After the place was secure, I sat in my car in front of the building, while Al Cruise, Russ Weklych and the Snohomish County detectives went in.

A uniformed Snohomish County deputy brought a transvestite and another guy out. He asked if he could put them in my car.

"No problem," I said.

They sat in my car for about a half hour while we sorted things out. I sat in the driver's seat making small talk with them. Eventually, we let them go back inside.

By the end of the night, our shooter was in custody, and we'd solved the Snohomish County murder we knew nothing about just a few hours earlier.

That, in a nutshell, is what's wrong with federal investigators. They aren't allowed to make decisions on their own; they can't think outside the box. If we'd listened to the US Attorney, the suspect in our murder would not have been arrested, at least not that night, and the other murder would probably still be unsolved.

The next day I got a call from Snohomish County. The transvestite who'd been in my car had sloughed a gun. The deputy that put him in my car hadn't patted him down.

I walked out to the car deck outside our office, to my car and lifted the back seat. Sure as shit, there was a fully-loaded handgun.

Needless to say, I was pissed. Both at the deputy that hadn't patted down the guy before putting him in my car, but at myself for trusting him.

That'll never happen again.

Several months later, the defendant's sister testified at trial about the horrible detective who made her do the rosary.

I just smiled.

Garry Boulden is a Victim Advocate attached to the Homicide unit. He's a retired Catholic Priest. After her testimony, he brought me a pamphlet about how to correctly administer the rosary.

What do I know? I'm Protestant.

Peanut's Playpen. Charles Jackson strangled Julie Sterling in this room. Note the bottles of urine on the dresser and coffee table.

Sterling's decomposing body was found near the shore of Lake Washington. The small remnant of a garbage bag on her back was a key to solving her murder.

Dewayne Lee Harris, AKA "Chilly Willy" confessed to and was convicted of killing Denise Harris, Olivia Smith and Toinette Jones. He tied them up with their own shoelaces. Harris claims to have killed many more women.

When Toinette Jones begged Dewayne Harris for her life, telling him she had babies at home, he replied, "You tell that to Jesus, when you see him in a minute," and then strangled her to death.

After Shannon Harps' murder, a witness helped develop a sketch of the suspect. William Ball had a history of violence against women, and looked just like the sketch. During his interview, he admitted being in the area of the murder, but said he "blacked out" when it happened. We thought he may be the killer. DNA proved otherwise.

Though witnesses had eliminated him the night of the murder of Shannon Harps, James Williams DNA was found on the knife that killed her. He confessed in detail to the killing.

183

Brenda Nicholas, (left) was a Gypsy, swindling millions of dollars from her marks. Patrick Fleming had a coin collection she wanted. She decided to kill him and take it. She convinced Charles Jungbluth, (center) and Gilda Ramirez,(right) to help her do it.

When Rosemary Garnett opened the door to Patrick Fleming's apartment in December, 2011, she found him dead on the floor.

Ian Stawicki enters the Café Racer in North Seattle, just before 11:00 AM on a Wednesday morning in May. He was about to shoot almost everyone there.

Stawicki, who was mentally ill, took out two .45 caliber pistols in the bar and opened fire.

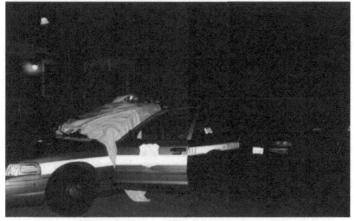

3-George-13, Officers Tim Brenton and Britt Sweeney were ambushed on October 31, 2009. Brenton's body was still inside their patrol car when I arrived.

This vehicle was captured on their dash camera moments before the shooting. It showed up on the cameras of several units racing to the scene to help their fellow officers as well.

A flag bandanna was found in the street north of the scene. It was later matched by DNA to the bombing of the police vehicles in the car shop, and ultimately, to the shooter: Christopher Monfort.

19

Most of the murders I have investigated in my career aren't interesting enough to write about. One gang-banger shoots another gang-banger. One is dead, the other is off to prison for years.

In April of 2004, I had one of those cases.

A known gang-banger named Damien Johnson was walking near Judkins Park in the Central area when he was gunned down. They make it sound so cool in the gansta-rap songs, but in reality, this is the cost of such a lifestyle.

Jason Kasner and I worked the case.

People sometimes say the police don't work hard on these cases because the victim was a gang-banger. Believe me, we work hard on those cases; sometimes harder than others. Because of the "don't snitch" culture, both on the street and in urban music, we have almost no cooperative witnesses. If we only worked murders where innocent people were killed, we'd have nothing to do.

We heard a rumor on the street that the shooter was Master Rat. We had no idea who Master Rat was. He reportedly belonged to a sub-set gang known as the Rat Pack.

We talked to guys in the Gang Unit, who told us that Master Rat was Master Anthony Jones. Master was his real name.

We worked the case extensively over the next two weeks. Finally, detectives in the Major Crimes Task Force called. They had an informant who had information about the murder. We met with the informant.

He told us that he was in jail with Master Anthony Jones, and Jones told him he'd killed a guy near Judkins Park. Now we had probable cause to arrest Jones for killing Johnson. He was charged in the case, but it was all based on the word of one informant. We needed to keep working to firm up the evidence.

Jones was being held at the Regional Justice Center in Kent, south of Seattle. The RJC is part of the King County Jail system.

As luck would have it, my favorite snitch, Paul, was in custody in the downtown jail.

I called the jail.

"I want you to transfer Paul to the RJC and I want him housed near Master Anthony Jones."

They agreed to move him.

A couple hours later, I got a phone call from Paul.

"They're transferring me to RJC!"

"Really?" I said.

"Did you do that?"

"Paul, why would I do that?" I asked.

"If you didn't do it, then why are they sending me there?" he asked.

"I have no idea," I told him.

I couldn't tell Paul what I was up to. That would make him my agent, and anything he found out would be inadmissible. I was just providing the opportunity for Jones to speak to him.

A couple of weeks later, I got a call from Paul.

"There's a guy in here named Master. He told me he killed someone."

"I'll be right down," I said.

The details Paul got from Jones were completely consistent with the information from the earlier informant.

Jones was convicted of the murder.

I was working nights in Homicide on February 18th, 2005. My sister Kim called.

"Gidget's been hit by a car. She's up at Harborview."

Gidget is my youngest sister. She was born in 1967, as evidenced by her name. I drove three blocks up the hill from police headquarters to Harborview.

I entered the emergency room through the back entrance, something I've done hundreds of times. I looked at the board to see which treatment room she was in, and then I went into the room.

A nurse was in there, along with a uniformed Federal Way police officer. They saw the badge clipped to my jacket.

A woman laid on a backboard on the bed, intubated, her face swollen. There was a problem. This woman had jet-black hair. Gidget had been blonde all her life.

"I think this is my sister," I said to the nurse.

"You're not sure?" she asked.

"I've never seen her with black hair."

"When did you last see her?" the nurse asked.

"She was at my house at Christmas," I said.

I pulled back the sheet at her ankles. Gidget had a tattoo of a butterfly on one ankle. The tattoo was there.

"This is her." I said.

I spoke to the Federal Way officer.

"She was in a bar and got into an argument with her boyfriend. She ran into the street. The first car stopped, but an SUV was in the second lane and didn't see her. He hit her."

Gidget was divorced. She had two daughters. Alex was 11. Whitney, her oldest daughter was 19 and living in Montana.

I called Doreen to tell her what happened.

"Where's Alex?" she asked.

"I have no idea."

Once again, the task of telling my parents fell on me. By that time, it was the middle of the night. I decided to wait until morning.

I went to their house first thing, to let them know what happened. They left immediately for Harborview.

As it ended up, Alex was with her dad Mike, Gidget's ex-husband. We called him. He said he'd drop her at our house. He came by and dropped her off, like it was a normal visitation coming to an end. He offered no support to his eleven-year-old daughter.

It soon became clear: Gidget would not survive. It was difficult for my parents to grasp, but her injuries were devastating.

We met with the hospital staff. There were people there to talk about organ procurement. They delicately tried to broach the subject. I spoke up.

"We want you to take every organ you can use."

They were taken aback.

"We may need to keep her alive for a couple days to do that."

"That's fine with us," I said. "We need to help as many people as possible, to make something positive out of this."

I got a call from Dave Delgado, an Investigator with the Medical Examiner's office a couple days later.

"Cloyd, I heard about your sister. I'm really sorry man. I'm handling the case here. Call me if you have any questions."

"I will, Dave. Thanks," I said.

A day later, Richard Harruff, the Chief Medical Examiner, called me. He was about to conduct the autopsy on Gidget.

"I just wanted to call and offer my condolences," he said.

I appreciated the gesture.

The United States Federal Courthouse in Seattle is at 700 Stewart Street; one block from SPD's West Precinct.

On the afternoon of June 20th, 2005, a man walked into the lobby of the courthouse, went around the metal detectors and stood next to a fountain. He wore a backpack turned around so that it was on the front of his body. In his hand was what appeared to be a hand grenade. He made no demands. In fact, he said nothing at all. Security called 911.

We got a call in the office, letting us know what was going on. This had officer-involved shooting written all over it.

Patrol responded, and called for SWAT. There was a foreign head of state in town. SWAT had been providing security, and at that time was seeing him off at the airport. There was only one officer in the SWAT office: Officer Tim Pasternak. I knew Tim well. He was a long-time SWAT-dog, as SWAT officers are called by their peers, and very competent. He responded.

By the time Tim arrived, patrol had taken control of the lobby of the courthouse. Bill Collins was an officer who'd recently left SWAT and went back to patrol. He and Pasternak took up a position across the lobby from the suspect. Pasternak was armed with an M-16. Collins had a shotgun loaded with slug rounds.

They yelled orders across the lobby to the suspect; he didn't respond.

The courthouse is ensconced in bomb-resistant glass. That's very helpful if the bomb is outside the courthouse. If the bomb is inside, it makes the problem exponentially worse. The glass would contain the concussion from an explosion, rather than releasing it through broken glass; a much deadlier situation.

The building was being evacuated, but employees looked over railings on the upper floors, down at the lobby and the suspect. If there was a bomb in the backpack around the suspect's chest, everyone in the lobby and railings above would be killed.

"I don't like this at all," Pasternak said to Collins.

Pasternak yelled one final order to the suspect. Getting no response, he fired one shot from his M-16, which went through the suspect's upper lip and back through his brain. Almost simultaneously, Collins fired his shotgun, striking the suspect in the chest. He was killed instantly.

Though he was down, because they didn't know if that was a bomb strapped to his chest that could possibly still go off, the scene wasn't secure.

The Bomb Squad had arrived. Detective Scott Kawahara entered the lobby adorned in a full bomb suit. He had to make sure any bombs on the suspect were rendered safe.

Kawahara discovered that the backpack worn backwards by the suspect contained only a wooden cutting board. The hand grenade he held was a shell; not loaded with gunpowder.

Never bring a fake hand grenade to a real gunfight.

Once the scene was under control, a rush of agencies began investigating. The FBI was involved, since this was an assault on a federal building. Jason and I were the primary detectives for the officer-involved shooting. On the surface, it seemed like a classic suicide-by-cop.

The ATF brought in bomb-sniffing dogs, checking the perimeter of the building. I was all for that idea. The first arriving dog handler walked up to me.

"Where do you want me to check first?" he asked.

"The area right around me," I answered, smiling.

An FBI supervisor stood on the corner, surrounded by other FBI agents.

"We need to get a search warrant for the suspect's apartment," he told the other agents.

"Why do you need a warrant?" I asked. "The suspect's dead. Who's going to challenge your search?"

He looked at me dumbfounded for a moment.

"Well, in case he had an accomplice," he said.

That, in a nutshell, is what's wrong with the way the FBI does things. They can't think on their feet. Check the lease; if there's no one else on there, there's no reason to get a warrant. I shook my head and walked away. If they want to spin their wheels, more power to them.

There was no accomplice. It was just a nut-job who wanted the police to kill him.

Wish granted.

March 25th, 2006 was a Saturday morning. I wasn't on call. None the less, my phone rang. There'd been a mass shooting at an East Precinct address. There were six dead at the scene.

I was on my way.

I arrived at the office, filled with survivors of the shooting, each needing to be interviewed. Everyone was covered in fake blood; they'd attended a zombie party the night before. That had caused a problem at the scene, discerning the real victim's from those covered in the fake blood.

After the zombie rave party, several attendees went to a house party on East Republican Street. Most of the people at the house knew each other. They were all friends in the goth scene.

One older guy showed up at the party. He was nice enough, talking with everyone. No one felt threatened by him.

At some point in the early morning hours, he excused himself and went outside. A few minutes later he returned, armed with a pistol and shotgun. He began shooting everyone he saw for no apparent reason.

One of the people killed was a 13-year-old girl.

I interviewed a boy and a girl.

"We ran to the bathroom and locked the door," one of them said. "We laid in the bathtub. He was shooting through the door. We could hear the bullets ricocheting off the side of the tub. I thought we were going to die."

When the first call came into 911, units were dispatched. An officer working alone in a car was the first to arrive. He came upon the shooter, later identified as Kyle Huff on the street in front of the house. When Huff saw the police car, he put the shotgun in his mouth and pulled the trigger, killing himself.

Huff had spray painted the word "Now" on the concrete steps leading up to the house from the street. No one knew what that meant, or why Huff had gone on the shooting spree.

We served a search warrant that evening on a North Seattle apartment Huff shared with his twin brother. The manager of the building was uncooperative and being a pain in the ass. He tried to keep us from entering the apartment, until we told him we'd be entering, just as soon as we booked his ass into jail. He backed off.

194

He stood near the front of the building, glaring.

Al Cruise and Russ Weklych were carrying boxes of evidence to our cars. Weklych looked at Cruise.

"Did you get that hand grenade?" he said.

Later that night, I got a call from a television reporter I know.

"Can you confirm that a grenade was found in the apartment?"

"I wouldn't go with that story," I told her.

We were working nights on the evening of April 25th, 2006 when a call came in of a fatal officer-involved shooting at Broadway and East John Street on Capitol Hill.

When we arrived, a white man lay dead on the sidewalk.

This guy had apparently been standing on a corner before the shooting. He told another guy standing nearby that he planned to shoot the next police officer he saw. Fortunately, that guy called 911.

When the officers got there, they found the suspect standing on the street. As they approached, he pulled a .38 revolver and pointed it at them. They opened fire, killing him.

I examined the scene. The suspect's gun was lying on the sidewalk a few feet from his body. It was an older revolver with a six-inch barrel.

I looked closely at the gun. I noticed an anomaly in the cylinder. I bent down for a closer look, shining my flashlight on the pistol.

An officer's bullet had gone the wrong way down the cylinder, striking a round in the gun. It was unequivocal evidence that the gun had been pointed at the officers when they fired. Had it not

195

been, it would have been physically impossible for the bullet to enter the cylinder.

The TV show Mythbusters did an episode on the shooting. They screwed it all up, claiming that the officer was armed with the revolver and that the shot entered an empty cylinder. In reality, the suspect was armed with the revolver, and the shot made by the officer entered into a cylinder loaded with a live round.

In the end, Mythbusters determined that the shot could have been made.

I know it could have been; I was there.

I've investigated a lot of murders where the suspect proffers a mental defense, claiming that because of mental illness, they are blameless. Most of the time, this is complete bullshit. Once in a while, though, I investigate a killing where the suspect is legitimately bat-shit crazy.

Medical insanity and legal insanity are two different things. A person can be medically insane, but legally sane. The test is if the person knew right from wrong at the time of the incident. The actions of the suspect give clues to whether the offender did or didn't.

Did the offender try to dispose of or otherwise hide evidence? Did he or she run or attempt to flee? These are things a person who didn't think their actions were wrong would not do.

Byron Thompson was bat-shit crazy.

He lived in an apartment in Yesler Terrace.

In July of 2007, we got a call of a shooting at the Terrace. There were two victims; Pedro Rodriguez was dead at the scene. Tina Johnson was critically wounded and taken to Harborview.

The shooter was Johnson's boyfriend, Byron Thompson.

We surrounded Thompson's nearby apartment. After I got a search warrant, we entered. Thompson wasn't there.

Aluminum foil covered his windows and the cracks in the doors.

In the business, we call that a clue.

Late on the same afternoon of the murder, I got a call from Sergeant Liz Eddy. Liz ran the Crisis Intervention Team, and regularly dealt with the mentally ill.

Harborview had called to say that a man had been checked in to the psych ward voluntarily after he told his father and brother that he'd killed someone. They didn't believe him, and thought he was crazy, so they took him to Harborview.

The patient was Byron Thompson.

Jason and I, along with a couple other detectives, went to Harborview and to the psych ward.

A nurse stood just outside the locked door.

I identified myself.

"We need to see Byron Thompson," I said.

"You can't see a patient on this ward," she responded.

About that time, someone exited the ward. I grabbed the now-open door.

"Sure I can," I said, as we walked in.

She tried to stop us; good luck with that.

We went to Bryon's room and arrested him. As we walked back past her, you should have seen the look on her face: Priceless.

We took Byron back to the Homicide office and put him in an interview room.

"They've been drugging and poisoning me for like four months," he said.

"Who's been poisoning you?" I asked.

"A combination of people," he said.

"Tell me about Tina Johnson," I said.

"She's the one who's drugging me," he said. "Vaguely, I remember going up there and playing cards, with Tina."

"Who else was there?" I asked.

"Her uncle, Pedro," he said.

"What time did you go over there?" I asked.

"I don't really know. They started drugging me, and I got really sick. They put it in Sky Blue Vodka."

As we carried on the conversation, Thompson seemed lucid. He didn't have any trouble carrying on a conversation, answered questions appropriately, and didn't say anything that was overtly nutso.

"Things were going okay," he said. "We were playing last card, then switched to twenty-one."

"Have you known Pedro for long?" Jason asked.

"Oh, yeah. I thought he was a good buddy of mine," Thompson responded.

"Why do you say that in the past tense?" I asked.

"Because he was drugging me," Thompson said. "You know, after I got drunk, I really…"

"How much did you have to drink?" I asked.

"I don't know, probably…quite a bit. My tongue has still got the, like, battery acid taste."

He talked about going to various doctors to see what he was drugged with. They couldn't find anything.

"Did you ever go to a psychiatrist about this?" I asked. "Has any doctor ever recommended that?"

"Everybody says that," he said.

"If you thought Tina and Pedro were drugging you," I asked, "why did you go over there?"

"You know, you want to face reality, and you don't want them to get away with it," he said.

"Were you confronting them about it?"

"No, I was just looking for evidence."

"Did you find any?"

"No, I blacked out, halfway through the bottle of…" he trailed off.

"Had you ever blacked out before?" I asked.

"Never."

"So this was the first time in your whole life?"

"Yeah."

"Why do you supposed you blacked out then?" I asked.

"Because they were drugging me," he said.

"You said they were drugging you before, but you didn't black out then."

"I didn't drink that much before."

"Where you drunk, or drugged," I asked.

"A combination of both."

"Did you get in an argument while you were there?" Jason asked.

"No," he said.

"Did you talk to them before about being drugged?"

"Yeah," he said.

"What did they say?"

"She said she knows I'm being drugged."

"Did she admit she was doing it?"

"No," he said. "But I ain't no fool."

He said he was sipping the vodka, but Pedro and Tina were drinking other things. He noticed a metallic taste, just before blacking out.

People who know that they did something very bad often say they "blacked out." It's a convenient way not to take responsibility for what happened. It's always bullshit and in my opinion, evidence that the person knew right from wrong. If they didn't, they would just say what happened, and have no problem with it.

We confronted him about telling his brother that he killed someone.

"You couldn't tell him that if you blacked out. You told him you shot two people. It's because you did shoot two people.

"Don't insult our intelligence," I said. "Just tell us what happened."

We changed our line of questioning.

"Where's your gun?"

"What gun?" he asked.

"Your .45?"

"It got stolen," he said.

"No it didn't," I said. "You used it this morning."

Again, his attempt to say that his gun was stolen is clear evidence that he knew right from wrong. A person who didn't think it was wrong would not make up a story that their gun was stolen.

"If it was stolen," I continued, "Why didn't you report it stolen?"

"Because every time I call the police, you guys act like I'm crazy," he said.

I wonder why?

"Byron," I said. "People saw you drive from the scene in your Olds Cutlass. They know you."

We pressed him on his "black-out" story.

"When did you wake up?"

"I ain't going to lie to you."

"Yes you are," I said.

He agreed to sign a release of medical records form after we promised to have his blood screened for toxins.

He continued talking about the victim's attempts to poison him.

"If you open my refrigerator, you'll see there's Freon leaking into the apartment. They're trying to do me that way."

"Do you think it's Tina and Pedro that are doing this to you?" I asked.

"A few weeks ago, I got something in the mail saying I won some money," he said.

"You mean like the Publisher's Clearing House?"

"I don't know," he said. "But Tina stole it."

"Do you think Pedro was involved," I asked.

"He probably was."

"Why did she move out of your apartment," I asked.

"I put her out," he said.

"Why?"

"I'd wake up and there'd be towels covered with blood all over."

"You didn't like her doing human sacrifices in your apartment?" I asked.

"After all this time, I just snapped," he said.

"You know, that's exactly what we think," I said. "You've been thinking these people are poisoning you, and you think they're going to kill you, so you went over there, maybe not with the intention of shooting anybody, but you took your gun with you."

"Why do you think I would do this," he asked.

"That's what we're trying to find out," I said.

"But you just think that I went in there…"

"Yeah," I said. "But maybe you have an excuse. Maybe you have a reason."

"You guys need to investigate that."

"Yeah, I know." I said.

"Is that the reason you shot them? I asked.

"I told you," he said. "I was blacked out."

"Is there a possibility that when you blacked out, you did it?"

"I don't think so," he said.

"Why would Tina say, 'Byron Thompson shot me'?" I asked. "She loved you."

"There's a possibility that she poisoned me so much, that I blacked out…"

"That you might have done this?" I asked.

"I might have went psychotic."

"Do you think this was a preemptive strike? That you got them before they could get you?"

"I don't know," he said.

"Byron," Jason asked. "Is it possible that when you were blacked out, you shot them?"

"If they drugged me enough," he said, "to make me go psychotic…"

"If a man's got to protective himself," Jason continued, "what's a man to do?"

"I'm tired of getting drugged," he said.

As Byron talked about the possibility that he'd done this, he cried softly.

"I never wanted to hurt no one," he said.

As the conversation with Thompson went on, he seemed completely lucid and sane, carrying on an intelligent conversation, until he spoke of gases being injected into his apartment from the upstairs apartment, though the refrigerator, and cracks in the doors and windows.

As we questioned Thompson, he was conversational, and had no problem answering our questions, unless it had something remotely to do with the murder, like where his car was parked. At those moments, he became conveniently muddled. If someone didn't know what he'd done was wrong, why would he do that?

Ultimately Thompson would only admit that he "could have done it," in a "psychotic state" brought on by the poison administered by the victims.

We booked him for the murder.

In the end, the prosecutor agreed to accepted a Not Guilty by Reason of Insanity plea.

Thompson was sent to a mental hospital.

20

The last several years of my career, I carried between ten and twelve weeks' vacation on the books. Because of that, I always took a week or two off at the holidays. That was the case in 2007.

On New Year's Eve of that year, we had several friends over. I was relaxed, talking to neighbors and other friends. I'd recently taught Doreen to make the perfect martini, a skilled she plied that night. I was working on my third, when my work cellphone rang. It was Jason.

"I would normally never call you on vacation for a homicide," he said, "but this isn't the usual doper murder."

"I'm up at 15th and Howell Street," he said. I knew the neighborhood well. It was only a few blocks from the East Precinct.

"This girl was stabbed to death in the outside stairwell of her apartment. She looks like a real innocent victim," he told me.

"I'm coming in," I told him.

Doreen stood nearby, listening to my half of the conversation.

"Oh, no you're not," she said. "How many martinis have you had?"

"This is my third," I said, "but I have to go to this one."

"Well, then I'm driving you," she said.

I was good with that.

Doreen drove me to the scene in her Volkswagen convertible.

On the drive downtown, I was on the phone with Jason, getting updates on the case.

We arrived at the scene, encircled with yellow crime scene tape.

"The victim lives in this building," Jason said. "She was going to a New Year's Eve party and had apparently walked to a nearby store. She was on her way back, and walked down the stairway to her basement apartment, when someone followed her and stabbed her several times. There were people standing on the corner near the apartment. They heard her scream. A guy walked out of the stairway and went right past them. They found her and called medics. They took her to Harborview, but she died."

Scott O'Toole from the prosecutor's office was there. He, Jason and I walked to a back street abutting the building.

"People said there was a weird guy sitting back here," Jason said. "He was sitting on the steps of Seattle Mental Health drinking beer. He was flipping Pabst Blue Ribbon caps into the street."

I looked at the steps this guy had been sitting on, and at the beer caps in the street directly in front of them.

There was a reusable grocery bag on the ground near the stairwell with receipts from two nearby stores. The most recent one was time-stamped at 7:09 PM, just a short time before the attack. It was walking distance from the scene. Her path home from there would have taken her right past the Seattle Mental Health building.

While we were examining the scene, we got word that patrol had stopped a guy a few blocks away. He was sitting in a bus shelter drinking Pabst Blue Ribbon beer.

Patrol brought the witnesses who'd seen the suspect to that location. They looked at the guy and told the officers he was not the suspect.

Jason and I talked about him.

"He was drinking Pabst beer, just like the guy on the steps," I said. "Maybe he was with the suspect earlier. Let's have him taken to the office for a chat."

Jason agreed.

We stayed at the scene for a while longer, and then headed in to the office to talk to this guy.

We went to the viewing area, on the other side of the one-way glass that looked into the interview room. We watched the guy for a little while. He'd been identified as James Williams. He was in his late forties, mostly bald with a moustache. He wore a clean blue and white jacket, and a sweat suit, with no blood stains that we could see. He didn't seem nervous.

We went in, taking our usual positions: me on the same side of the table as Williams, Jason across from him.

"I was at the bus stop drinking beer, when this police dog came along. The officer said, 'You'd better watch out, you're going to get bit'," he said.

"Did you know what was going on?" I asked.

"Some guy was in the bus stop with me a few minutes earlier. He said something about some girl getting stabbed."

"Were you sitting up at Seattle Mental Health earlier, flicking bottle caps into the street?" I asked.

"No, I wasn't," he said.

Jason and I looked at each other.

"Do you mind if we swab the inside of your cheek?" I asked.

"No, that's fine," he said. "I just got out of prison a few months ago," he said.

"What were you in for?"

"I shot a guy on the street ten years ago."

Our witnesses had eliminated him as the suspect, but I had a feeling he'd been the guy flipping the bottle caps. Why wouldn't he admit that? He was drinking Pabst beer just a few blocks away. What are the odds? Pabst isn't that common of a beer brand to be drinking in this area. At least by swabbing his cheek, we could eliminate the beer caps lead.

Buccal mucosa is the lining on the inside of the cheek. We collected cells by swabbing the inside of his cheeks with a swab similar to a long-stemmed Q-Tip and let him go.

New Year's Day, we were in the office working the case.

By that time, the victim had been identified as Shannon Harps. I sent an email to the Department of Licensing, asking for Harps' driver's license photo.

I always want a photo of my victim in life, first to remind me that they were a real person, and also, in case I need to show someone a photo to identify who I am talking about with them, if they don't know the victim by name.

This case received a lot of local media attention, especially since it appeared she was an innocent person murdered on the street. Tips began to pour in. Some sounded promising, but all the early tips were dead-ends.

I also did a part of the job I don't like but have to do. I called Harps' family in Florida. I spoke to Ron Harps, her father. He'd been notified the night before about the murder. Needless to say, he and his family were devastated.

During our conversation, there were frequent pauses; he tried to control his crying but was having a lot of difficulty.

I told him that Jason and I were the primary detectives tasked with getting whoever did this. I gave him our direct contact information, as well as the numbers for the victim advocates, who would help them through the process.

I asked if Shannon had a boyfriend, or ex-boyfriend, eliminating the obvious reasons why this may have happened.

"I spoke to her on Christmas Day," he said. "Everything was fine. As far as I know, she didn't have a boyfriend."

He'd received an email from her that morning; she'd apparently been planning on a trip to Chile in February with two friends.

She worked at the Sierra Club, an organization dedicated to the environment, particularly forest land.

I asked about close friends she had in Seattle that could help me figure out what was going on in her life. He knew her friends, but in his emotional state, he couldn't think of their names. I asked him to call me later if he remembered them.

It's always hard talking to family members so soon after their loved ones are killed. I try to present myself professionally, but empathetically. When family members call me "Detective Steiger," I tell them to call me Cloyd. It really hits home the burden that I have to find the son of a bitch that did this.

He called an hour later with two friend's names. He gave me a phone number.

I got a call an hour or so later from the regional director of Sierra Club, who identified himself as Martin Leblanc. He and his wife were close friends with Shannon.

I asked about boyfriends and the like. He said she was not in a relationship and had not been recently.

The next morning, I went to the Medical Examiner's office for the autopsy. Scott O'Toole was there too.

Harps had been stabbed four times in the torso and once in the arm. The chest wounds severed her aorta. She bled out in seconds, and hadn't stood a chance of survival.

When the autopsy was complete, I went to my office to learn as much as I could about her.

She'd been employed by the Sierra Club for a year; she'd moved to Seattle from Ohio because she loved the mountains and forests here.

She'd been invited to a New Year's Eve party that night and had gone to two different stores.

We looked for surveillance video from the stores and from the route she likely took from her apartment to each of them, which were in opposite directions.

We were able to get video from the Safeway store she went to first. We saw her enter and walk around the store. It didn't appear that she interacted with anyone, and no one appeared to follow her from the store.

Shannon's family flew to Seattle.

On January 3rd, we met with her mother, father, and sister.

Meeting with the family of a murder victim is always hard; this was no exception.

Losing a child is the worst thing that can ever happen to a person in their life. Nothing else comes close; it's unnatural. As I spoke with Shannon's family, I promised them I'd so everything I could to find out who did this to their daughter. I meant it, but inside I hoped that I'd be able to get this guy. Sometimes it takes years. I told them that.

It's good for us to meet with family members. We work murders every day. They are cases to us, and we become jaded. It's a good grounding experience to remind me that what I think of as a job has a huge effect on the loved one's left behind after a murder; it's a huge burden, meeting with families, but they're just as much victims of homicide as the person killed.

Later that day, I drove Ron Harps and his wife to the scene to show them where this happened. I tried to explain the unfathomable to them. I do that by speaking in personal and simple terms. No police lingo or officious talk. It's difficult; these people are suffering.

I pulled my unmarked detective car to the curb next to the stairwell where Shannon Harps drew her last breaths. Ron sat in the front seat next to me and Angela, Shannon's mother, in the back.

"There's one thing I really have to know," Ron said. "Did she suffer?"

I answered him honestly.

"I've spoken to a lot of people over the years that had been stabbed. Pretty much all of them told me the same thing: they didn't even realize they were being stabbed. They just thought they were being punched. It wasn't until later that they realized what happened. I'm sure it was the same with Shannon. She didn't know she'd been stabbed. She just passed out from lack of blood."

I called Betty Kincaid, my favorite composite sketch artist, and made arrangements for her to come in and meet with one of the witnesses the killer had walked right past after the attack.

She met with the witness, and the two of them developed a sketch. The witness scored it a nine out of ten as looking like the person he saw. That's a good rating.

The sketch depicted a thin-faced young man with black hair under a knit cap, and a beard.

The knife used to murder Harps was recovered in a planting strip near her building. The lab tested it and found, in addition to Harps' DNA, the DNA of an unknown male contributor, whom they referred to as Individual A on the handle. They'd run the DNA profile through CODIS and hadn't received a hit. CODIS is populated with the DNA of convicted felons. Presumably, our suspect had not been convicted of a felony, at least since they started taking DNA samples.

I sent a bulletin, including the sketch of the suspect, to every police agency in the state. We also decided to give it to the media, who were clamoring for something to put out. Someone may recognize this guy.

A couple days later, I got a call from an officer from the Department of Corrections.

"I've got a guy on my caseload," he said, "that looks just like the sketch. He has a psych history and has been violent toward women in the past."

The guy he was talking about was William Ball. He also went by the name William Torrito.

I pulled up a recent jail booking photo for Ball/Toritto. He could have posed for the composite sketch.

I found from the DOC that Ball was in violation of his probation for drinking alcohol. They agreed to issue a warrant for his arrest.

I called Randy Moore, a Seattle Detective assigned to the US Marshall's fugitive task force, and asked him to find Ball and bring him in.

Ball was living in DOC provided housing on Summit Avenue on Capitol Hill. We went there looking for him.

We brought the manager to his door and knocked but received no answer. We had the manager open the door and went in. Ball wasn't there.

The manager said that he'd seen Ball on January 2nd. Ball seemed to be drunk. The manager thought that he'd relapsed.

By 10 o'clock that night, Ball was in custody. We'd been working all day, and were about to leave, but those plans were quickly quashed. He was being transported to our office.

When Ball arrived at our office, we had him put in an interview room. Jason and I went to the viewing area to watch him through the one-way glass for a few minutes. He was calm and content, never asking why he was there. There were scratches on his face.

After a while, we went in for the interview, again, taking our usual places in the room.

"How'd you get the scratches on your face?" I asked.

"I got them hiding in the dirt," he said.

"Who were you hiding from?"

"My parole officer," he said.

We made small talk for several minutes, asking his background and things like that. Finally, I steered the conversation toward New Year's Eve.

He admitted being on Capitol Hill that night. He went into great detail about his movements early in the evening. At some point he said that he'd "blacked out," and didn't remember what happened.

How convenient that he "blacked out" right when our murder occurred. I've heard that dozens of times from guilty people.

We've got him, I thought. Then he said something that really got me pumped that this was the guy: "I remember seeing police cars driving around; I hid from them."

He still hadn't asked what this was about, or why he was there. Finally, I broached that subject.

"William, aren't you wondering why we have you here, questioning you?" I asked.

"I was wondering," he said.

"We're investigating the murder of a girl that happened while you were up on Capitol Hill."

"Oh, no," he said. "I didn't murder anyone."

"How do you know, if you were blacked out?"

We'd given him gum to chew and a soda to drink while we interviewed him. Before taking him to jail for the probation violation, we had him spit the gum out. We collected that,r and the soda can.

After we completed the interview, I left the room. Scott O'Toole had been watching in the viewing room. He walked around to meet us.

"What do you think?" he asked me.

"I would have told you for sure he was the guy when he put himself up there, admitted hiding from police cars and said he

212

'blacked out'. But he was pretty adamant when I mentioned the murder."

"I'm glad you said that," O'Toole said. "I just don't know either."

We submitted the gum and soda can from Ball to the lab, so they could develop a profile and compare it to Individual A, the contributor of the DNA on the knife handle.

A few days later, I got a call from Amy Jagmin in the crime lab.

"William Ball is not your guy."

I was a little deflated. Ball had been promising. He looked just like the sketch, had admitted being in the area the night of the murder, even hiding from police cars, and having a black out. It just goes to show; you never know.

We were back to square one.

We followed up other leads. I submitted the DNA swabs from James Williams to see if they matched potential DNA from the bottle caps.

Several leads seemed promising, but each faded away, unrelated to this murder.

On January 25th, I left my house in the suburbs to come into the office. I was in a Starbucks drive-through when my cell phone rang. It was Amy Jagmin from the lab.

"I need to read you my lab report," she said.

My ears perked up. When someone at the lab says they need to read you a report, something big is happening. I'd talked to Amy a lot since this murder happened. She just told me what she had. She'd never said she had to read me a report.

"Items submitted as buccal swabs from James Williams were developed for DNA…" She continued to read all the lab-esque language about the process of developing DNA. Then she got to the meat of the matter.

"The DNA extracted from the swabs from James Williams match the DNA developed from the knife submitted and the DNA profile identified as Individual A."

What the fuck?

"Williams is the guy?" I asked her, incredulous. Williams was a convicted felon. His DNA should have been in CODIS. Also, witnesses looked at him the night of the murder and eliminated him as the suspect, and he looked absolutely nothing like the sketch of the suspect our witness had helped develop.

I jumped my police car over the curb to get out of the Starbucks line, and raced downtown. I called Jason on the way to tell him what was going on.

When I arrived in the office, things were buzzing. We were gearing up, getting ready to go find Williams and bring him in. He lived in an apartment on Summit Avenue, (coincidentally, only a block from William Ball).

We were just about ready to leave the office.

"Just a minute," I said, and walked to my desk. I checked Williams' name in the jail booking systems.

"He's in jail," I told the others.

I've been burned before, chasing all over town looking for a suspect, only to find they were in jail the whole time. Glad I checked.

After taking off our bullet-proof vests and putting our other gear away, Jason and I walked through the tunnel that connects Seattle Police Headquarters with the downtown jail. We retrieved Williams and brought him to our office.

By that time, it was getting close to dinner time in the jail. I knew we'd be several hours, so we got Williams a burger, fries and shake.

We left him in Interview Room #1, the same one we'd previously interviewed him in, and let him eat.

214

Finally, we entered the room, assuming our usual places.

We started off playing softball.

"We just want to go over the things you told us the last time we spoke with you," I said.

Williams began recounting what he told us before. The only problem was, the story he told wasn't at all the story he'd told before.

When a person recounts the truth, it's easy. You remember, for the most part, what happened, and can recite it over and over again. There may be small omissions, but generally, the story is the same.

The story Williams told was hugely different than the one he told before. It's because he made it up as he went along last time, and now couldn't remember what he said. We just went with it, reeling out the rope with which he would eventually hang himself.

"Tell me about the guy who told you someone had been stabbed," I said.

He had no idea what I was talking about. Of course not; he'd completely made that up. Both interviews were audio and video recorded, so we had them memorialized.

We asked about his mental illness.

"I think God is punishing me," he said.

"Why do you say that?" I asked.

"I was in prison," he said. "My dick started burning real bad. I was going to cut it off, and then a guy said, 'Your dick doesn't burn anymore,' and it didn't. How the hell could he make my dick stop burning?"

Like many mentally ill people I've dealt with in the past, Williams blamed most of his problems on the psych medications he was taking.

"They're controlling my mind; they're poisoning me."

"How many knives do you own?" I asked, completely changing the subject.

"I have four knives in my apartment," he said.

"Where are they?" I asked.

"They're in a drawer in my apartment."

"So, you had five knives," I said.

"What?" he asked confused.

"You have four in your apartment, and we found one right here," I said, pointing to a diagram of the Harps crime scene. "We didn't just find a knife. We found your knife. Do you know how we know?"

"No," he barely squeaked.

"Because we found your DNA on it. Do you know about DNA?"

"Oh, I know about DNA," he said, his voice barely above a whisper.

"Then you know DNA is a done deal," I said. "DNA does two things; it absolutely exonerates the innocent, and it absolutely verifies when someone isn't innocent." (I intentionally didn't use the word guilty.)

Williams picked up the coffee we'd given him and look a long drink.

"Can I have some more coffee?" he asked.

"Sure," I said. Jason got up to get him more.

Williams became melancholy.

"All my life, people have been fucking with me," he said, again, barely above a whisper. "Like I said, I think God's punishing me."

"Maybe it's not God," I said. "Maybe you're blaming the wrong guy."

Tears welled in Williams' eyes.

I scooted closer to him.

"James," I said. "It's okay if you want to cry."

As if on cue, he wept softly. I knew then, he would confess to this murder.

When I teach interview and interrogation, I often use the analogy that a good interrogator is like a time-share salesman. Only we sell timeshares in Walla Walla, Shelton, Monroe and the sites of other prisons around the state.

I let Williams cry uninterrupted for a few moments. Finally, I spoke.

"James, I know you think your life is over, but there's one thing about being on the very bottom: there's nowhere to go but up."

"Who's got a life?" he asked.

Shannon Harps hasn't got a life, I wanted to say.

"It may seem like that now," I said instead, "but what people want to know, is you're sorry for what happened. They won't say, 'Oh, it's okay, James. You can go.' That's not going to happen. I'm not going to sit here and bullshit you. But if you tell them you're sorry, they can look at you and say, 'James is a tortured soul. We can't ignore what happened, but we can understand it.' "

An interrogation, at a point like this, requires the skill of a good fisherman. Reel him in slowly. As he starts to drift off, let out some line, but then slowly reel him back.

"I've been trying to kill people for a long time," he said.

"You mean you've wanted to?" I asked.

"No," he said. "I've actually tried to kill about ten people."

217

He digressed into stories of all the people he's tried to kill over the years. Then we steered the conversation back to this murder.

"I need to protect myself," he said.

"So, you carry a knife for protection?" Jason asked. "That makes sense, because you can't carry a gun. Where do you normally carry it?"

"In my coat pocket," Williams answered.

"She walked right past you, didn't she?" I asked.

He lowered his head and almost imperceptibly nodded.

"What happened?" I asked, my voice barely above a whisper.

"I just snapped," he said so softly I had to ask him to repeat it, so I was sure the microphone caught it. "She went by, and I followed her. She walked down the street and turned on Howell. I kept following her. She went into a stairwell. I just started stabbing her."

"What did she do?" My question still just above a whisper.

"She put her hands on my shoulders," he said, then paused. "And said 'get off me.'"

"What did you do?" I asked,

"I said, 'Die, bitch,' and kept stabbing her."

He described just walking away when he was done.

"Have you seen the coverage of this on the news?" I asked.

"When I saw who she was," he said, his sobbing increasing, "I realized we like the same things. I mean, I want to protect the environment and everything.

"I realized I'd killed my soulmate!"

We returned Williams to jail, rebooking him for murder.

A couple days later, we needed to talk to him again.

Several jailers surrounded him from his cell to the sally port where we picked him up. He wore a white "Ultra Security Prisoner" suit.

He was out of control, and just as they passed him off to us, he spat in the face of a jailer.

I sat with him in the back seat of our car.

"James," I said to him. "You know they're going to kick your ass when you get back for that."

"I know," he said calmly.

Williams was a near out-of-control prisoner; the type that shits in his hand and flings it at guards. He wasn't like that with Jason and me. He liked us. We were nice to him.

A few months later, against his attorney's advice, James Williams pled guilty to the murder of Shannon Harps.

At sentencing he received a life sentence.

Ron Harps, Shannon's dad came up and hugged me.

"You're a good man, Cloyd," he said.

That meant a lot to me.

On February 21st Jason and I were called in the middle of the night to a murder in the Greenwood area of North Seattle.

I spoke to the patrol sergeant at the scene, Sammy Derezes. Sammy came on the department a couple months after me, and I knew him well.

"People saw two men fighting," he told me. "One person walked away, but the other guy stayed down. They called 911. Medics came and took him to Harborview, but he died there."

219

The only evidence at the scene was a blood stain on the sidewalk where this happened.

"I'm going to Harborview and look at the victim," I told Jason.

I entered the treatment room where the victim's body laid, awaiting the arrival of the Medical Examiner. He was covered with a yellow blanket. I pulled it back to look at him.

"Holy shit!" I said to myself. I called Jason.

"It's William Ball."

After a couple days, we were able to track down the guy who'd killed Ball.

He was sobbing as he told us what happened.

"I just met that dude that night," he said. We were just talking, and he went off and attacked me. He picked up a wooden sign and was smashing me with it. I had a knife in my pocket. I took it out and swung it at him. I didn't even think I hurt him. I just ran.

Knowing what we knew about Ball's propensity for violence, this guy's claim of self-defense sounded reasonable. Prosecutors agreed.

He wasn't charged.

21

I'd just arrived in my office on a Monday morning in mid-April of 2008 when we were called to a dead body.

The scene was a construction site in downtown Seattle, just east of Interstate 5 on Madison Street, only a few blocks from police headquarters.

An office tower was being built there. When the construction crew arrived for work that morning, more than sawdust and drywall awaited them.

Patrol officers at the scene led us to the middle of the site on the first floor. The body of a white man in his 20's was lying there.

He'd obviously been beaten severely about the head.

I noticed right away: He was dressed in a Batman suit. (I'm a trained observer).

Russ Weklych and Al Cruise were the primary detectives on the case.

"You'd better put a bulletin out right away," I said to them. "This is obviously the work of the Joker."

Little did I know at the time; I wasn't far off.

We found 2x4s and rebar stained with blood. That's what he'd been beaten to death with.

We were at the scene most of the day. In the afternoon, my cellphone rang. It was the assisted living facility where my parents lived. My dad, who was 82, had fallen and broken his hip. He was at a hospital near my house.

I still had work to do at the scene. I told them I'd get to the hospital as soon as I could.

It was just the beginning of a very busy spring and early summer.

When I was finally able to get away, I drove to the suburban hospital near my house. I went to the emergency room, and back to the treatment room where my dad was.

He was resting comfortably. He'd been in the apartment he and my mother lived in. My mom started to fall. He tried to grab her to break her fall, when they both went down she landing on him, breaking his hip. She was unhurt.

"We're transferring him to Virginia Mason Hospital," the nurse told me. That was two blocks from the murder scene I'd been at all day.

They took him by ambulance. I followed in my unmarked police car.

He went into surgery right away; a partial hip replacement.

I waited through his surgery. They took him to his room late that night. I sat with him for an hour or so after he got there. I left to go home at about 1 o'clock in the morning. It'd been a long day.

I was back in the office in the morning. Weklych and Cruise were working the Batman murder. They'd developed suspects: Followers of the group Insane Clown Posse.

I didn't know a lot about ICP at that time, but I learned. They're a cross between a musical group and a gang. Their followers, known as Juggalos, wear clown makeup.

It was the Joker after all.

The murder victim had been developmentally delayed, Cruise and Weklych learned. The Juggalos thought he'd molested a girl. There was no evidence he had. They took him to the construction site and beat him for more than an hour, killing him.

Another stupid murder.

The suspects were arrested, and eventually convicted.

Since my dad was in a hospital only a few blocks from my office, it was convenient to visit him while I was working.

A few days after his surgery, they transferred him to a nursing home near my home.

I went to see him one day.

The staff gave him physical therapy. He needed to be up and walking, but he wasn't cooperative. He was depressed, wanting to go back to the assisted living facility with my mother. I told him the only way that was going to happen was if he could get around on his own, and he needed to do the therapy for that to happen.

I thought that if he could spend time back with my mom, he'd be inspired to do the work to get well enough to move back.

On weekends, both Saturday and Sunday, I checked him out of the nursing home and took him back to the apartment with my mother. He enjoyed the visits and his attitude improved. He was more upbeat and took part in the physical therapy.

I juggled all this with my busy work schedule; people were still killing people all over town.

In early July, I had to go to San Jose for a case. A suspect fled there.

My dad was in the hospital; he'd developed a slight fever. I stopped by there the night before I was going to leave.

He was in good spirits. I told him about the case I was going to California for. He always liked hearing about the cases I was working.

"I'll be back in a couple days," I told him.

"Okay," he said. "I'll see you when you get back."

I was in San Jose over the 4th of July. We arrested the suspect and interrogated him. He confessed to the murder. It was a very productive trip.

I was in the airport in San Jose on the morning of July 6th, getting ready to fly home. I called Doreen.

"They moved your dad to a different nursing home," she told me. "I went to see him this morning. He's not happy at all. He wants out of there."

"I'll go see him this afternoon when I get back," I told her.

When I got home, I dropped off my suitcase and jumped on my Harley to ride over to see my dad. It always perked him up when I rode my Harley over. He'd owned several Harley's as a young man and loved to ride. He nearly took my mother to the hospital to give birth to me on a Harley, but a friend gave them a ride.

"There's only one thing wrong with that bike," he said the first time he saw my shiny new Electra-Glide Ultra Classic.

"What's that?" I asked.

"I'm not on it."

I would have loved to have given him a ride on it, but with his hip, there was no way until he got better.

I parked my bike in the parking lot of the nursing home and walked in. I went up to the nurse's station.

"Can you tell me which room Cloyd Steiger is in?"

Two women behind the counter stared at me, wide-eyed.

"He's dead, isn't he?" I said.

They didn't answer.

"What room is he in?"

They told me. I walked down the hall to the room. It was quiet. His body laid on the bed, covered with a sheet. I lifted the sheet to look at the lifeless body of my father.

I called Doreen to tell her. She was shocked; she'd just been to see him a few hours ago.

Death is part of my normal life. It sounds weird, but I wasn't upset. I kind of went into work-mode. I called a funeral home, and then called my two surviving sisters. I did what I had to do.

When the woman from the funeral home arrived an hour or two later, I walked her to the room.

She was a small woman. Though my dad was no longer the big man he once was, I knew she'd struggle to get him out of there. I offered to give her a hand.

I helped put my father's body into a body bag.

I went to the assisted living facility where my mother lived. I told her.

I finally went home. I sat in a chair, and the reality of losing my dad finally hit me.

I cried.

22

I was watching an address in West Seattle in May of 2009. It was a beautiful morning. I sat outside an address trying to contact a not-so-cooperative witness to a murder I was investigating. The police radio in my car was tuned to the frequency that covers the South and Southwest precincts.

I listened on the radio as officers in Rainier Valley were dispatched to a report of a dead body at an address off of Rainier Avenue South.

Reports of a dead body are in themselves no big deal. Several occur every day in Seattle. The vast majority are not homicides.

When the first patrol cars arrived, they seemed to be acting differently than the normal dead body call.

I called the Chief Dispatcher's direct line.

"What's up with the call in the Valley," I asked.

"It looks hinky," the CD said.

"I'm going to head that way," I told him.

I drove to the Rainier Valley address.

I arrived to find the exterior stairway of the apartment building enclosed in yellow crime scene tape; my instincts were working fine.

I approached a patrol officer.

"The victim is on the second-floor landing," she told me. "He apparently shared the apartment with another guy. They were involved in some sort of dispute overnight, and the police were called. The officers who responded took him to the station, but later released him.

"People in the building called when they found this guy lying in the hallway outside his apartment."

I walked up to the dead guy. He'd been stabbed through the eye.

I called the Homicide office.

"I'm going to need a scene response here," I said. "Including CSI."

Jason and I were next-up for a murder; this would be our case.

The roommate was in the wind. The patrol officers had his cellphone number.

I called Randy Moore on the Fugitive Task Force.

"I've got a murder," I told Randy, "and I've got a suspect in the wind."

I gave Randy the suspect's cellphone number.

"I'll get on it and call you back," Randy said.

We spent the day interviewing witnesses, including officers who had responded to a disturbance there the night before, trying to figure out what happened between the victim and his roommate.

At about two PM, I got a call from Randy.

"Your suspect is driving through Sacramento right now," he said. "I called the Fresno Task Force. They're jumping on it."

I got another call from Randy an hour later.

"We got him," he said.

The next morning, Jason and I were on a plane to Fresno. We met with the US Marshal task force guys who got him.

"We got the call that he was on I-5," they said. "It was rush hour and we were an hour from the freeway. Once we got to the onramp, I asked my partner, 'what was the description of the car?' He told me it was a Mazda pick-up with Washington plates. Just as he said that, I looked up, and the guy was, driving right past us!"

They followed the car and asked for back-up. They had California Highway Patrol cars and a helicopter in the air, when they pulled him over.

"I walked up to him and said, 'Do you know why we're pulling you over?'"

"He said, 'I killed my roommate'."

Jason and I went to the jail. He confessed.

That's a wrap.

In late July of 2009, I was working nights. Like most months when I worked nights, I'd been at work all day too. There are things you can't get done on night shift.

I'd been helping other detectives on a notorious murder that had occurred while I was out of town. Two women were in the home when a stranger broke in. He held them both for a long time, raping them. He killed one of the women. The other jumped through a plate-glass window to get away; the suspect fled and was at that time still unidentified. It wasn't my case, but there was more work to do on the case than the assigned detectives could do.

It was a beautiful summer night. By that evening, my ass was dragging. I sat in my office trying to make it through the last few hours before I could go home. The main line into the Homicide office rang. It was the Chief Dispatcher.

Jason and I were next-up for a murder. This can't be good.

228

"There's a shooting in the 700 block of 32nd Avenue South," he said. "There's one dead at the scene. The suspect may be holed-up in a house. There's a SWAT response also."

This had all the makings of a world-class cluster fuck.

"We're on our way," I told the dispatcher.

I dragged my butt out of my chair, my dreams of going home evaporating like a spilled latte on a hot Seattle sidewalk.

A few minutes later, we arrived at the Leschi neighborhood address. The street lined with million-dollar homes was not the usual venue of a shooting such as this.

A car was stopped in the street, its rear window shot out. The body of a young black man lay on the ground next to the car, remnants of his brain staining the driver's seat.

Up the street to the north, a beehive of activity, patrol officers with shotguns out surrounding a house awaiting the arrival of SWAT.

The scene wasn't secure. We couldn't investigate it quite yet. I spoke to a patrol sergeant. There were two other people in the car with the victim when the shooting happened. He got some of the story from them.

"There was a group of friends at Leschi Beach," he said. "Another group of kids showed up. These guys all went to high school together and were friends, but apparently there was some sort of feud or something, supposedly over a girl.

"The first group left, and the others followed them. They all showed up here at the house up the street. A guy named Tristan Appleberry lives there. They were driving away when Tristan came out with a rifle and fired one shot. The bullet went in the back window, right past the two in the back seat and hit the driver in the head."

I walked to my car, a block south, to get a piece of equipment. An older man stood on the sidewalk near my car.

"Excuse me," he said. "I don't know where my wife is."

I reassured him. "Don't worry," I said. "The victim is not a woman."

"This is ridiculous," he said.

"Yes, it is," I agreed. I turned to walk back to the scene.

"No, I mean all these guns the police have out."

I stopped and turned around; "You're a fucking idiot."

I walked away.

Only in Seattle.

Tristan's mother eventually came out of the house. She said that Tristan wasn't there, but she was evasive and not being cooperative otherwise. SWAT didn't want to take a chance on entering. They gave several warnings over the Public Address system, and then commenced lobbing tear gas inside.

After about fifteen minutes, SWAT entered. The house was empty.

We had to get a search warrant to process the house for evidence. Once that was done, CSI started working on the scene.

The victim was Aaron Sullivan. He'd been struck in the back of the head with a bullet fired from an AK-47-like rifle. The round had actually only grazed his head, making a "key hole" type of wound, but because of the energy the round had, it created a vacuum, which sucked the brain matter out, killing him instantly.

Aaron was the adopted son of a doctor.

Another stupid murder about nothing.

We worked all night long.

We found out that Tristan may be with his girlfriend in West Seattle. By 6:45 that morning, we had him in custody.

I had him in the interview room. He had that perpetually stoned look of a chronic marijuana user, his words slow and slurred, his eyes only half open. At some point he mumbled that he wanted to call his lawyer.

"Who's your lawyer," I asked.

"I don't know her name," he said.

"Do you want to call a public defender?"

"No, I want to call my lawyer."

"I don't know who you lawyer is, and you don't seem to know. How can we call her?"

I finally looked up the lawyer from his last charge, a marijuana possession. I told him the name.

"Is that your lawyer?" I asked.

"I think so," he said through blurry eyes.

I found a number and called. His lawyer answered.

"We have Tristan Appleberry under arrest," I told her.

"What's the charge?" she asked.

"Murder."

There was a long pause. I smiled to myself. This was way out of her wheelhouse.

"I'll be right down."

"Actually," I said. "I have a warrant to have his blood drawn. We're taking him to Harborview."

"Can I be there for the blood draw?" she asked.

There's nothing that says I need to let her be there for the blood draw, but hey; I'm a nice guy.

"Sure," I said. "We'll be up there in about a half-hour."

We walked in the ER entrance at Harborview. We told the triage nurse what we needed, and they put us in a treatment room.

I walked to the public waiting room. His attorney wasn't there. We waited for another fifteen minutes. Still no attorney.

"Go ahead and do the draw," I told the nurse.

We had Tristan back in our car and were driving to the jail when my phone rang. It was Tristan's attorney.

"Are you guys almost here?" she asked.

"We're already done," I told her. "We waited and waited, but we didn't see you, so we went ahead and did the draw."

"I've been sitting here in the lab," she said.

I rolled my eyes. I forgot. This was out of her league. Like we're going to walk this guy, accused of murder, into the lab and sit him next to people getting their cholesterol checked.

"We don't go to the lab. We have it done in the ER."

"We're taking Tristan to jail now. You can see him there."

After booking him into the jail, we went back to our office. Because we had our suspect in custody, we had to get a lot done so the judge would hold him at First Appearance.

We worked until about five PM. I'd been at work 32 hours.

I was getting ready to leave for home when my cellphone rang. It was Doreen. She worked in a dental office, and was attending a dental convention in Bellevue, east of Seattle.

Our oldest son Casey's wife, Tawnie, was very pregnant.

"Tawnie's in labor!" Doreen said. "I'm heading to the hospital. I'll see you there."

"Oh no you won't," I said. "I've been up a long time. I'll be lucky if I can make it home. This is Tawnie's first baby. She'll be in labor for a while. I'm going home and going to bed."

I made it home and went straight to bed. I slept until eight the next morning.

I got up, took a shower, and then jumped on my Harley and rode it to the hospital.

I walked in the door, and twenty minutes later, my first grandson Keaton was born.

I'm a pro.

Tristan pled guilty to murder. He was sentenced to 18 years in prison. That's as long as he'd been alive, but a pretty short time for killing someone.

23

Halloween night of 2009 started out fun. It fell on a Sunday that year, so I didn't have to rush home from work.

My grandson Keaton was three months old. It was his first Halloween. He was adorably dressed in a pumpkin suit. Casey and Tawnie brought him over at about 5 o'clock to trick or treat. Really, it was just an excuse to show him off to our neighbors.

At about six-thirty, Casey had to leave for work. He was working 3rd Watch, which is 7:30 at night to 4:30 in the morning, in the East Precinct. Tawnie and Keaton stayed at our house for a while visiting with Doreen and I as well as Doreen's sisters Andrea and Glenna, my mother-in-law, Jeanette, and my father-in-law, Joel. We were all doting over Keaton when my work cellphone rang in the kitchen. I was next-up for a murder, so I was pretty sure my evening at home was over.

Mark Worstman, a sergeant in Homicide, was on the phone.

"Cloyd, we have an officer-involved shooting with an officer down at 29th and East Yesler."

Shit. An officer-involved shooting is no big deal, but an officer down means an officer's been shot.

"I'm on my way," I told him, hanging up.

29th Avenue and East Yesler Street is in the East Precinct, right where Casey was working. I grabbed my gun and keys and headed for the door, glancing over at Tawnie and Keaton as I did, my stomach churning.

"What's going on?" Doreen asked.

"I have to go to work," I said.

She had two sons working patrol in Seattle that night. I didn't want to tell her what was going on.

"What happened?" she asked.

"It's an officer-involved shooting," I answered. I wasn't about to tell her there had been an officer shot.

"Where?" she asked.

"I don't know," I muttered, still walking to the door, trying to appear calm on the outside, holding back the fear and angst in my heart.

She gave me a puzzled look. I always knew where I was going when I was called in, and she knew that.

At that moment, my cellphone rang again. I looked at the screen; it was Casey. I could finally breathe.

Casey had been one of the first officers to arrive at the scene.

"He's dead, dad," he said.

My heart sunk. I last worked a murder of an officer in 1994. I had no desire to work another one.

Doreen could see by the look on my face that something really bad was happening.

"What's going on?" she insisted.

"An officer's been shot and killed in the East Precinct," I said. "Casey's fine. That was him calling. He's at the scene."

All the women in the room burst into tears. They were the lucky ones this time; some other officer's family's whole world had just collapsed.

I got into my detective car and tore off, lights flashing, siren screaming.

I pulled up to the scene, the first detective to arrive.

It was surreal; thirty patrol cars at the scene, fifty more desperately scouring the streets nearby looking for the shooter, helicopters overhead, and the stony faces of officers, who only a couple hours earlier had attended roll call with the dead officer, laughing and joking, with no idea of what the evening held for them.

As I walked to the scene, I spoke to an officer.

"Who is it?" I asked.

"Tim Brenton," he said.

I didn't know him.

"Is he related to Boyd Brenton?"

Boyd had been an older officer when I was a rookie working out of Georgetown. He was in a different squad than me, but I knew him from work.

"That's his dad," the officer told me.

Shit. He had a son following in his footsteps, just like me. He hadn't been as lucky as I'd been.

Yellow crime scene tape surrounded the actual shooting scene. I walked to it and ducked under. I approached the marked Seattle Police car, parked at the curb southbound on 29th, just north of East Yesler Street, its engine idling. The cacophony and chaos of the scene outside the tape faded away, and I was very alone, standing inside the yellow tape, with no one near me or the inner scene; it seemed incredibly quiet. I looked in the window and saw Officer Timothy Q. Brenton, seated on the passenger side of the car, slumped over, his head hideously shaped from what I later discovered where four .223 rifle rounds striking it, a blood-stained Starbucks coffee cup in the cup holder between the seats, more of his life-blood spattered in the front passenger area of the car. The weight of the situation wore on me. Jason and I would have to find the fucker that did this. At this point, I had nothing at all to go on.

Though I didn't know Brenton, I'd almost certainly responded to scenes he'd been on; we'd probably spoken before, perhaps he gave me a briefing at a different scene.

Over the next few years, I would come to learn who Tim was, and to know his family even more.

I ducked back out of the crime scene tape and to a patrol sergeant.

"Who was in the driver's seat?" I asked.

"He had a student officer. She's in the back of the medic unit," he said, gesturing to a fire department rig parked nearby.

A student officer is an officer who recently graduated from the police academy and continues their training on the street in real-life situations called Field Training. They are trained by officers known as Field Training Officers, or FTO's.

I walked to the back of the medic unit and opened the door. Inside there was a uniformed female officer, Miki Mann, a paramedic I knew, and another female, wearing only a t-shirt and uniform pants. She was sobbing hysterically.

"I'm Cloyd Steiger from Homicide," I said. "What's your name?"

"Britt," she muttered between sobs.

"Britt," I said, "you're safe now. I'm going to talk to you more later, but right now, I just need you to take a deep breath and tell me the basics about what happened."

"We made a traffic stop earlier," she said, still sobbing, "and we parked here so Tim could go over the stop with me. We were talking about it when I became aware of a car next to us. I didn't really see it, I just knew it was so close, I couldn't have opened my door.

"I don't know why, but I ducked. There were loud bangs over and over. Then the car backed away. I got out and shot at the car. I don't know how many times, or even if I hit it. Then I saw that Tim was dead. "

With that statement she sobbed uncontrollably again. I waited while she regained her composure.

"I didn't know if the guy was coming back. I went and hid behind cars in the parking lot of the apartments next to us."

It had only been her second night working with Brenton. She'd been out of the academy one month. We later determined that she'd fired 10 rounds at the fleeing suspect vehicle.

"Listen to me," I told her. "You did fantastic. I know a lot of veteran officers that wouldn't have done as well as you. Just try to relax. I'll be up at the hospital later to talk to you more."

I jumped out of the medic unit and walked back to the scene. By that time, Mark Worstman, the sergeant who'd called me to the scene had arrived.

"Cloyd," he said. "Let me know if you need anyone else called in to help on this."

"I want everyone called in," I told him. "The whole unit."

"Done," he said, and pulled out his phone.

I called several of the other guys in Homicide myself. One of the guys I called was Rolf Norton. His phone went to voicemail. I left a message.

A few minutes later, Norton called me back. I told him what was going on.

"I'm in Dallas with the Seahawks," he said. I'd forgotten. Several guys worked on the side for the team. The director of security for the Seahawks, Rick Ninomaya, had retired from SPD Homicide to take the job.

Rolf felt bad.

"That's right," I told him. "I forgot. Don't worry."

Rolf would become very involved in the case when he got back.

Jason Kasner and I were the primary detectives in the case, but Russ Weklych and Al Cruise, also in our squad, joined us as the key investigators.

Steve Wilske had become the lieutenant in Homicide just a week before. He'd been the SWAT commander before that. His background was in operations; he had no investigation experience. Despite that, he was the best lieutenant I ever worked for in Homicide.

He understood that he didn't know the minutiae of homicide investigations just because he commanded the unit. Like all good commanders, he knew his job was to make sure his people had what they needed to do their jobs. He was a fast learner, and eager to do it. This was trial under fire for him.

Deputy Chief Jim Pugel was at the scene.

Jim was a friend, and I'd known him all his career. He'd been a student officer on my watch when I was in patrol and had worked a car with Clark Kimerer in the next precinct over. We'd meet up with them near the border between our two precincts. Kimerer himself later rose to Deputy Chief. I wonder what went on in that patrol car?

Pugel approached me.

"Why are we leaving the body here?" he said.

"We need to process the scene first," I said, and then walked away.

A little while later, Wilske approached me.

"They want to see you in the command post," he said.

He and I walked to the command post, inside a large, new truck, flat-panel televisions lining the walls, all sorts of communications equipment, and a large conference room.

Captain Mike Washburn was the scene commander. I knew him casually, but not well. We'd never worked around each other.

239

"What's your position about moving the body?" he asked.

There was an ill-thought-out policy in place at the time that if an officer is killed, his or her body is to be removed from the scene immediately.

"Well," I said. "We can do this the emotional way, and fuck this thing all up, or we can do it the right way, and get this motherfucker."

Washburn was somewhat taken aback.

"Okay, then," he said. "We'll do it your way, but we're going to have to change the policy."

"That's a good idea," I said, and then got up to leave.

A few weeks later, Washburn was named the Captain of the Violent Crimes Section, of which Homicide is a part. He was a great captain to work for, and we became friends.

When I approached the crime scene tape again, Casey came up to me.

"One of the guys we work with told us that last night a car pulled up alongside his patrol car. He pulled away and got the license number, but the car got away."

"Where's that officer now?" I asked.

"He's off tonight," he said.

"Call him and tell him to come in."

Casey walked away to get ahold of that officer.

I was intrigued. Maybe this guy tried it last night or was making practice runs.

Casey walked up again.

"He's not answering his phone," he said.

"Where does he live?"

"In Kent," Casey said.

Kent is in the suburbs, south of Seattle.

"Go to his house and get him," I said.

"I need to get that approved by a sergeant," he said.

"Bullshit," I said. "I just approved you. Go."

He and another officer left to go there.

Other detectives arrived, and we detailed them to interview witnesses and take statements.

A witness who lived in the condo complex directly adjacent to the scene, the one in whose parking lot, Britt had hidden, was out on his deck which is directly over the patrol car, when the shooting occurred.

He described the suspect vehicle as an older, Toyota Corolla-type vehicle. It was a hatchback, with louvers on the rear window.

The CSI detectives processed the scene.

I stood back surveying the scene. I noticed something in the street, north of the area where the shooting took place. I walked up to take a look.

It looked like a small American flag. (It turned out to be a flag-patterned bandanna.)

Nine days earlier, the Charles Street shops, where police cars are worked on, had been bombed. Someone lit a mobile command post on fire, and placed pipe bombs with time-delayed fuses under police cars in the lot. The bombs exploded as police and fire department units arrived for the fire.

I wasn't involved in that case, but I'd spoken to detectives in the Intelligence Unit who'd been assisting with that investigation. I knew that a large knife had been punched through the roof of a patrol car that was there, and an American flag was attached to it. Also, there were several "manifestos" taped on the property, talking about police brutality and referring to police deaths.

When I saw the flag, I wondered if this could be related to that event.

John Castleton arrived from the King County Prosecutor's Office. John is assigned to the unit in the prosecutors that handles all murders in the county. It was policy for one of them to respond to the scene of every murder.

I hadn't worked with John at that point; he was relatively new to the unit, but he'd gained a good reputation in our office. We discussed the facts of the case as we knew them at that point, the enormity of it not lost on either of us.

As the scene was being processed, Jason, Russ, Al and I went over what we knew. The ballistic evidence at the scene suggested the shooter had used a .223 caliber, (5.56mm NATO) round, like is fired from an M-16, or its civilian cousin, the AR-15. It was serious firepower.

We called the Medical Examiner's office. I was glad to see Richard Harruff was the pathologist to respond, along with his investigator, Jane Jorgenson. Jane was also a friend I'd known for years.

Richard examined the scene. He agreed that based on the evidence, it looked like a .223. He examined Tim's body as it sat in the patrol car. The wounds were devastating, and death had been instantaneous.

As the time came to remove Tim's body from the car, a group of paramedics approached.

"He's not going to the M.E.'s in the back of their truck," one of them said. "We'll take him in a medic unit."

If cops are brothers and sisters, then firefighters and paramedics are our first cousins. It was a kind gesture that was greatly appreciated by everyone.

They lined up with us at the front passenger door of the patrol car. Tim's body was slowly lifted and placed on a gurney.

We loaded Tim's body into a medic unit. An impromptu procession formed. About forty police cars, red and blue lights flashing, escorted the medic unit bearing Tim's body the mile and a half to the Medical Examiner's office. Jason and I were the last car in line.

When Tim's body arrived, the sidewalk in front of the building was lined with uniformed officers standing at attention. As the medic unit approached, they saluted. It was an awesome sight.

Bob Vallor, my sergeant, was waiting there as well. When things settled down he, Jason and I walked across the street to the emergency room at Harborview.

The first person I saw when I walked in the door was my daughter-in-law, Leah. She's married to my son Landon, also a Seattle Police officer, and worked in the ER at Harborview.

"Where's Britt Sweeney?" I asked her.

She led us to her room.

Britt had calmed down considerably since I saw her before at the scene; she was still upset but could at least communicate clearly.

She was surrounded by Ted Buck, an attorney retained to represent officers in shootings, and Seattle Police Officer's Guild President Rich O'Neill.

We questioned her more at length about what happened. She tried to tell us more, but she didn't know much more than she'd told me at the scene. It all happened so fast.

"You did really well," I told her again. "Nothing can prepare you for something like this. You did great."

We got back to the office at about 5 a.m. I was exhausted.

I have a motorhome I keep at the police range south of Boeing Field. It's much closer than home. I went there to sleep a couple hours. At 8 o'clock, I was at the Medical Examiner's office for the autopsy.

Autopsies aren't usually done on Sundays, but Dr. Harruff was there, along with autopsy technician Jessa Wubbles. John Castleton and Steve Wilske were also there.

I've attended hundreds of autopsies in my time in Homicide. This one was different.

Surreal is the only word that can describe the sight of a uniformed Seattle Police Officer on an autopsy table. It didn't take a Forensic Pathologist to see; horrific wounds had caused his death.

Some detectives never attend autopsies. They think it's a waste of time. I couldn't disagree more. There are things I learn by attending that I could never understand by having someone recount the facts to me over the phone. I want to see it all; the wounds, the evidence recovered. Everything. It's part of the job and a disservice if you don't take the time to go.

I returned to my office to find the message light on my desk phone flashing. It was Tim Greely. Tim was an old friend I'd known most of my career. He was also my neighbor and lived down the street from me. He worked in the East Precinct Community Police Team. He'd been working at the ad-hoc memorial that had been set up at the scene of the shooting. Many people were coming by, leaving flowers and expressing their sorrow about what had happened.

A woman had approached him. She thought she may have information about the shooting.

On the night of the shooting, she told him, she'd been walking her dog near Martin Luther King Boulevard and East Cherry Street, when she saw a police car with its lights on. Her dog was new, and she was trying to orient it to urban living, so she walked up to the police car.

While letting her dog experience the police car, she noticed that a car had pulled up in the park across the street on the grass. The car appeared to be watching the police car.

She walked the dog a few blocks back to her house. Just as she got home, she heard several loud bangs that sounded like gunshots.

It seemed likely that she'd walked to the stop that Brenton and Sweeney had made shortly before the shooting. I liked the tip; I liked it a lot.

I asked Russ Weklych and Al Cruise to follow up and interview the woman.

After talking to her, they called me.

"She said the car was a white or light-colored Toyota-like car with a hatchback," Cruise told me.

That matched the description the people living near the scene had given.

We ordered the dash-cam video from the traffic stop they'd been on.

Once we received the video, we all huddled around, watching each car that passed. One car matched the description we'd been given. We slowed the video and watched as it passed. It looked like an eighties model Toyota Supra or similar model car. The right headlight was either burned out or misaimed.

We ordered the dash-cam videos from every car that responded to the shooting. A lot of cars had responded, so it was a big order. The Video Unit put their personnel on overtime to accommodate our requests.

We watched the videos of officers racing at hair-raising speeds through the city streets, trying to get there to help their brother and sister officers who were in a desperate situation.

Casey had been working a one-man car that night. I watched his in-car video. He drove incredibly fast and fell in behind another unit racing to the scene. His police radio blared in the background. Britt Sweeney could be heard saying over the radio in a meek, defeated voice, "My partner's dead."

"Fuck!" Casey yelled to himself as he drove to the scene.

The Video Unit is at a building south of downtown near Safeco Field known as the Park 90-5 complex, where Traffic, SWAT, the Bomb Squad and Evidence Unit, among others, are housed, not in the headquarters building. At that time, in order to see the videos, they had to copy them to DVD, and we picked them up. (Now those videos can be viewed online at any time). The Video Unit called when they had a group of discs ready to the picked up. We'd drive there to get them.

One night at about 10 p.m., I made the run to the Video Unit to pick up a new batch of discs. I drove southbound on I-5. I sped to their office, taking the exit at high speed.

What am I doing? I thought to myself. It then occurred to me: I'd been watching so many cars race down the street on the videos that I unconsciously did the same. I slowed way down the rest of the way to their office.

Watching the videos paid off.

We watched as a car from the South Precinct responded northbound on 14th Avenue South. As the patrol car approached East Yesler Street, a white SUV turned south on 14th. Right behind the SUV, a small car crossed westbound on Yesler; it was the same car that had passed Brenton and Sweeney's traffic stop on Martin Luther King Way before the shooting. The car's location and direction was the opposite way it had been going when it passed their stop.

We found another video from a car that was going east on Yesler before the car crossed 14th Avenue. We saw the white SUV traveling westbound; the suspect vehicle was nowhere to be seen.

"Rewind it to the part where the SUV passes," I said to Al Cruise, who was controlling the video, "and advance it frame by frame."

As the rear of the SUV passed the patrol car whose video we watched, I caught a glimpse.

"There it is," I said.

To the right of the SUV, there was the tail light. There was no lane to the right of the SUV; it was one lane each direction. This guy was trying to hide from the oncoming police car by pulling alongside the other traffic.

This was definitely our guy.

There's a computer program the police department has, where a map of the city shows all patrol cars in motion, tracking their location. We asked that the response to this incident be captured, so we could show all the units responding and the routes they took. We knew the route the suspect took to flee. We could then isolate our search for video to those cars who took the same streets to get there that the suspect took to flee.

Lt. Ron Rasmussen copied and delivered the mapping software and data.

We watched units in the entire city on routine patrol. There was no audio, or synchronization with radio traffic, but at once, cars from all over the city raced to the East Precinct in response to the "Help the officer" call that was broadcast citywide.

We identified the cars that probably passed the suspect vehicle on the way to the scene, and then picked up those units in-car video.

We traced the shooter's car on Yesler Way to Boren Avenue, and then northbound on Boren, where we lost it.

We had detectives identify all private video surveillance in that area, including building security and ATM video. On a recording from Swedish Hospital, north of the last place we saw the suspect vehicle on the police video, an interior security tape that partially recorded out a door caught the suspect passing by.

There were red light traffic cameras on a couple intersections near that area. Those cameras record passively all the time, but only take snapshots and actively record when a vehicle runs the light. They were maintained by a company in Phoenix, Arizona.

Airlift Northwest is a service in the Seattle area that uses helicopters to fly the severely injured to hospitals, usually Harborview. They also have a Lear jet. They volunteered the use of that jet.

Detective Nathan Janes, a detective in Homicide, went to Boeing Field, jumped on the jet, and flew to Phoenix. He retrieved the red-light camera video and returned to Seattle.

No video of use came from that footage, but it demonstrated the help we received from the community at-large in the early days of this case.

We had video of who we believed to be the suspect vehicle in this case. The video didn't show an angle where we could read the license plate number of the car.

Patrol car video, like the red-light cameras, also passively records all the time. It only actively records if either an officer turns the record function on in the patrol car, or the emergency red and blue lights are activated. During either of those cases, the video records back a cache of one minute of video to show why the recording was activated.

We sent the hard drive from Brenton and Sweeney's patrol car out to retrieve the passive video recordings. We got it back the following Wednesday.

Detective Monty Moss worked in the Intelligence Unit. He was the one who sent the video out. When it came back, he summoned us all to the Intel offices.

We were in a dark room with a large flat-panel television on the wall when Moss played the video. The view on the screen was out the front windshield of Brenton and Sweeney's patrol car.

We watched as the car drove to 29th and East Yesler. They drove eastbound on Yesler, and turned left on 29th, making a U-turn to face southbound. As they made the turn, I noticed that the flag bandanna that I'd seen in the street south of the scene

248

was not there; the suspect had clearly dropped it. That convinced me that this case was related to the Charles Street bombing.

After they parked, a few cars passed by. As those cars approached, we could see the distinct pattern of two headlights on the ground in front of them and reflecting off a stop sign at the intersection.

After a few moments, a car approached that only shone one headlight pattern on the ground. The car passed their position; it was the same car that had passed their traffic stop; it was the same car that had driven westbound on East Yesler Street; it was the same car that drove northbound on Boren Avenue; it was our suspect vehicle. Since the headlights of Brenton and Sweeney's patrol car where off, the license plate wasn't illuminated. It was unreadable.

The car turned right, westbound on Yesler.

A few moments later, that same single-headlight pattern shone on the street again, and on the stop sign again. This time, it didn't pass, but stopped.

Brenton and Sweeney's car rocked, and blood spattered on the front windshield. Then the headlight pattern backed away. A moment later, Britt Sweeney was on the video, in front of her patrol car, gun in hand, talking into the microphone from her portable radio, clipped to her left shoulder. She ran out of the frame to the right, from the bedlam she'd experienced to the asylum of a nearby parking lot of the condo complex. Less than a minute later, her salvation in the form of other police cars arrived at the scene.

Now we had, as they say in the legal world, prima facia evidence that the car we were looking at was our suspect. But what to do with that information?

We needed to nail down the make and model of the car we were looking for.

We sent a team of detectives to find an expert who could identify the type of car this was. They identified a junk car dealer in Bellingham, about 120 miles north of Seattle. The detectives came back with precise information.

"This guy looked at the car," said Dave Redemann, one of the detectives we sent up there. "He used calipers and measured the car precisely. He said that the car is a 1980 to 1982 Datsun 210. Not a Datsun B210, but a 210. It's an entirely different car."

We made a request to the Department of Licensing to give us a list of all Datsun 210's registered in the state of Washington. When we got the list, we assigned them out to the scores of detectives we had running down leads.

"Put eyes on all the cars," we told them. "Find a reason to eliminate the car you see as the suspect vehicle."

With that, we sent them out.

We heard back on several cars right away. There weren't that many of these cars still on the road. Many were hulks.

I said a silent thank you to the moron who'd used a relatively rare car to commit this crime; a more common car would have made this much more difficult.

During that week, I got a lot of calls from local reporters that knew me. One female reporter practically begged me.

"Give me anything I can put out," she said. "We can help you get this guy."

"I can't do it," I told her. "Anything I say to you, I'm whispering into the ear of the suspect. He's following the news coverage of this closely. If I tell you what I know, it may cause him to destroy evidence. Maybe in a couple days we'll release something, but not now."

Every day that week there was a meeting with the Chief of Police, our Bureau Chief and command staff. We discussed how the investigation was going at that point, and also what to release and not release to the media at the daily press conferences. That was a good idea on paper, but invariably, things we said we didn't want out got released; It was frustrating.

On Wednesday morning we had the information about the car we were looking for. Jason and I talked about it; I approached Steve Wilske before the morning command staff meeting.

"We think we should release the suspect vehicle information to the media," I said. "We're creeping along on this; we need to kick-start something."

"It's your call," Wilske said. "Whatever you want to do."

"That's what we want to do," I told him.

That day we released still photos of the actual vehicle, and the make and model that we believed the car was. In the meantime, teams continued to track down every Datsun 210 in the state.

Friday, November 6th was the day of Brenton's funeral. We had the usual morning command staff meeting.

"Are we going to shut down the investigation for the funeral?" asked Investigations Bureau Chief Jim Pugel.

"No," I said. "Jason, Russ and Al are going to the funeral. We need to keep pressing this case."

I remembered working on the murder of Officer Antonio Terry while the funeral went on.

Doreen and Tawnie, (Casey's wife) along with my youngest son Dylan, were going to the funeral. Casey and Landon went with their respective squads. Parking would be a nightmare.

"I'll pick you up at the firing range," I told Doreen, "and drive you to Key Arena, (where the funeral was being held.) "I'll drop you off and then pick you up afterward."

Security was a big issue at the funeral. The shop where police cars were repaired had been bombed, pamphlets left threating the lives of police officers, and then the ambush murder of Brenton. In addition to the thousands of officers and others attending the funeral, there were hundreds of others working security in and around the perimeter, including SWAT snipers, and bomb dogs. If someone wanted to go on a suicide mission to attack the police, there would be no better place.

When I got back to my office, there was a message on my phone from Rick Wyant, a firearms and tool mark scientist at the crime lab. I called him back.

"I analyzed the bullet fragments you submitted," he said. "The weapon you're looking for is a .223 caliber, a Colt, Bushmaster, or weapon with similar characteristics. "

A little later that day, Tim Renihan, a detective in the Intelligence Unit, approached me.

"Cloyd, I got a call from a lady I know from another investigation. She manages an apartment complex in Tukwila," (just south of Seattle). "She said she has a tenant in the building who owns a car just like the one we put out in the news. He never covered it before, but the last couple days, he put a car cover over it."

My ears perked up. Why would someone who owns a piece of shit car like that all of the sudden cover it?

"The guy's name is Christopher Monfort," Renihan told me.

I ran Monfort's name. He had no criminal history. I retrieved his driver's license photo; there was the smiling face of a mixed-race male.

Immediately after this incident, we were inundated with tips phoned in by well-meaning citizens and police officers from all over. So many we had to develop a system, so as not be overwhelmed. None came to the core detectives investigating the case, (myself, Jason, Weklych or Cruise), without having been screened through other detectives and then a homicide sergeant, who would determine the likelihood that the tip was good. Despite that, each morning I read the tips that came in. In the first days after the shooting, I read a tip. It was from a woman who had been driving in the area the night of this incident. She saw all the police cars racing to the scene. She

252

was near Boren Avenue and East Yesler. A small white or light blue car pulled alongside her. The driver looked like a mixed-race or Hispanic man. She commented to the person she was with that he was probably who the police were looking for. Looking at Monfort's photo, I was reminded of the tip. Perhaps he was the person she saw.

My phone rang. It was Sarah Atterbury from the crime lab; she'd developed DNA from the flag-patterned bandanna recovered at the Brenton shooting scene. It matched DNA developed from an American Flag at the Charles Street bombing.

Now we had a scientific link; the two crimes were committed by the same guy.

I walked with Tim Renihan, the Intelligence detective who brought me the tip, into Steve Wilske's office.

"I like this tip." I told Wilske. "I like it a lot,"

"I'll have SWAT sit on the car," he said.

Bob Vallor was in the room too. He, Gary Nelson and Rolf Norton left to go the apartment. They would sit on the car until SWAT arrived. I stayed behind to get a search warrant.

John Castleton, the prosecutor assigned to the case, was at the funeral. I called Jeff Baird, Castleton's boss.

"We have a hot tip on the Brenton case," I told him. "I need you here. We're going to get a search warrant."

"I'm on my way," he said.

The prosecutor's office is in the downtown King County Courthouse, just a block down the hill from police headquarters. Baird was in my office in a couple minutes

Brenton's funeral was playing on a flat-panel TV mounted on the wall over my desk.

Baird and I sat at my desk, just starting to draft an affidavit for the warrant. Wilske came running out of his office, a portable radio in his hand.

"We've got shots fired at the Tukwila address!" he said.

Baird and I ran to the parking deck to my car. Jason was at the funeral. I called his phone.

"Get back here! Things are breaking!"

We raced down the parking structure from the 7th floor level that detective cars are parked on, emergency lights on, my siren echoing off the concrete walls.

It was rush-hour on a Friday. The traffic on I-5 southbound was stopped. We shot up the shoulder past the clogged traffic and raced to Tukwila, Baird's hands both on the dash as we passed the other cars. I made another call to Jason as I drove, giving him the address.

Brenton's funeral was just ending when events in Tukwila erupted, and word quickly spread about what was going on. When we arrived at the scene, there were scores of police cars from several jurisdictions there. They left the funeral and responded.

Baird jumped out of my car and ran toward the scene. I saw several officers, rifles pointed into the complex. I grabbed Jeff by the back of his shirt.

"The scene's not secure yet," I told him. "We have to wait. Get down"

We crouched behind a patrol car until we heard the situation was contained, and then walked into the inner scene.

Paramedics brought Christopher Monfort past us on a stretcher. I recognized him from the driver's license photo I'd seen earlier. There was a bullet hole in his face and he was unconscious. He'll probably die, I thought to myself.

Monfort lived in an upstairs apartment in the rear, off an exterior walkway. SWAT tried to enter the apartment looking for other suspects but saw what looked like bombs inside. They backed out and called the Bomb Squad.

I thought that SWAT had been the ones who shot Monfort. That wasn't the case.

Bob Vallor, Gary Nelson and Rolf Norton, who'd come to sit on the car while I applied for a search warrant, encountered Monfort. Norton, who'd been in Dallas with the Seahawks the night of the shooting, approached him, holding up his badge.

"Police," he said. "We need to talk to you."

"Fuck that," Monfort said, and ran into a nearby stairwell. Nelson went into the stairwell after him. Monfort was waiting. He put a pistol in Nelson's face and pulled the trigger.

Click.

Monfort hadn't loaded a round in the chamber. If he had, Nelson would have been killed.

Monfort ran up the stairs, racking a round into the chamber as he did. Vallor, Norton and Nelson, now back out in the parking lot fired two rounds each at him when he pointed his weapon at them. He was hit and went down.

We waited for hours for the apartment to be secured. The Bomb Squad finally made it safe; they removed several home-made bombs from inside, including homemade hand grenades, large balls of explosives, wrapped in duct tape, with wire and other shrapnel inside, which had been laid on the kitchen stove, their fuses touching the element. All Monfort had to do to set them off was turn on the stove.

We finally entered the apartment late at night.

Monfort had stacked tires just inside his living room. There was a .223 rifle, shotgun and handguns behind the barricade; some of the grenades had been found there also.

An ink-jet printer sat next to a computer on one wall. In the document tray, we found a copy of the manifesto Monfort had posted around the Charles Street bombing scene.

A flag lay draped across the bed in a back bedroom; there were several other flags still in packaging nearby. Monfort had intended to strike again.

Jeff Baird, John Castleton, Jason and I returned to our office at three in the morning. It had been a week of long hours, and little sleep; we were exhausted.

We have a tradition in the Homicide Unit after an arrest, especially on a major case like this.

I pulled a bottle of good bourbon from a bottom drawer in my desk. We poured drinks all around.

By the time I got home, it was after 5 o'clock in the morning.

My assumption that Monfort would die of the wounds he received was a little too optimistic. He survived, though he was a paraplegic.

Unlike on television and movies, the case doesn't end when the suspect is arrested. In fact, it really just begins. There is a lot of investigating still to do trying to build evidence for trial. In this case, the investigation went on for 5 years before the case went to trial.

Dan Satterberg was the elected prosecutor of King County. He charged Monfort with Aggravated First-Degree Murder for the killing of Tim Brenton, as well as a myriad of other charges including three counts of Attempted Murder, (one each for Britt Sweeney, and Gary Nelson, and another for the collective officers he'd meant to kill at Charles Street) as well as Arson charges.

The crime lab matched the .223 rifle in his living room ballistically to the bullets that had killed Brenton.

Monfort was an enigmatic person, described by those who knew him as socially inept. He had a bachelor's degree in Criminal Justice, and applied to become a police officer at least once. He held radical opinions about the police. Searches of his computer files showed he'd planned the crime for months. We found a lot of Google searches about where Seattle Police officers eat, where they hang out and the location of the Seattle Police union. There were also searches about where Los Angeles Police eat, etc.

I called LAPD and told them what I was investigating, and about the searches on Monfort's computer. We found information on the computer that'd he'd travelled to Los Angeles the previous spring. I wanted to make sure there were no attempts to commit the murder of an officer there.

The detective I spoke to couldn't find any record of anything like that happening there.

We got search warrants to search Monfort's cars. In the Datsun, we recovered a receipt for a liquor store on 4th Avenue South. The receipt was dated November 2nd and indicated that Monfort purchased a bottle of Laird's Apple Jack at 1:10 PM.

I knew that liquor store; it's right across the street from the offices of the Seattle Police Officer's Guild, the union that represents officers, detectives and sergeants on the Seattle Police Department.

I went to the liquor store. They had several surveillance cameras in and around the store. The store was new, however, and none were hooked up to a recording device yet.

I thought it likely that Monfort had been in his car watching the Guild offices. I went to their offices and spoke with Rich O'Neill, the SPOG president. I showed the staff Monfort's photo and asked if they'd ever seen him. They thought he looked familiar but didn't know for sure.

It seemed likely that Monfort thought about striking again there, but never got the chance.

We also found two receipts from Shucks Auto Parts. One was for a store in downtown Renton, another suburban city south of Seattle. He'd purchased Bondo there, with which he filled in the bullet hole from one of the rounds Sweeny had fired that hit his car. There was a second Shucks receipt for a different store, east of town for the car cover Monfort had put over the Datsun.

257

I went to each of the stores looking for surveillance video. Neither store had video.

I spoke to the salesman who sold Monfort the car cover. He told me that Monfort was acting very oddly, asking for a car cover, but not telling the clerk the type of car he wanted to cover. Ultimately, Monfort bought two different sizes.

I believed Monfort went to this store to get the cover rather than the one he bought the Bondo in, which was much closer to his home, so no one could identify him later.

Unfortunately for him, the clerk could easily identify Monfort, whom he recognized; they lived in the same apartment complex.

We got a search warrant for Monfort's cellphone records. When we searched them, we found that he'd made a phone call on the night of the murder. We traced the number he called to a man in Port Hadlock, a small town on the Olympic Peninsula near the scenic tourist town of Port Townsend.

I called Bob Gebo, an old friend and retired Seattle Homicide detective. He worked part time for the Jefferson County Sheriff's office, where Port Hadlock is located.

I told Gebo we'd be coming over to interrogate the guy who Monfort called. He made arrangements for us to meet at the Sheriff's office, where he'd have an interview room available for us.

We took the ferry from downtown Seattle to Bainbridge Island, and then drove to Port Hadlock, and to the Sheriff's office. We checked in there, and then headed out.

The address where this guy lived was in a trailer park. At that point, we didn't know what we were dealing with. This guy could be a co-conspirator, as far as we knew. We just knew Monfort had called his phone after he killed Tim Brenton.

We surrounded his trailer, dressed in bullet-proof vests, guns out.

"Seattle Police!" we yelled as we pounded on the door. "Open up!"

The door opened, and a thin, disheveled and unshaven man appeared. We grabbed him and pulled him from the trailer.

We took him to the Sheriff's office and put him in an interview room.

Jason and I went in for the interview.

He told us he was an oyster raker, working on the oyster beds when the tide was out.

"Do you know what this is about?" I asked.

"Is it about the dope?" he squeaked.

"No, it's not about the dope," I said.

He let out a breath like he'd been holding it an hour, a look of relief on his face.

"Then I don't know what it's about."

I told him we were investigating a murder.

"I don't know nothing about no murder," he said.

"You got a phone call on your cellphone on Halloween, the night of the murder right after it happened," I said. "The call was from the killer."

He had a puzzled look on his face, not sure what we were talking about.

"It was from a 425 area code," I said.

"Oh, wait!" he said. "I was in a bar on Halloween and I did get a call from a 425 area code phone. My boss's wife has a 425 phone, so I thought it was her. I answered, but it was the wrong number."

I was sure this guy was telling us the truth. As we lead him to the door, I resisted the urge to say, "Actually, it is about the dope."

We let him go.

A trace of the rifle used in the murder showed that it was purchased at Cabela's Outfitters, near Chehalis, Washington, about 90 miles south of Seattle. Jason and I, along with Bob Vallor, Al Cruise, Russ Weklych and Detective Rik Hall from the Intelligence unit drove there. On the way down, we stopped the Western Washington State Fairgrounds, in Puyallup, a small city east of Tacoma. There was a gun show in progress that weekend, and we found documents that Monfort had become a member of this show, which is required to make purchases, in the months before the murder.

We spoke to several dealers at the gun show. They were all very cooperative. Many recognized a photo of Monfort as having been there before.

One dealer specifically remembered Monfort and thought Monfort had made purchases from him. Rik Hall had worked a lot on the bombing at the maintenance shops at Charles Street. We found fusing that this vendor sold that was identical to fuse found in Monfort's apartment.

We then proceeded to Cabela's. We went to the gun counter. We gave them the serial number of the rifle, and they retrieved the paperwork from the sale. It was sold in June of 2008 to a local man. They gave us his address.

We went to the man who'd purchased the weapon's house, but he wasn't home. We set up surveillance there. After a couple hours, he came home.

We identified ourselves and told him why we were there.

He confirmed that he purchased the rifle at Cabela's. He explained that after he had the gun, he didn't like it. He knew a man who traded weapons and he went to that man and traded the rifle for a different one.

He said he traded the weapon to David Delvenney and gave us Delvenny's address. It was an address in rural Lewis County, near the foothills of the Cascade Mountains, not far from Mount St. Helens. We met with Delvenney.

Delvenny said he was willing to cooperate, but I had the feeling he was hiding something. He admitted that he received the rifle but claimed he didn't know what happened to it. He said that he doesn't have a Federal Firearms License, so he's precluded from selling weapons; he just trades them. He said he goes to a lot of firearm shows. We showed him the photo of Monfort. He denied recognizing him. I didn't believe him.

We left.

A few months later, Delvenny was arrested by the ATF and charged with the illegal sale of firearms. He was convicted and given a jail term.

I had a court order to take a DNA sample from Monfort. I went through the tunnel connecting police headquarters to the downtown jail. I wheeled Monfort in his wheelchair back to my office.

"Do you remember the TV show, 'The Blue Night?'" he asked me as we traversed the tunnel.

"Sure," I said. "George Kennedy played Bumper Morgan. I read the book by Joseph Wambaugh too."

"Now, that was community policing," he said.

You know that's fiction, right? I thought.

The case went to trial in January of 2015. It lasted more than five months. Monfort was convicted. The jury did not find that he should receive the death penalty.

Judge Ron Kessler was the judge in the case. At sentencing, he said, "The court sentences Mr. Monfort to spend the remainder of his natural life in prison, and to die there an insignificant death."

On January 18, 2017, guards found Monfort dead in his cell at Walla Walla State Penitentiary. It was later found that he had been hoarding medication, and then committed suicide by overdose.

An ignoble end to an ignoble life.

24

The morning after Thanksgiving, 2009, I got a call from my mother-in-law Jeanette in Spokane.

"What the hell's going on over there?" she asked.

I didn't know what she was talking about.

"I heard on the news that four police officers in Tacoma were shot and killed!"

I still didn't know what she was talking about, and I told her so.

I turned on the television. There it was: Four Lakewood police officers had been ambushed in a coffee shop. All four were dead. Lakewood is a suburb of Tacoma.

After having made the arrest in Tim Brenton's murder just three weeks earlier, it was hard to fathom.

I was familiar with the coffee shop where the shooting occurred. I owned a rental house not far from there and passed it many times while going to do work on that house.

The Pierce County Sheriff's Office was leading the investigation into the shooting. Later that day, they issued a statement. They identified the suspect in the shooting as Maurice Clemmons. His photograph was released. A heavy-set black male, he had a distinctive mole on his face.

When I got back to work that week, it was surreal. Five local cops had been killed in ambushes in less than a month. Nothing remotely like that had ever happened in my career.

Calls continually came in, reporting sightings of Clemmons in Seattle. We drove around, three or four detectives per car, guns on our laps chasing down the reports. I was worried for officers in patrol, easily identified, unlike us in plain clothes and in unmarked cars. I was especially concerned for my two sons.

The last quarter of 2009 and the first quarter of 2010 had seven local police officers killed in the line of duty. An unprecedented number.

In the very early morning hours of December 1st, we staked out a location in Renton, south of Seattle related to a murder other detectives in our unit were investigating. Our radios were tuned to the frequency for the South and Southwest Precincts.

At about 2:30 in the morning, a patrol car in Rainier Valley broadcast that he had shots fired. He said that the suspect in the Lakewood shootings had attempted to approach him. The officer reported that he'd fired on the suspect, who'd fled.

A moment later, the officer broadcast that the suspect was down. In police jargon, that meant that the suspect had been shot.

We abandoned our stakeout and headed that way.

Jason and I were detailed to head to the office to meet the officer, who was being taken there, which is policy in officer-involved shootings.

The shooting officer was brought in by other officers. His name was Ben Kelly. I didn't know Kelly at all at that time. I spoke to him in the same casual tone I always use with officers who had been in shootings. He was a little shaken. I offered him something to drink, had he and the other officers go to the conference room at the south end of the Homicide office.

Once he was settled, there was no reason for us to stay there. We left for the scene.

When we got there, Clemmons' body was in the back of a medic unit. Patty Mann is a paramedic I'd known most of my career. She was working on the medic unit Clemmons was in. When I walked up, she gave me a hug. She has a lot of friends on the police department and knew what stress we'd all been under lately.

I stepped into the back of the unit and looked at Clemmons' body. I stared for a moment at the lifeless face that I and every police officer in the region had scoured the streets for the last several days.

He was handcuffed, his eyes in the vacant stare of death, duct tape around his torso, applied, as it turned out, to cover a gunshot wound that one of the Lakewood officers had managed to get off while fighting a losing battle for his life. Clemmons had that officer's pistol on him when he was killed by Kelly.

I called Casey and Landon telling them both that Clemmons was dead. They were relieved that he'd been stopped before hurting anyone else.

The Medical Examiner arrived. Dr. Aldo Fusaro was with ME Investigator Alison Myrabo.

Dr. Fusaro conducted the preliminary scene investigation, examining both new and old gunshot wounds on Clemmons' body. He and Myrabo removed the body from the scene.

Valentine's Day was on a Sunday in 2010.

I read the news on my computer. A story dominated the local news sites: A Washington State Patrol trooper had been shot overnight in the sleepy coastal community of Long Beach, Washington. With all the recent shootings and murders of law enforcement officers in the area lately, I read the story with interest.

Troopers had made a DUI arrest. While they were towing the suspect's car, someone walked up and shot a trooper in the head. The shot glanced off the side of the trooper's head, and he was able to return fire, but the suspect got away. The trooper was taken to the hospital but was stable.

A couple hours later, my work cellphone rang. It was Mark Worstman, one of the Homicide sergeants.

"Cloyd, I don't know if you heard about the trooper getting shot in Long Beach, but they're asking for our help on it. Are you available to go over there?"

I'm always available.

"You, me and Dana (Duffy) are going over," he told me. "We'll meet you in the office."

After meeting, we left the office for the two-hour drive to Long Beach.

We arrived at the Pacific County Sheriff's office at about six o'clock in the evening. A briefing was just beginning. The room was filled with about twenty State Patrol detectives. I sat in the back of the room and listened. The trooper detective giving the briefing was someone I'd gone to high school with.

Small world.

I was dismayed by what I heard. They were looking for the boogie man. WSP detectives work mainly on crimes dealing with vehicles, like auto theft, and vehicular homicides or assaults. This was way out of their wheelhouse. I could tell by the leads they talked about following up on in the briefing; they had no idea how to handle a case like this and were obviously shaken by the shooting of one of their own. They needed perspective.

One of the troopers at the front of the room looked back at us.

"Are you guys from Seattle?" he asked.

"Yeah, we are," I said.

"What do you think?"

I'm glad he asked.

Because of the recent rash of police officers being shot, like Tim Brenton and the Lakewood officers, they had assumed the worst.

"You've got to stop looking for the boogie man," I said. "The guy you're looking for is just a regular guy. He's not someone

266

who turns into smoke and seeps under doorways. This isn't a random ambush where he's just looking to assassinate an officer. This is Long Beach, not a populated urban center where something like that may happen."

"Tell me about the DUI," I said. "What was the woman doing before being stopped?"

"She was at a bar with her husband and another couple. Her husband left early, and she stayed with the others. She was stopped when she left the bar. This was her third DUI."

The trooper that made the stop transported the woman to the station for a breathalyzer. Another trooper, Scott Johnson, came by to help with impounding the car.

"The tow truck driver was hooking up," he continued," when a guy walked up and asked why they were towing the car. Johnson told him that the driver had been arrested for DUI. The guy pulled a small handgun and put it to Johnson's head. A moment later, it went off. Johnson fell to the ground and the guy ran off. Johnson was able to shoot at him a couple times. The guy turned around and shot back at Johnson and the tow truck driver."

"Have we interviewed the tow truck driver?" I asked.

"We did."

"Let's get him back in here. I want to interview him."

I was sure that this wasn't random.

"This guy had something to do with that car" I said. "Who are the males in this woman's life?"

"She has her husband, Martin Jones, but we've already cleared him. She also has an adult son."

"How did you clear the husband?" I asked.

"We talked to him at his house," he said. "He was on his couch with his wife and another woman."

"We don't clear people at their house," I said. "We clear people at our house. Let's get him and the son in here.

"Also, you need to get a search warrant for Jones' house. You'll be looking for guns and ammunition, and clothes that match what the shooter was wearing."

The tow truck driver arrived. I went to a back room to interview him.

"I've known Scott all my life," he said. Johnson had worked in Pacific County his entire career. "I have a video camera, and I video a lot of things I do. I taped some of this."

My ears perked.

"Where's the video now?" I asked.

He pulled out a small digital video recorder.

"Right here."

He played the video for me. It jostled around. Johnson's voice could be heard calling for back up, and the tow truck driver asking Johnson if he was okay, but there was no image of the shooter.

The tow truck driver was trying to be helpful. He was trying too hard to be helpful. Some of the things he said didn't match the evidence.

I thanked him and sent him home.

While the troopers looked for the husband and son, I went out to follow up on phoned in tips. At about one o'clock in the morning, my phone rang.

It was Worstman.

"They found Jones," he told me. "He was hiding in a house at the north end of the peninsula. His wife does housecleaning there, and the owners were out of town."

"Good," I said.

"They want you to interview him," Worstman told me.

"Me? I've only been involved in the case for a few hours," I said. "Okay, I guess."

I arrived back at the sheriff's office. Jones was in an interview room. I went in with a State Patrol detective.

Jones was all over the board during our three-hour interview. He made conflicting statements, contradicting himself over and over. There was no doubt: This was our guy.

"I didn't even know anything was going on," he said.

His house was right off the main highway going in and out of town.

"There were dozens of police cars racing by your house all night, with lights and sirens on. Are you telling me you didn't hear any of that? This is a quiet town. Hearing that many sirens on a late Sunday night in February isn't normal."

Jones was a business owner with no criminal history. He was way out of his league.

"I have a theory, Marty," I told him. "You left your wife at the bar and went home. She'd already had two other DUIs. When you heard she was arrested again, you got pissed. You left your house, for whatever reason, with a gun. You'd been drinking too, so you weren't thinking straight. When you put the gun to the trooper's head, you didn't mean to shoot, but the gun accidentally went off. You panicked and ran. If it was an accident, you have to tell us. Otherwise people will think you tried to assassinate the trooper, and that won't be good. It's the difference between a short sentence or the rest of your life in prison.

"That's what happened, isn't it?"

Jones stared at me without saying anything. He was thinking it over. Should he bite? I could see on his face that he was considering it.

He took a deep breath.

"I don't know anything about it," he said.

Of course, even if he admitted it was an accident, when he ran and then fired back at the trooper and tow truck driver, all bets were off. I didn't tell him that, of course.

Throughout the interview, Jones made equivocal requests for an attorney. An equivocal request is one in which the subject of the interview says, "I think I need a lawyer," or "Maybe I need a lawyer." Case law on that is clear: It's not an exercise of the right to counsel.

Finally, at one point, Jones said, "I want a lawyer."

There was nothing unequivocal about that request.

"Okay," I said. "Then we're leaving. I'm not going to listen to your side of the story anymore."

As I stood up to leave, Jones put his head in his hands.

"I just want this to all go away."

I'll bet he did. What he did do was reinitiate the conversation. The interview continued.

In a pre-trial hearing with Jones' attorney, in which he sought to have the statement suppressed, he questioned me about whether Jones reinitiated the conversation.

"Are you saying if he says anything after asserting his right to counsel, he is reinitiating the conversation?"

"If he says something about the case, yes," I said.

Obviously, if he asked what time it was, or what happens next, or if he could use the restroom, that would not be reinitiating the conversation. But when he asks a question or makes a statement directly about what he is being interviewed about: In this case, "I just want it all to go away," he reopens the door.

Ultimately, the state got in all of the statements from Jones they wanted to use.

When I ended the interview with Jones, I walked out of the room. His wife was in another room nearby. Needless to say, she was very upset.

I told her my theory that it had been an accident, and that Marty was hurting himself by not saying so.

"Can I talk to him?" she asked.

My initial reaction was to say no, but I thought about it.

"Sure," I said and led her to the room.

The room was audio and video monitored. We watched as she spoke to him.

"Marty!" she pleaded. "You have to tell them it was an accident. You didn't mean to do it!"

Jones stared at the table, with no reaction. Finally, he looked up at her.

"There are some bills on the counter you need to take care of."

What the hell?

If I was wrongly accused of something like this, and my wife came in pleading with me to claim it was an accident, I'd say, "But I didn't fucking do it!"

The case was moved to Pierce County Superior Court in Tacoma and was prosecuted by the State Attorney General.

Jones was convicted. He was sentenced to 50 years in prison.

Told you so.

25

I had an intern for the summer of 2010. Steve Sargent was in the master's program at Florida State University. He really wanted a career as a police officer, and ultimately as a homicide detective.

I'd had interns before, and when they start I always ask them the same thing.

"Do you want to spend your summer making copies and doing menial tasks, or do you want the full meal deal?"

"What do you mean," Steve asked.

"Do you want to see what being a homicide detective is really all about?"

"I do want that," he said.

I remembered how I felt before I was hired on the police department. I wanted it so badly; I'd do whatever it took to get it. I was an old, jaded detective now, but I wanted to give back to people who were where I was back then.

We were in the office one day when Randy Moore of the Fugitive Task Force called.

"I'm bringing a guy in. He's wanted for murder out of Arkansas. They're flying detectives up here to talk to him right now. Can we hold him in your office until they get here?"

"No problem," I told him.

I told Steve what was going on.

"You're welcome to stay if you want, but you're not getting paid. You can just go home if you want. I won't rate you down for it." (I did weekly evaluations on him that I faxed to Florida State.)

"No, I want to stay," he said.

I knew he would.

Randy arrived with the suspect, and we put him in an interview room.

I knew it would be a long time before the detectives from Arkansas got here, so I got him food. They arrived in our office at three in the morning.

They gave us the details of the murder.

"The woman who got murdered was elderly. Her dad founded a church. She stopped by one day and didn't come home. They checked the church and found her. She'd been beaten to death with a crucifix."

They'd identified the guy Randy had arrested as the suspect; he was a transient. They found out that he was traveling to the Seattle area. They'd called Randy, who, along with his team, tracked the guy down in Bremerton, across Puget Sound from Seattle, and arrested him.

"The interview room is audio and video recorded," I told them. "When you're done, I'll burn the file to a DVD."

"Great," they said, and entered the room.

Steve and I went to the viewing area for the interview rooms to watch.

The suspect was itching to confess. There was no problem. Except the detectives tried to write down everything he said. They continually stopped him, so they could catch up.

"Watch what these guys are doing," I told Steve, "and when you become a detective, don't ever fucking do it."

I wanted to scream at them. Why are you writing everything down? This is being recorded. Look at him, engage him in conversation. Let him tell the story! If you think you need to write everything down, (you don't), do it from the recording later. They were lucky this guy didn't get frustrated and decide he wasn't going to confess after all. Fortunately for them, that didn't happen. He patiently waited for them to catch up, and then continued his story.

I have a credo about situations like this: Act like you've done this before.

During his confession, he said he'd been in a park in Seattle and had thrown the victims identification and credit cards in the bushes. From the description he gave, I thought it was probably Volunteer Park on Capitol Hill.

By the time the interview was over, the sun was up. I was dog-tired, but I offered to drive them up to the park to look for the evidence. I told Steve he didn't have to go if he didn't want to, but he did, of course.

I drove to the park, and to an area I thought he was describing. We came upon a copse of trees and bushes like those he'd described. Steve jumped out of the car and ran in.

"Got it!" he yelled.

Are you kidding me? What are the odds? But we got out and walked back there; sure as shit, there was the victim's ID and credit cards.

Steve finished his master's that next year. He was hired by the Bellevue Police Department, just across Lake Washington from Seattle.

Steve got what he wanted that summer: the full meal deal. I think the exposure to the cases we worked will make him a better officer, and someday, a better detective.

26

Just after one in the afternoon in late October 2010 we were called to a suspicious death in a Belltown apartment. A man was found dead, blood covering most of the floor of the entire interior of his apartment.

We walked to the second-floor unit. The male victim lay on the bed in the studio apartment. A towel was wrapped around his throat, which had been cut. Jason and I were next-up for a murder. It looked like this was going to be ours.

I looked at the floor, almost completely covered in blood. There was no blood in the hallway. That was curious. If he'd been killed inside, one would think the killer would have tracked at least some blood into the hall.

The only other way out was through the window. It was only on the second floor, but it was on a busy downtown sidewalk in the middle of a weekday; someone would have been seen jumping out the window.

Don Raz was the prosecutor who was next-up for a murder. I gave him a call.

"We're at this scene in Belltown. This guy's got his throat cut, but I'm not convinced it's a murder yet."

"I was just heading out anyway," Raz told me. "I'll stop by."

I stood at the doorway to the apartment and took in the scene. A laundry basket with clothes, including towels, recently laundered and neatly folded sat just inside the door. There was low-velocity blood spatter on a towel at the top of the stack of laundry. It had a vertical orientation.

There are three different types of blood spatter: High velocity, usually from a high-caliber gunshot wound, or something like a power saw, it's mist- like, or has fine droplets. Medium velocity is a little larger, and is usually caused by a hand-held weapon, like a club or a bat. There is often cast-off spatter in those cases, when blood on the weapon is hurled against a wall or ceiling when the assailant reels back for another strike. The third type of spatter is low velocity. Low velocity is blood that is propelled by gravity alone, like a dripping wound. If the person is moving when the blood is dripping, the droplet will have a tail pointing in the direction of the movement. Vertical low-velocity spatter leaves a drop that has no tail indicating movement. It's usually a stellate shape with spikes going in all directions. That's what I saw on the laundry. To me, that indicated that the victim was bleeding, having already had his throat cut, and leaned over the laundry, likely to get the towel that was on his throat as he lay dead. He was not struggling with anyone, or thrashing about, as you would expect in an attack.

"I think this is self-inflicted," I told the other detectives.

Cutting your own throat seems pretty difficult to do, and it is, but I've seen it a few times before, mostly in people with serious mental issues.

The one sticking point in this case was that we didn't see the weapon he'd used if he did cut his own throat. That's a problem. That issue was resolved a few minutes later when officers spotted the knife he'd used on the sidewalk outside his window.

It looked like he'd used a knife to cut his own throat, which of course caused him to bleed profusely. He tossed the knife out the window, walked to the laundry, leaned over to pick up a towel that he put on his throat, and then laid on the bed and died.

Elementary, my dear Watson.

I was just about to call Don Raz back to tell him not to bother stopping by, when we heard a report of a shooting on the radio frequency that covers downtown. A few moments later, officers had arrived and said they needed Homicide to respond.

I was getting my murder today after all.

I walked downstairs to my car. Raz had just pulled up.

"This is going to be a suicide," I told him. "but we've got a shooting at 2nd and Pike. They're asking for Homicide. Leave your car here and just ride with me."

We were only about eight blocks from the scene, but it was just after 4 in the afternoon, and a Friday. Traffic was a mess. Seattle has some of the worst traffic in the nation. I turned on the blue and red lights in my unmarked car and activated my siren.

It was Don Raz's turn to go on Mr. Toad's Wild Ride.

Pike Street is one-way eastbound. I drove to Pine Street, which is one block north of Pike and one-way westbound. Because of the shooting and police cars blocking off streets, what would have normally been bad traffic was now gridlock.

As I tried to drive on Pine, all lanes were stopped. There was nowhere for cars to pull over and get out of my way. I used an extra lane, put there just for me: I drove down the sidewalk.

My siren screamed as pedestrians jumped out of the way. I was only going about five miles per hour, but Raz muttered, "Oh, God."

When we got to 2nd and Pine, there were six or seven patrol cars stopped, I thought I might have misunderstood. Maybe the shooting was at 2nd and Pine. I parked in the street. Raz and I walked up to an officer. He had a rifle out.

"Is this the scene?" I asked.

"No, we think we have the shooter holed up in a restaurant here. The scene's at Pike."

"Don!" I called to Raz, who had walked further up. "This isn't the scene. Get back in the car."

Once again, lights flashing, siren blaring, I tried to make my way to Pike Street.

"Sounds like they have the shooter. Sweet: this'll be a grounder."

A grounder is jargon we use to describe an easy case, where the suspect is arrested by patrol on the day of the murder. A nice easy toss to first.

I pulled up at the correct scene on Pike Street, just a block from the famous Pike Place Market.

Medics were still treating the victim in the back of their medic unit. He was a black male in his 30s and had been shot in the head. I could tell by looking at him; he would not survive.

He still had a slight pulse, so the medics had to transport him, but he was dead on arrival at Harborview.

A patrol officer at the scene filled me in.

"The victim was standing on the northwest corner of 2nd and Pike, when a guy came up behind him, and without saying a word, shot him in the back of the head.

"He was in a crowd with tourists and people going home from work, and a lot of them got blood spattered on them.

"There was a Community Ambassador on a bicycle, and he saw it happen. The shooter walked casually north on 2nd and turned left on Pine, and then went into a restaurant mid-block. We have that place shut down."

Community Ambassadors either walk or ride bicycles in the downtown corridor. They're there to help people, mostly tourists, find things they're looking for.

After a few minutes, I heard officers broadcast over the radio that they had the suspect in custody and were taking him to the Homicide office.

They recovered a pistol inside the tank of a toilet in the restaurant.

Jason arrived at the scene.

"I'm going to the office to talk to the shooter," he said, getting back in his car and driving off. I stayed at the scene to interview witnesses, and to look for surveillance video. This is a busy intersection. There would likely be lots of video.

I wasn't wrong.

On Pike Street, east of 2nd Avenue, we found a camera pointed toward the scene. It belonged to a parking garage. I went to the security office to view the tape.

The scene was a little distant, but it captured the entire murder; the victim standing on the corner, oblivious to what was about to happen, the suspect approaching from behind, reaching up toward his head, something in his hand, a puff of smoke, the victim dropping instantly, the others on the corner aghast.

A couple hours later, I was in the office.

The suspect was Tomas Aferworki.

"He lawyered up right away," Jason told me. Since he'd asked for a lawyer, Jason couldn't interview him.

By 7 o'clock we were ready to book him into jail.

As we walked down the hall from the Homicide office to the door to the parking garage, Afeworki, looked at me.

"How old are you?" he asked.

"I'm 52," I told him.

"Man, I'll be as old as you when I get out of prison."

That's what we call in the business an admission against interest. He said, "when I get out of prison". It's an admission that he's going to prison; because he did it. An innocent person would never say that.

The gun recovered in the toilet tank was ballistically matched to the murder.

Afeworki was convicted a year later in a trial in which he represented himself after firing several attorneys.

He was wrong; he'll be much older than I was at the time before
he gets out of prison.

27

I was just thinking about going to bed about 10 o'clock in the evening on a December night, when my phone rang. I was next up for a murder again. Guess who's working all night?

"Hey Cloyd."

It was Mark Worstman. His squad was working nights that month.

"We're up here at the Four Freedoms House. We've got a murder."

The Four Freedoms House is an assisted-living facility for elderly residents. I didn't need the address. I'm very familiar with the Four Freedoms. I'd been there several times before. I grabbed my gun and badge and headed out the door.

The Four Freedoms is way up north. I live way down south. I went flying up Interstate 5, lights on, siren wailing.

Several patrol cars were parked in the lot when I arrived.

The building is a security-entry building, but the doors were unlocked. Anyone could walk right in. The scene was on the seventh floor.

The elevator opened to a seating area. Several uniformed officers milled around, and detectives from Worstman's squad were talking to potential witnesses.

Mark was there.

"The victim's in his apartment," he told me, pointing down a hallway. "His lady-friend was with him until about 7 o'clock. She lives in a different apartment on this same floor, but down a different hallway. She went back to her place at about seven. She realized she forgot something in his apartment, and she tried to call him, but there was no answer. At about 9, she went back down to his place. She found the door ajar, which was unusual for him. She opened it and found him dead on the floor. There's blood everywhere in there. It looks like he may have been beaten to death."

Jason and I went to the apartment door and looked in.

It was a studio apartment, a hallway leading to the main room passing a bathroom on the left, the bed directly ahead. On the floor between the door and the bed lay the lifeless body of Francis Patrick Fleming, on his back, blood pooled around his body, his lifeless blue eyes staring into oblivion, his mouth agape.

I walked closer. It was hard to judge what had happened to him. It could have been bludgeoning or something else; we'd have to wait for the medical examiner to know for sure.

There was a men's boot print on the carpet near his head.

"Did the Fire Department come in here?" I asked the patrol officer at the door. The print could have come from their boots.

"I don't think they went in that far," he said. "They just looked in the door and said he was dead."

They hadn't left the print, I thought.

Tiny droplets of blood stained the carpet leading to the door. It was either Fleming's blood, dripping from a weapon, or the killer had bled. I prayed for the latter.

I looked around, taking in the scene. The apartment had been ransacked; there were drawers opened and overturned, and cabinets stood open. Clothes in the closet were meticulously lined up by shade of color, many pairs of immaculately shined shoes lined up in a row. This guy wasn't sloppy. He was probably OCD.

There was a folding metal chair leaning against the wall to the left. The kind that come with a card table, with a padded cloth seat and back rest. It was out of place. Blood stained the back rest. It was probably the victim's blood; I hoped not.

I walked back out of the apartment. In the hallway, and older man approached me. He flashed a badge. It said, "Private Investigator."

"Jerry Delia," he said. "Retired P.I."

Jerry was, as they say, a character.

"Hi Jerry," I said. "Do you live on this floor?"

"I live just down the hall," he said. "He was a real quiet guy," he said, referring to Fleming. "He kept to himself. He wouldn't even say hi if he passed you in the hall. The last few months he'd been seeing this lady who is pretty quiet too. That's her down there." He pointed down the hall to a woman being interviewed by night shift detectives. She was the woman who'd called 911.

"He collected silver and gold coins," Delia continued. "That's the only time he talked, when he talked about that stuff."

I walked down the hall to where the woman was being interviewed by Dana Duffy and Frank Clark from the night shift.

"This is Rosemary Garnett," Duffy told me. "She found the victim."

I introduced myself to Rosemary.

"Tell me what happened," I said.

"Patrick and I were engaged," she said. "He hadn't given me a ring yet, but I expected to get one this Christmas.

"I was out running errands all day, and I got home at about 5:30. When I got back, Patrick wanted to hear about everything I did.

"We watched Fox News on TV. The O'Reilly Factor. At about 6:45 or seven o'clock, I went back to my apartment. I had to take my medications. When I got there, I realized I'd forgotten my orange juice in Patrick's refrigerator.

"I tried to call him on the phone, but he didn't answer. I thought that was odd."

"Tell me about his coin collection," I said.

"Yes, he's a numismatist. He kept a lot of money in his apartment. I don't think he told anyone but me."

She talked about a man named James who used to live in a different apartment on the same floor.

"He used to take Patrick on his rounds, like going to stores and the bank. Patrick loaned him 50 dollars a day, until it got up to about seven hundred dollars, then Patrick cut him off."

James was in his 80s, she told me, but had a son in his 50s.

That was intriguing to me; Fleming wasn't killed by another elderly resident of the building. There'd been a lot of force used in this murder.

"Then there's Sylvia," she continued. "She visited Patrick all the time. She'd go to his apartment to watch television. She sometimes brought her niece with her."

Rosemary said that Sylvia moved out of the building a few months ago. Recently, she'd been calling Patrick, asking to borrow money.

Sylvia was an elderly woman. She hadn't done this to him either.

Carla Carlstrom and Sean O'Donnell from the Prosecutor's office arrived. I filled them in on what we knew at that point.

The Crime Scene detectives got to work processing the scene.

There were a few scattered loose coins, but no collection like Rosemary had described was in the apartment.

A little while later, Dr. Micheline Lubin and Investigator Bill Barbour from the Medical Examiner's office arrived. Dr. Lubin started her examination of Fleming's body.

She quickly determined that this wasn't a bludgeoning at all; Fleming had been stabbed to death. There were deep stab wounds to his throat, almost to the point of decapitation.

When she lifted his shirt, she also saw several superficial stab wounds to his torso. They were consistent with torture. She found defensive wounds to his hands; he'd fought desperately for his life.

He lost.

They took possession of Fleming's body and transported him to the Medical Examiner's office for an autopsy that would take place in the morning.

Gary Jackson, the primary CSI detective who'd processed the scene, called me the next morning.

"The Latent Print people processed the scene. They didn't find any prints. They said it looked like the place had been wiped down."

Most of the time, I try to attend the autopsy of a murder I'm investigating. Sometimes I'm too busy with other things and can't make it. Carla Carlstrom from the prosecutor's office attended. She called me from the Medical Examiners. She confirmed what we surmised at the scene. Fleming's throat had been cut, nearly to the point of decapitation.

Jason and I sent a bulletin out state-wide. We wanted to know about anyone trying to sell coin collections or sheets of uncut US currency, which was also missing from the apartment.

Virginia Merceri was the manager at the Four Freedoms. She called me later that day.

"I got a call from a woman, claiming to be Patrick Fleming's wife. We have no record of him being married."

She gave me the phone number of the woman who'd called, who'd given the name Melba Fleming.

I called the number, and Melba answered.

She told me she worked for the City of Seattle and was actually in a building next door to police headquarters.

I asked her to come to my office.

"We were married in 1983," she told me when she arrived. "Patrick was in the Vietnam War. He was a sailor on a riverboat."

I had an uncle who fought on a riverboat in Vietnam. It was a dangerous assignment.

"Patrick earned two purple hearts and a bronze star," she said. "He suffered from PTSD. We couldn't live together because of it, but we had a joint checking account and he sent me money every month."

She'd last seen him two weeks before his murder, on Thanksgiving.

She had photo albums with her, containing pictures of her and Patrick from over the years. In almost every photo, Patrick was dressed in camouflage, or some other form of military clothing.

"He had a large collection of coins," she told me. "I told him it was dangerous to keep them in his apartment, and that he needed to put them in a safe deposit box. He told me he could defend himself and no one was going to take his collection."

A woman called me from Four Freedoms later in the day.

"I moved in a couple days ago," she said. "On the day this happened, I was downstairs in the basement, near the laundry room. There was a young man down there. He looked really suspicious."

"What time were you down there?" I asked her.

"It was about 6:45," she said.

That was only 15 minutes before Patrick was last seen alive.

I set her up with Betty Kincaid to produce a composite sketch of the man she'd seen.

She and Betty met in my office. They worked together, producing the sketch. I put it in a bulletin, and then sent it out to police agencies state-wide, trying to identify the person who'd been in the building shortly before the murder.

Jason and I went back to the Four Freedoms. We wanted to look for credit card bills, so we could flag his accounts, in case the cards were taken.

While we were there, we went to see Rosemary Garnett again.

"Patrick had a handgun," she said. "I never saw it, but it was a .38 revolver."

This is the first we'd heard of a gun. None was found in his apartment.

"He also had a briefcase that he kept his important papers in," she continued. "My passport was in it too."

The briefcase hadn't been in the apartment either.

We left the Four Freedoms, heading back downtown. Our police radio was on the frequency that covers that part of the city. We heard a patrol car radio that they'd stopped a person who looks similar to the sketch I'd put out. We drove to where the guy was stopped, not far from the Four Freedoms.

We arrived at the strip mall where the stop had taken place. The guy was seated on the sidewalk. After speaking to the patrol officer who'd stopped him, we approached the guy. He looked a little like the sketch.

"Do you have ID?" I asked.

"It's in my wallet," he said, gesturing to the patrol car parked nearby. His wallet was lying on the trunk. I walked over and picked it up, taking out his ID. There was a credit card behind the ID. It had a woman's name on it. I walked back over to him.

"Whose credit card is this?" I asked.

"I found it," he said. "It's not active."

How the hell did he know it's not active, unless he tried to use it? He'd just given me probable cause to arrest him.

"We're taking you downtown to our office," I told him.

287

At the office, I put him in an interview room.

"Okay, I found the card in the parking lot," he admitted, "and I did try to use it, but it didn't work. I don't know nothing about no murder."

I showed him a photo of Patrick Fleming in life.

"Oh, God, I know that guy!" he said. "I'd see him in the Burger King up the street. He always bought me coffee. He told me I needed to join the military to get my life straight. He told me he'd served."

He was tearing up.

"He was a good guy. I can't believe someone killed him!"

This guy definitely wasn't the killer. But he could be useful. I turned him into an informant.

"Whoever did this is probably someone off Aurora," the major arterial that ran a couple blocks from the Four Freedoms. "I'll let you walk for now on the credit card fraud, but you're going to work for us. We want you to snoop around all the street people out there and see what you can find out about this. If you try to stiff us, we'll have a warrant issued for the fraud."

"I'll do it," he said. "That guy didn't deserve to be murdered."

We drove him back out to where we'd picked him up and released him.

Over the next few days, he called us, or we went out to find him.

"Nobody seems to know anything about this," he said. "The people I've been talking to would at least know about it. I don't know what to think."

I didn't think he was lying to me.

Over the next several days, we developed other leads. Many looked promising, but like most whodunit cases, one by one, they petered out.

Murder investigations are a process of exclusion. You have a virtual pot of everything that "could have" happened. They can't all be true, so the early part of a case like this is throwing out all the things that didn't happen, or the people who didn't do it. Hopefully, in the end, you'll be left with the actual solution.

On January 13th, I got a message to call Tara Roy from the crime lab.

She'd analyzed the DNA evidence we'd submitted.

"Most of the blood belongs to Fleming," she said. "But I found male DNA that wasn't his."

That was the bombshell I'd hoped she'd drop. Whenever there is an unidentified contributor of DNA, they are referred to as Individual A.

Individual A's DNA was found on the cloth from the folding metal chair that had been against the far wall in his apartment, as well as on carpet samples leading to the door. The killer had been cut. That's pretty common in stabbing cases. The knife gets covered with blood and gets slippery. The killer cuts themselves. She also found smaller samples of Individual A's DNA on the swabs taken from Fleming's fingertips.

"I entered the DNA profile into CODIS", she said, "but I didn't get a hit."

That meant, in theory, that our killer had never been convicted of a felony. I say "in theory" because I've had cases, like Shannon Harps' killer, James Williams, who had been convicted of felonies, and in Williams' case, actually went to prison for quite a while and had been released, and though DNA samples were taken, they were never processed and entered into the database.

Having DNA from at least one of the killers was huge. Now I just had to swab the correct cheek to get a match.

A couple weeks later, I got a call from Jerry Delia, the "retired PI" I'd spoken to on the night of the murder.

"I thought of something I forgot to tell you," he said. "On the day of the murder, I was in the seating area just off the elevators on the seventh floor. These three women got off the elevator. They really looked out of place. They were dressed really trashy, like they were trying to look high class, but it was way too much.

"They sat in the chairs there. One of them went down the hall toward Patrick's room, while the other two stayed seated. They made a point not to make eye contact with me or anyone who walked through. They were really strange."

He said he'd spoken to a couple other residents who'd seen them as well. He gave me the name of one woman who'd also seen them.

"I also wanted to tell you about the guy who lives across the hall from Patrick," he continued. "He disappeared for a couple weeks after the murder. He just showed back up here. He's been telling people he heard screams from Patrick's apartment the night of the murder. He knew Patrick had been stabbed."

That was intriguing. The night of the murder, the residents all believed he'd been bludgeoned.

Delia said he thought the guy may have a criminal history.

After hanging up, I called the office at Four Freedoms. They gave me the name and date of birth of the guy who lived across from Patrick. I ran his criminal history. I found a charge, more than twenty years old, of "harassing children." We decided to pay him a visit.

Jason and I went back to Four Freedoms and knocked on the door across from Patrick's apartment.

The man opened the door and invited us in.

"Where were you the night Patrick was murdered?" I asked.

"I was home," he said. "I was taking a bath, when I heard screaming. Someone was pounding on my door. By the time I got there, the person was gone. I looked through the peephole.

Patrick's door was open, and I could see him lying on the floor. I went out and stood by his door. I saw blood everywhere. I went back into my apartment.

"I was looking out the peephole again when the Medical Examiner was there. I heard her say he'd been stabbed."

He mentioned someone who'd been trying to get money from Patrick.

"Her name was Sylvia. She used to live here."

That was the second time Sylvia's name had come up. As a general rule, when a name comes up from more than one source, you should probably look closer.

"Do you mind if I swab the inside of your cheek?" I asked.

He didn't have a problem with it.

"I don't think that guy had anything to do with it," I told Jason after we left his apartment.

"No, neither to I," he said.

We'd still submit his cheek swab, just in case.

Since we were there, we walked to the apartment of the woman Jerry Delia told me about, who'd seen the strange women in the seating area.

"I saw three people," she told us. "I was going to do my laundry, and they were sitting in the area by the elevators. They were acting strange, not making eye contact. They were dressed really garishly, like they tried too hard to be fashionable."

Back in the office, I submitted the cheek swab from Patrick's neighbor to the crime lab.

We concentrated on finding out who Sylvia was. Once again, I called the Four Freedoms office. They gave me Sylvia's name and date of birth. Jason ran her in the computer systems.

"She's the victim in an elderly exploitation fraud case," he said. "It's being investigated downstairs in the Elderly Exploitation detail."

That unit is housed one floor down, on the sixth floor at headquarters. We walked down to ask about it.

Pam St. John was the detective assigned to the case.

"Sylvia is a retired school teacher," St. John told us. "She was pretty wealthy because of good investments she'd made.

"She lost a life-partner a few months ago. She was at a street fair in Chinatown. She went into a tent giving palm readings. There was a woman in there who called herself 'Lady Monica'. She told Sylvia that she had a dark aura about her, and she could see that Sylvia was troubled. She told Sylvia she could help her, but it was going to cost money. She told Sylvia she had a friend, a Father Thomas. He could help her clear her aura, if she would cooperate. Sylvia was more than happy to."

St. John told us that Sylvia met with Monica several times over the next several months. Whenever she did, Monica gave her a pill she said would help calm her. Sylvia gave Monica money. A lot of money. Sylvia owned several thousand shares of Microsoft stock; she sold them and gave Monica the money.

By the time she realized she'd been scammed, she'd given Monica over a million and a half dollars.

"I haven't been able to identify Monica," St. John said. "I've showed her a lot of pictures of people I thought could be her, but she hasn't identified anyone."

"How does she get a hold of Monica when she needs to?" Jason asked.

"She has a phone number," St. John said, and gave Jason the number.

We went back up to our office. Jason ran the phone number in several databases we use.

"It comes back to a man's name," he said. "But it's also associated with a woman named Brenda Nicholas."

He searched her name and found that Kirkland Police, a suburban city across Lake Washington from Seattle, had investigated her for theft and fraud.

Now it was getting interesting.

Kirkland PD served a search warrant on a house in Lynnwood, north of Seattle. There was a list of the evidence they seized from the warrant.

"Holy shit!" Jason yelled. "Listen to this! In a bedroom closet the detectives found a brown briefcase containing papers with the name Francis Patrick Fleming on them!"

"Holy shit is right!" I said. "These are our people. We just have to figure out who the male was, whose DNA we have."

I called Kirkland Police and spoke with detectives there. They didn't know anything about this murder, or that Fleming had been the victim.

"We arrested Nicholas, and another woman, Gilda Ramirez," the Kirkland detective told me. "There was a guy there named Charles Jungbluth, but we didn't have anything to arrest him for."

Jason got a photo of Nicholas and went to visit Sylvia. He included the photo with five others in a photomontage.

"Oh, my God!" she said, looking at the photo of Nicholas. "That's Monica!"

Now that Monica was identified, and we believed she was involved in Patrick's murder, we needed to find her.

When we ran her name in other computer systems, we found out that she was on active probation for a theft conviction out of California. Her Community Corrections Officer, the new phrase for what used to be called a Parole Officer, was in Seattle. Jason called him.

He confirmed that Brenda was on his caseload. She came to his office from time to time. In fact, she had an appointment to see him next week.

Perfect. We'd be there.

The Corrections officer's office was near Safeco Field, home of the Seattle Mariners. On the day of Brenda's appointment, we staked out the parking lot of his office.

Jason and I were in an unmarked pickup truck, Al Cruise and Russ Weklych were in another car, and Bob Vallor in another. We took up spots across the lot from each other.

After a while, Brenda arrived. She was a passenger in a car driven by a man. A teenaged boy sat in the back seat.

We watched Brenda go in.

The man driving, and the boy waited in the car. The man was smoking and throwing his cigarette butts out the window.

After a half hour, Brenda came back out and got in the car. They drove off. We followed, heading toward North Seattle.

Following people in a car is a lot harder than television shows make it out to be. You can't just pull right in behind the car you're following; you don't want to be obvious.

People generally have their heads up their asses and don't see anything going on around them, but you can't assume the person you're following will be quite so oblivious.

We traded off in a relay-like technique, staying a couple cars behind them, and then one of the other cars switching places.

At one point, we came upon a road construction site. They made it through, but an officer working traffic control motioned for us to stop. I recognized the officer, Bob Hoff.

"Bobby!" I yelled out the window. He walked to the side of the truck. "We're following that car. We need to go." He held up traffic and we sped through. Luckily, we were able to catch up and didn't lose them.

The car pulled into the lot of an espresso place on Stone Way North. We set up surveillance across the street where we could watch them. Cruise and Weklych set up on the other side.

After a while, the teenaged boy that was with them walked out of the coffee place to a building across the street. That's when I saw the sign: Palm Readings. This was Brenda's shop.

We set up surveillance on that building. Eventually, Brenda and the man who'd been driving left the coffee place, and drove across the street to the Psychic shop and went in.

We watched for a little while, and then went back to the office. We knew where to find them now.

I called Sergeant Verner O'Quinn who worked in the Intelligence Section.

"Verner, I need some pole cameras put up." I gave him the address on Stone Way North.

Pole cameras are cameras mounted on utility poles. We wanted one mounted on each side of the building.

Detectives dressed as utility workers went to the scene with a cherry-picker truck and mounted the cameras. They're disguised in boxes, so they don't look like cameras. Once they were up, we could access them over the internet. They can be controlled by whoever is monitoring, panning any direction. They also have a powerful zoom capability, so the operator can get a really close look at anything in their field of view. You can record anything you want or take snapshots.

Once the cameras were set up, I logged into them from the computer at my desk in the office. I had two monitors, so I kept the cameras on one at all times. As cars came and went, I zoomed in so that only the license plates showed on the screen and took snapshots of each one. A lot of different cars came and went, many driven by the same people. It seemed they only used a car for a couple days, and then changed to a different one. I ran each new license plate that showed up. None of their registrations were current.

I could also monitor the cameras from home. I constantly had the camera on my laptop.

On a Friday evening, I was home, the psychic shop on the screen on my computer. My mother-in-law and father-in-law visited from Spokane.

My mother-in-law, Jeanette loved cop shows and was kind of a cop groupie. When Doreen was growing up, her mom was constantly listening to a police scanner. When she found out her daughter was marrying a cop, she was ecstatic.

"What's this?" she asked, looking at my computer monitor.

"I'm watching this place as part of a murder I'm investigating."

"Oh, my God!" she said, plopping down in front of the computer, staring at the monitor.

"Tell me if anyone shows up," I said, sipping from a glass of wine.

I had free help.

Brenda Nicholas was a Gypsy. I didn't know much about Gypsies, other than one time investigating a family of Gypsies for a child molestation case when I was in the Special Assault unit. It was a nightmare. They lied about everything. If I asked on a Monday what day it was, they'd say Wednesday; they were incapable of telling the truth about anything, no matter how innocuous the question.

Dan Stokke had retired the previous year after working the Intelligence Unit for years. He specialized in Gypsies. I called him.

"I know Brenda Nicholas," he said, "and her husband, Archie Marx. Archie runs a used car scam."

That explained all the different cars.

"I had a couple good informants in the Gypsy community. I can hook you up with them."

I met up with them the next week. I got a crash course in the Roma, (Gypsy) way of life. I learned a lot about the Roma and Gypsy cultures.

"Roma is the culture," they told me. "Gypsy is the criminal element of that culture."

They didn't know anything about the murder but knew a lot about Brenda and Archie.

"They're into sweetheart scams," they said. "Brenda will get close to some old guy who they think has money; they usually drug the guy and get him to give them money."

I thought of Brenda giving Sylvia pills to "calm her down."

"They're also into palm reading scams," they told me. "They drug victims there too. They have access to pharmacists who they pay for the drugs."

I'd captured photos of several people around the psychic shop with the pole cameras. I showed them photos.

They identified Brenda and Archie, as well as Archie's father and Brenda's two teenaged sons. There was another woman they couldn't identify.

"She's not Roma," they said.

I also showed them photos of Charles Jungbluth, who'd been at the house in Lynnwood when Brenda had been arrested. They didn't know him either.

We had male DNA from someone involved in the murder. My guess was it was going to be Archie Marx.

Watching the video from the cameras, I learned that Archie always came outside to smoke. He stood next to a 3-foot-high concrete wall that ran along an alley beside the building. He did that several times a day.

We sent Intelligence detectives back out there.

One of the detectives, Sam DeJesus, put on a reflective vest like a city worker and walked into the alley. He had a small broom and dust bin. He swept up all the cigarette butts in the area where Archie smoked.

We sat back and waited. We didn't have to wait long.

A few minutes later, Archie came out. He leaned against the concrete wall and smoked. When he was through, he tossed the butt down and went back in the building.

We zoomed the camera on the discarded butt, recording as DeJesus came back and picked up that butt. There could be no issue that Archie was the one who discarded that cigarette butt; he had just cleaned all the others out of the area.

One of Brenda's sons was outside when DeJesus picked up the cigarette butt and placed it into a plastic bag. He looked at Sam with a curious expression. Sam walked away.

He brought the butt directly to me. I packaged it and placed into evidence. I sent a request that the lab process it for DNA.

I got a call from Tara Roy from the lab a few days later. She was able to develop a DNA profile from the cigarette butt. Archie was not Individual A. She also eliminated Patrick's neighbor from across the hall.

We were back to square one in our attempt to identify Individual A.

We needed to put a stick in the hornet's nest to stir things up. We met with St. John and formulated a plan. We would arrest Brenda, Gilda and Charles Jungbluth for the scam they pulled on Sylvia.

I called Randy Moore at the US Marshal's Fugitive Task Force. I told him what we were up to. Randy doesn't usually work property crimes, but because this was being used to forward a murder, he was on board.

I showed him the video feed of Brenda's shop.

"We'll sit on the place. When she shows up, we'll arrest her."

I sat in my office, watching the video feed from Brenda's shop. Brenda and Gilda left in a car. Randy wasn't in place yet. I called him to let him know what happened.

A couple hours later, Brenda and Gilda returned. I watched as Randy and his team swooped in. They arrested them both.

Archie walked out and tried to interfere. There was no audio, but I watched as Randy put him in his place. Archie backed down.

A few minutes later, Randy arrived in our office. We put Brenda and Gilda in interview rooms. Randy left, only to return a while later, Charles Jungbluth in tow.

Pam St. John went into interview Brenda. Jason and I watched through the one-way mirror.

I was surprised by Brenda's high-pitched, squeaky voice. This was the brains behind this operation?

She asked for a lawyer right away and had nothing to say.

A few minutes later, St. John interviewed Gilda. She spoke with a strong Hispanic accent, denying any knowledge of the theft.

Lastly, she interviewed Jungbluth.

As we watched the interview, I looked over at Jason.

"This can't be our guy; he's way too much of a wimp to have done this."

After St. John was through with Jungbluth, we decided to talk to him. He was the weak link in this whole chain.

We walked in an introduced ourselves. We didn't tell Jungbluth we were investigating a murder.

"What's your relationship with Brenda Nicholas?" I asked.

"I'm her driver."

"Does she pay you to be her driver?"

"No," he said. "She just gives me money for gas."

"Why would you drive her around for nothing other than gas money?" I asked.

He shrugged.

"I got nothing else going on."

"Have you ever been to Four Freedoms House?" I asked.

"I've driven Brenda there, but I always wait in the car in the parking lot."

"Do you know Sylvia?"

"Yes, I know her," he said.

"Didn't you help her move out of the Four Freedoms?"

"Yeah, I guess I did."

"Why did Sylvia suddenly want to move out of the Four Freedoms?"

"Some guy was harassing her, I guess," he said.

I laid down a photo of Patrick Fleming

"Have you ever seen this guy before?"

Charles looked at the photo.

"No, never."

I threw down a photo of Fleming from the murder scene, covered in blood, mouth agape.

"Maybe he looked like this when you saw him.

"I never saw that," he said.

We asked Charles what he knew about Brenda's involvement in thefts. He said he thought she was involved in some thefts, but he didn't have any specific information.

"We're investigating the murder of the guy whose photo we showed you," I told him. "Have you ever heard Brenda talk about coin collections, or uncut sheets of currency?"

"I was driving Brenda one time," he said. "Sylvia was in the back with her. They were talking about a guy. Brenda told Sylvia she really needed to get close to that guy. I think they talked about coins or something."

He talked about a different time at the house in Kirkland.

"Brenda told Archie that she knew an old guy who had a really nice coin collection. She told Archie she really wanted the collection, but didn't know how to get it. They walked into another room and closed the door. I didn't hear anything that was said after that."

Charles added some very important information.

"I was at the house in Lynnwood before the police raided it. Brenda had a bunch of coins, some of them in bags. She was selling them."

He'd seen many of the coins, he said, and could identify them if he saw them again.

Jason went to get photos we'd gotten online of collections similar to the ones Patrick had. Charles identified about two thirds of them as ones he'd seen before.

We were happy with how the interview went. We now had a witness who could put Brenda with the property stolen during the murder. With Patrick's briefcase being recovered in Brenda's bedroom during the search warrant, we had the right person. We needed to get a little more to make the murder case stick.

"Charles, do you mind if we take a cheek swab from you?" I asked.

"No, that's fine," he said.

We used two long Q-tip like swabs to take a buccal swab of his inner cheeks. We placed the swabs in a petri dish.

We booked him for the theft charge. He was released after a couple days.

A couple weeks later, I received another call from Tara Roy at the lab.

"I processed the swabs submitted from Charles Jungbluth," she said. "The DNA profile for Charles Jungbluth matches the DNA profile from Individual A. The chance of finding a matching profile at random from the public is one in ten quintillion."

That's ten, with eighteen zeros after it: A big-assed number.

Apparently, he wasn't as much of a wimp as I'd thought.

I put out bulletins state-wide for the arrest of Charles Jungbluth. His last known address was in Lake Stevens, north of Seattle in Snohomish County.

My phone started ringing right away.

A Seattle patrol officer called.

"I live right down the street from that address," he said. "I've seen that guy around the neighborhood."

I also got a call from members of a Snohomish County Sheriff's task force.

"Do you want us to go arrest this guy?" he asked.

"Yes," I said, "but don't mention the murder."

Twenty minutes later, I got another call from the Snohomish County guy.

"We've got him," he said. "We told him it was about a hit and run. We're on our way in."

Jason recently had shoulder surgery, so he was off for a while. I was on my own.

It was a hot summer day. When Charles arrived, he was bare chested. Not a pretty sight.

I put him back in interview room #1.

After letting him stew for a while, I went in.

"I want to go over some things you told us before, Charles."

"Okay," he said.

I laid out photos he'd signed in our first interview, of Brenda, Archie, and Gilda.

"Tell me again about when you heard these guys talking about wanting to get the coins," I said.

"I just heard 'em saying they wanted the coins. I didn't hear nothing else.'

"You didn't know who they were talking about getting the coins from?"

"I didn't know who they were talking about," he said.

"Remember that picture I showed you before?" I asked.

Charles nodded.

"Are you sure you've never seen that guy before?"

"No," Charles said, almost in a whisper.

"You said you'd never been in his apartment."

"No," he said, again, almost a whisper.

"Ever."

"No."

"Not to visit or anything?"

He shook his head.

I had him on the line, but like a good fisherman, I slowly let the line out. Let him go with it a while. Charles was getting nervous.

"Were you ever with Brenda when she went to see…"

"I don't even know where he lives," he interrupted. "I didn't know the guy with the coins lives there."

"Didn't Brenda want Sylvia to get closer to him?"

"She wanted Sylvia to get closer to him, to get money from him, because he's supposed to have a lot of money."

"And you've definitely never been in his apartment."

"No, I haven't."

"Did Sylvia ever seem a little loopy to you when she was with Brenda?" I asked.

"Yeah."

"Did you ever hear or suspect that Brenda may be drugging Sylvia?"

"No, none whatsoever."

I shifted the focus briefly to throw Charles off guard.

"Are you right handed or left handed?"

"Right handed."

"Oh, okay."

"I never knew her to give Sylvia drugs at all," Charles said, apparently eager to change the subject.

"Did you ever know her to have prescription drugs other than any she takes herself?"

"She was taking stuff for her heart, heart pills and stuff like that," he said. "Now you've got me wondering."

"You don't know?" I asked.

"I have no clue. I thought I knew this woman, but I don't know the woman."

"First of all," I said. "Let me say something. I'm not here to investigate these thefts and things you're charged with. I don't give a shit about any of that. I'm not trying to say that you were involved or not involved in those cases, because I just don't care.

"I'm here to investigate this murder, so it's really important that you're completely honest. Don't minimize what you know. That can only hurt you in the end."

"Right," Charles said, nodding.

"Go over what you heard Brenda talking to Archie about."

"Just that she knew a guy that had a big coin collection, and she wanted to get it."

"Did you know who she was talking about?"

"No, I had no idea who she was talking about," he said.

"What happened when she told that to Archie?"

"They closed the door."

Charles tried to explain the dynamic of his relationship with Brenda.

"When I was around, and Brenda talked on the phone, she'd walk into another room, so I couldn't hear what she was saying.

"When she was talking to Sylvia, I wasn't around; it was just her and Sylvia."

"Except when you were driving them around," I pointed out.

"Yeah, sometimes I'd be driving them around, or if we went out to lunch and I was sitting at the table with them, but sometimes I'd sit at a different table."

"Why were you even doing this for her?" I asked.

"I liked her. She was a friend of a good friend of mine."

"Yeah," I said. "That would be why you'd give her a ride once in a while. But you were basically her bitch when it came to driving."

"Well, yeah," he said. "But like I said, I didn't have a business at the time, so I didn't have anything else to do."

"Did you know Brenda to go by any name other than Brenda?"

"No, um…"

"Did Sylvia call her Brenda?" I asked.

"Sylvia called her Monica."

"Why would Sylvia call her Monica?"

"I don't know. I thought it was her last name, er, uh, middle name."

"Did Brenda tell you that?"

"No."

"You didn't wonder why Sylvia was calling Brenda Monica?"

Charles paused for a moment. This was way too much intellectual heavy lifting for him.

"I thought it was kinda weird, but you know, who am I?"

"Did you ever call her Brenda in front of Sylvia?"

"Sometimes."

"Did Sylvia ever say, 'Who's Brenda?'?"

"No, she never said that," he said.

"But she was kind of loopy," I added.

"Yeah, and Brenda never said anything about it."

I went back over things he said in the earlier interview, including seeing Brenda with various coin collections. He tried to hedge the answers he'd given the last time. Especially about whether these were the coins Brenda had expressed interest in getting, and about what knowledge he had of Brenda's scams.

"Your earlier interview was recorded," I reminded him.

I steered the conversation back toward Patrick Fleming.

"Just to be clear, you've never met him in your life, right?"

"Right."

"You've never even seen him or been in his apartment."

"No."

"Do have any idea where in the building he lived?"

"No."

"Do you remember before, when we showed you pictures of him after he was killed?" I asked. "How would you describe those pictures?"

"Bad."

"Pretty gruesome, huh?"

"A lot of blood. A lot of blood."

Charles stared at the table, saying nothing.

"Do you remember when OJ Simpson was arrested?" I asked him.

"Yeah."

"There was a lot of blood there too. Do you remember the issue of him cutting his finger?"

"Yeah."

"And leaving blood at the scene?"

"Right."

"Let me see your right hand," I said.

I leaned forward to look at his hand.

"You see, what happens," I said, scooting my chair up close to Charles—so close it made him uncomfortable, just like I wanted, "is that when the knife gets covered with blood, it gets really slippery; that's what happened to OJ, and to a lot of people. Their hand slips down to the blade and they cut themselves. Do you understand that?"

"Yeah," he barely squeaked.

"Have you ever heard of that happening?" I asked.

"No, not really," he said, chuckling nervously now.

"Not really? Come on, Charles."

He chuckled nervously again, likely trying not to shit himself.

I leaned forward, very close now.

"Not only does it happen," I said, "it happened to you, Charles."

"No," barely above a whisper, my face less than four inches from his.

"Yeah," I said. "See you cut yourself, and you bled. You bled on the chair that was in the room, the folding chair. And you dripped your blood."

"What are you talking about?" he asked.

"This is what I'm talking about." I picked up a paper from the table. "This is a lab report from the State Crime Lab. It's dated today.

"Do you remember the last time you were here, I swabbed the inside of your cheek?"

"Yeah."

"What did I tell you that was for?"

"You told me DNA."

"Right," I said. "So, I submitted those swabs to the crime lab."

I read him the parts of the report dealing with what was tested and compared to his DNA. Then I read the punch line.

"The blood left at the scene matched the DNA sample from Charles Jungbluth to a probability of one in ten quintillion.

"Quintillion," I said for emphasis. "That's a big-assed number, Charles."

Earlier I'd given Charles a can of soda. He took a big slug of it now.

I read the other parts of the lab report to him listing all the places we found his DNA.

"You were dripping blood as you walked out the door," I told him. "There were drops of your blood on the carpet in the hallway."

Charles sat, hands on his hips, staring at the report, taking more swigs from the soda can.

"Here's the question, Charles. Are you going to go down for this by yourself?"

"Now you're telling me I need a lawyer," he said.

"Do you need a lawyer?"

"You're telling me my DNA's…"

"That's right."

"This is where I tell you I need…I'm probably going to need a lawyer."

"You're probably going to need a lawyer, okay, so if you want to take this all by yourself, and not take anybody with you, if you think you probably need a lawyer, you'd better think about that. But before you make any rash decisions, you'd better think. Because you're fucked, okay?

"The only way you can help yourself here, to make anything happen, the least you have to do is cooperate and take the other people down."

Charles fidgeted in his chair as I spoke, looking at himself in the one-way mirror, a group of detectives and prosecutors watching him in the other side, and scooted his chair away from me. He was nearing panic; the reality of his situation smashing him in the face like an eight-pound sledge.

"You didn't plan this, Charles. You were put up to this, and you were sweating it.

"You're going down for this, Charles. It's a done deal. So, I don't need to hear anything from you. I didn't even need to speak with you, but I know you didn't plan this. You were put up to it. There were other people involved, and I know you don't want to be the only one going down for it. You were the patsy."

I leaned in close again, placing my left hand on his right shoulder, and spoke quietly to him.

"You were the patsy, Charles. They set you up, and they knocked you down, and if you want them to get away with that, it's up to you. Do you want them to get away with that? Because, you, Charles, are going down. No question. The only question is how long you're going down for, and the thing that matters is whether you're willing to tell us the truth.

"And if you just sit there and say, 'I don't know nothing. I don't want to talk'," I pounded the lab report on the table. "We already know what happened.

"One in ten quintillion, Charles" I continued. "That's ten followed by eighteen zeros.

"Do you know how many people are on the planet right now? Between six and seven billion. Do you know how many people have ever lived on the planet since the beginning of time? A few more billion. That leaves a whole bunch of zeros unaccounted for. That's how unlikely it is that you didn't do this.

"You could go to the store every day for five days, and buy a lottery ticket every day, and win every day. The odds wouldn't be that bad for you.

"So, Charles, you're the patsy. Brenda set you up and knocked you down. Has she called you or done anything for you since you got arrested last time?"

"She can't. She's in jail."

"But Archie could have," I pointed out. "And she could have called you collect. She could have had somebody else reach out to you.

"We listened to her phone calls to Archie from jail," I said. "They talked about you. She wasn't at all sorry she got you wrapped up in this. They used you from the beginning; you were their bitch. That's what they do to people. Now do you want to just let them throw you away? You've never been in serious trouble before, but you're in big trouble now. You're a little league player in a major league game. You can help yourself by telling the truth."

"I have a problem," Charles said.

"What's your problem?" I asked,

"My attorney told me not to talk to you guys at all, but I need to talk to him, but he's not here."

"I'll get you a phone," I said.

Charles waffled back and forth about wanting an attorney. Like I explained in an earlier chapter, it was an equivocal request for an attorney. Determined by courts not to be a valid exercise of his right to a lawyer.

"I'll call an attorney for you," I said. "The attorney's probably going to tell you not to talk to me. If that's what you want to do, I'm just going to book you for murder."

Charles hemmed and hawed. He picked a photo of Brenda up off the table, then put it down, only to pick it up again.

311

"Brenda didn't just walk in and say, 'we need to kill this guy', she did it slowly. She groomed you, just like a child molester grooms his victims."

"We did have a relationship," he said. "Maybe I need to take the fall myself."

"Why would you do that," I asked. "Do you love this girl or something?"

"I have feelings for her, yes."

"Even now, after what she's done to you?"

"Love is blind," he said. "Whether she played me or not, I don't know."

Charles squirmed, and evaded, trying to not answer questions.

"What do you want to know," he said, finally.

"I want to know what happened, who planned it, who was there and what went down."

Charles picked up photos of Brenda and Gilda Ramirez. He scooted them to me.

"There you go. These two."

"Tell me about the first time you heard about this plan," I said.

He described a time they were leaving the Four Freedoms. He was driving. Brenda was in the back with either Gilda or Sylvia. They talked about the coins.

"Brenda couldn't believe he had that many coins," he said.

Another time they were in a restaurant when Brenda brought up the coins.

"She told me she really wanted them," he said.

"Did she tell you how she planned to get them?" I asked.

"No."

"When did that conversation take place?"

"About a month before," he said.

"Did you ever hear her talk to anyone else about the coins and that she wanted to get them?"

"Yeah," he said.

"Who did she talk to?"

"Gilda and her son, Kevin."

"What did she say to them?"

"Just that the guy had a bunch of coins, and she wanted to go get them."

"What was Gilda's reaction to that?" I asked.

"She would do anything for Brenda."

"At some point, she broached the subject of you being involved in helping her get those coins. Am I right?"

"Yeah."

"How did she do that?"

"She just said, 'You've got to help me get those coins'."

"What did you say," I asked.

"I asked her, 'How in the fuck are we going to get the coins?'"

"Did she ever get more specific about what she wanted you to do?"

"Yeah."

"What did she say?"

"She said 'We gotta go in there and kill him'."

"What was your reaction when she said that you had to kill him?"

"I thought she was losing it," he said. "I didn't think she was serious. But she kept talking about it. Talking about killing him and taking the coins."

"When you had these conversations about killing him, was anyone else present?" I asked.

"Not most of the time. Gilda was there a couple times."

"How many times were the three of you together when you talked about killing him?"

"About five or six times."

"Was anyone else there?"

"Kevin was there a couple times."

"Kevin, her fifteen-year-old son was there a couple times while you talked about killing him?"

"Yeah."

Charles described the day of the murder.

"She came to me and said 'We gotta do it today, I'm out of money'.

"Me and Brenda went to Goodwill to buy clothes to wear, and butcher knives we were going to do it with."

"Were you wearing women's clothing?" I asked him. The witnesses described three women in the sitting area.

"No," he said, barely above a whisper.

"You wore men's clothes?"

"Yeah". He stared at the table as he answered.

"Were any of you wearing wigs?"

There was a long pause.

"No."

He'd been dressed as a woman but didn't want to admit it. It didn't matter to me. I moved on.

"You drove to the Four Freedoms?" I asked.

"Yeah."

"What happened when you got there? Did you go straight to his apartment?"

"No, we stood in the hallway for a little bit, and then…"

"The hallway, or the seating area? You know the one just off the elevator? Did you sit there for a while?"

"Yeah," he said. "We sat there for a while because there were people coming and going."

That was the corroborative statement I was looking for. When someone is confessing to a crime, you need to get something that corroborates the evidence as you know it. There can be no claim of a false confession if those factors are there.

"We went down to his apartment. It was down a hallway to the left. His apartment is three or four doors down on the left."

Another corroborative statement.

"What happened when you got to his apartment?" I asked.

"Gilda went in first."

"Did she knock on the door first?" I asked.

"She knocked and went in."

As Charles described the actual crime, he crossed his arms across his chest and stared at the wall, not making eye contact with me. He tried to gloss over the key parts.

"Charles, you have to say the hard parts too." I told him. "You can't just say, 'that was it'."

"I walked in. He asked who I was," Charles said.

"What did you say?"

"I didn't say anything."

"Did you have your knife out?"

"It was behind my back."

"What happened next?" I asked.

"Brenda went up and stabbed him."

"Where?"

"She tried stabbing him in the stomach. He grabbed her."

"What did you do?"

"At first, I did nothing. Then we all three got him down on the ground. He was hurting her."

"Hurting who?" I asked.

"Brenda. He grabbed her by the throat. That's when I went to help."

"Did you knock him to the floor at that point?"

"Yeah. We all three knocked him to the floor and that was it."

Whenever he didn't want to talk about the actual murder, he'd say, "that was it." Sorry, Charlie. You don't get away with that.

"You have to describe your actions." I said.

"I tried stabbing him in the front of the throat…"

"You tried, or you did?"

"I tried. The knife wasn't working too well."

The statement that he stabbed him in the throat was another corroborative statement. His assertion that "the knife wasn't working too well," is corroborative also. Killing someone is a lot more difficult than television and movies would have you believe. It takes a lot more force than most people realize.

"And then Brenda and me both did it," he continued.

"Were you stabbing, or more slicing?"

"It was more slicing."

That was consistent with the wounds Patrick had suffered.

"Where was Gilda during all this?"

"Gilda just disappeared. I didn't know where she was."

"Once Patrick was dead, or at least unconscious, what did you do?"

"Oh, he was dead," Charles assured me.

"What happened then?"

"We started getting his coins and putting them in duffle bags."

"Once you had all the coins and everything you were going to take, what happened?"

"We left."

"How did you leave?" I asked.

"We walked to the elevator, took it down, and walked out to the car."

They went back to Brenda's house. Brenda's 15-year-old son was there, anxious to hear all the gory details of the murder.

"Did you get anything for being involved in this murder?" I asked.

"She gave me gas money."

"Nothing else?"

"No."

Where you worried about being caught for this?" I asked.

"I was kind of hoping I'd be caught," he said.

"Yet you didn't call to turn yourself in, did you?"

"Um, well…no."

I booked Charles into the King County Jail for Investigation of First Degree Murder.

Next up the food chain was Gilda.

After Gilda was released from jail for the theft charges, she hadn't gone back to the psychic shop. I found out that she was staying at a women's shelter downtown.

I sent the dogs out for her. I heard back shortly thereafter.

I got a call from Bob Vallor.

"We've got Gilda. We're bringing her in."

I put her in the same interview room Charles had been in.

After advising her of her rights, I interviewed her.

"No, officer," she said in a heavy Hispanic accent. "I don't know anything about a murder."

"Let me play something for you," I said. I had a laptop on the table. I played a segment of Charles' confession.

"Stop playing that," she said. "Okay, I'll talk."

Gilda recounted the murder consistent with the story Charles told, though she denied having a knife herself. (Charles said she had.)

She added a story that Charles forgot to mention. Patrick hadn't been the only target that night. They'd gone to an address in the Sand Point neighborhood where an elderly man lived. He also had a lot of money. Brenda wanted his too. Brenda told Gilda the plan: Gilda would knock on the door and say that she'd moved in next door and needed to use his phone to order cable. Brenda and Charles, armed with knives, waited around the corner.

She knocked on the door.

"I just moved in next door," she told the man. "Can I use your phone to order cable?"

The guy wasn't stupid. Everyone has a cellphone nowadays.

"No, you can't come in," he said.

Gilda tried to insist. She pushed on the door as Brenda had instructed.

"I have a gun!" the man said.

Gilda turned and ran. Charles and Brenda fell in behind. When they got to the car, she told Charles to drive to Four Freedoms.

At the Four Freedoms, the story was consistent with the one Charles told. They sat in the area near the elevators.

When the time came, Brenda told her to go to the apartment.

She knocked on the door. Charles and Brenda were lined up along the wall out of Patrick's sight.

"I just moved in next door," she told Patrick when he answered the door. "Can I use your phone?"

"No, you can't use my phone," Patrick said, and went to close the door.

Brenda pushed her way in, her knife out.

Brenda and Charles had Patrick up against the wall.

"I couldn't handle it," Gilda said. "I ran in the bathroom."

She watched through the open door as Brenda and Charles stabbed Patrick to death.

When they were done, Brenda called to her.

"Gilda!"

Brenda told her to help load up the things they were taking. They put the stuff in duffel bags and left the apartment.

They went to a hotel in Kirkland and got a room. Brenda spread all the loot on the bed. She was very happy.

Like Charles, Gilda didn't get anything.

A couple weeks later, they took the coins to a coin shop in West Seattle where they sold them.

Still a few weeks later, Archie told her to come with him. He had retrieved the clothes they'd been wearing when they committed the murder, along with the knives they'd used. They drove to a spot in Ballard, part of northwest Seattle. He burned the clothing in a barrel, and threw the knives, as well as military medals they'd taken, into the Ship Canal.

After completing the interview, I left the room. I returned about a half-hour later.

"Can I talk to you?" Gilda asked.

I sat down.

"I have to tell you how I ended up here," she said. "I was an architect in New York. I was working in Astoria, Queens. I just had a baby, and my boyfriend left me.

"I was walking on the street when I came upon a woman. She said that she could see I was troubled. She said she was a psychic. She could help me. She gave me her card.

"I'm Columbian, in my culture, we strongly believe in psychics and things like that. I called her back. She said she could help me, but it would cost money. She said she had a friend named Father Thomas. He could help me heal, but it would take money.

"I started sending her money. Just a little bit at first, but she needed more and more. I sent thousands of dollars. I was borrowing from friends. My parents took a second mortgage on their house. I sent it all to her. Then I was out of money. I got fired from my job because I borrowed so much money from coworkers.

"I called her and told her I was broke. I had nothing left. She had moved to Seattle and told me to come to her. She and Father Thomas could help me here. I came with my son.

"I have lived like a slave in her house. I do everything.

"When she asked me to do this, I was in a daze. I just went along. But when it came time to do it, I couldn't.

"When I got arrested for the theft, I was in jail, and I read the papers. I realized that she was doing the same thing to Sylvia that she'd done to me. When I got out, I went to get my things. I would not return to them."

Her son had been sent back to New York to live with her parents.

A few months later, Gilda's attorney made a deal with the prosecutors. Gilda would testify for the state against Brenda. In exchange, she would plead guilty to Robbery and Burglary charges and serve eight years in prison.

Almost a year after the murders, Gilda and her attorney showed Jason and I the spot where Archie threw the knives into the canal. She stood on the shore and demonstrated how they'd done it.

A couple days later, Jason and I went to the Harbor Station, where the police boats are housed. We boarded one of the boats and took them to the spot Gilda had shown us.

One of the boats dropped anchor, and police divers went in the water.

The anchor that had been dropped actually landed on one of the knives, causing it to stick up at a 45-degree angle. Both knives and a honing rod were recovered.

At trial, both Gilda and Charles testified.

Charles made a deal with the state: His testimony for a guilty plea to First Degree Murder and a twenty-five-year sentence.

Gilda, who had not participated in the murder, pled guilty to Robbery charges and was sentenced to eight years in prison.

Brenda Nichols was convicted of First Degree Murder with a Deadly Weapon enhancement for the murder of Patrick Fleming.

At the sentencing, Brenda's attorney told the court that she had been raised since childhood to be a criminal. I think he was looking for sympathy, but at some point, you're an adult; you make your own choices.

She was sentenced to 35 years in prison

28

May 30th, 2012 was a Wednesday. At about 1130 in the morning, a man walked into the Café Racer, a small coffee shop and bar on Roosevelt Way Northeast, not far from the University of Washington campus.

He was a regular at the café, but had been causing problems recently, and had been told not to come back.

"You're not supposed to be in here," the barista behind the counter said to him.

"I just want a cup of coffee," he answered.

"I'll make you one to go, but then you have to leave," the barista told him.

He took a seat at the end of the bar nearest the door. Other people sat next to him at the bar; a young woman read her book at a table behind them.

The man next to him at the bar got up to leave. He said goodbye to his friend, seated next to him, and then turned for the door.

He didn't notice the man slide off the bar stool as he did. The man reached inside his jacket, pulled out a .45 caliber pistol and shot the man in the back of the head.

The shooter had a second .45 pistol, and pulled it too, and began shooting the other people in the café.

Bob Vallor and I were at the Medical Examiner's Office. We were at a weekly case review. I try to attend these as much as I can.

My phone rang.

A few moments later, I was racing north toward Roosevelt Way.

The scene was a madhouse, with a dozen police cars in the street, along with fire engines, medic units and other emergency vehicles. Several victims were being treated in the back of the medic trucks.

"There are three dead inside," a patrol officer told me, "Two more are being treated by medics. I'm not sure if they're going to make it."

I stood at the front door to the business and looked in. The trendy café and bar, had a blue tile floor and green countertop now mixed with red from pools of blood. What had been a pleasant and orderly setting just an hour ago, now told the story of the chaos that had interrupted the otherwise normal weekday late morning. Chairs were overturned, and bodies were visible in a back hallway, the victim's having tried desperately and in vain, to escape the horror inside. The familiar metallic smell of blood was in the air

A couple minutes later, Bob Vallor walked up to me.

"There's another shooting downtown, and patrol's calling for Homicide. Can you go handle that one?"

Because of this homicide, I was next up; I got in my car and took off. Jason had gone home early. I called him while I drove.

"Things are going to shit here," I said. I told him about the Café Racer, and that there was another possible homicide downtown.

"The downtown shooting's at 8th and Seneca," I told him. "I'll meet you there."

The downtown scene was in the parking lot of a building called Town Hall. I'd never heard of it before but learned that it hosts music and art events weekly. I pulled my car to a stop in the street on Seneca.

Yellow tape surrounded the lot. I ducked under and approached a patrol officer.

"What've you got?" I asked.

"The victim is a woman in her 50s," he told me. "She was apparently heading to a meeting in Town Hall and had just parked her car. A guy walked up to her and just shot her in the head. No words, no argument, nothing. He took her car and drove off.

"Medics took her to Harborview, but she was DOA."

The vehicle was a black Mercedes SUV. The patrol officers broadcast a description of the vehicle for other officers to watch for.

I walked over to the spot where the victim had been shot. There was one .45 shell casing lying on the ground.

I called Bob Vallor.

"Was that a .45 used up there?" I asked him.

"I think so, but I'm not sure. We haven't gone in yet," he said.

"Let me know if it is," I said. "I wonder if these two cases are related?"

Vallor called me back a little while later.

"These are .45s."

Jason arrived. I filled him in on what we had so far. He was inspecting the scene when an officer walked up.

"They found the victim's car in West Seattle on Delridge Way."

Jason and I took off for that location. Al Cruise and Russ Weklych went as well.

We arrived to find the car legally parked facing southbound. Like the other scenes, dozens of patrol cars swarmed the area; other officers were on foot, guns drawn, checking the yards of nearby houses, but he was nowhere to be found.

The driver's door to the car stood open. A .45 semiautomatic pistol lay on the driver's seat.

A patrol officer approached me.

"The guy that lives there," he said, pointing to the house in front of which the car was parked, "saw the guy get out of the car."

I walked to where the guy stood in front of his house.

"What did you see?" I asked.

"The guy was a white guy," he said. "I didn't really pay much attention to him, but he walked across the street to the bus stop."

I called the Chief Dispatcher.

"I need someone from Metro Transit Police here."

The King County Sheriff's office has a section that act as transit police officers for the region. After a short time, a sergeant from that unit arrived.

"Our shooter may have been picked up at that bus stop," I said, pointing across the street. "It would have been in the last hour. I need you to see if any driver picked someone up there, and if there's video aboard the coach."

"I'll take care of it," he said, and walked away.

We had the car impounded to the vehicle processing room where the CSI detectives could later search it for evidence. They were busy with two homicide scenes now, so it'd have to be tomorrow.

We went back to the Homicide office to regroup and discuss what to do next.

Jessica Berliner is a prosecutor. She was assigned to our homicide. She met us in the office. Carla Carlstrom was the prosecutor for the Café Racer case. She was also there.

"I think these cases are the same guy," I said. "Both cases involve apparently random shootings of innocent people, and both involved a .45."

We talked about whether the shooter could have gotten to the downtown scene so fast after the Café Racer shooting in the north end with busy weekday traffic.

The Café Racer was equipped with surveillance video. The detectives up there were able to recover it. It captured the entire shooting. By that time, the shooter was identified as Ian Stawicki by other employees who'd rushed to the scene after hearing the news. Still photos from the video were sent to all patrol cars. Shortly thereafter, the information was released publicly, so citizens could watch for him too.

"They think they have the suspect in West Seattle," someone yelled out.

I switched a radio on my desk to the frequency for the Southwest Precinct.

"Shot's fired!"

We all ran to the car deck. Jessica Berliner got in a car with me. It was her turn for Mr. Toad's Wild Ride.

When we arrived, there was a medic unit on the scene. A white male was in the back. He'd been pronounced dead. I stepped into the back of the unit to look at him. I couldn't tell for sure if he was Ian Stawicki.

There was a backpack on the planting strip next to a pool of blood. Lying next to it was another .45 pistol. Stawicki had used two .45s at the Café Racer scene. I was pretty sure that was who was dead in the back of the medic unit.

Jim Cooper is another detective in Homicide. He'd stayed at Café Racer and saw the video up close. He thought he'd be able to recognize Stawicki. He climbed in the back of the medic unit.

"That's him," he said.

Detective Scotty Bach of the Intelligence Unit had been driving in the area in an undercover vehicle and spotted Stawicki walking down a residential street. He got on the radio and asked for a patrol unit. Officer Scott Luckie was working by himself and was in the area. He approached Stawicki walking down the street. He stopped behind him and ordered Stawicki to stop. Stawicki knelt on the ground and shot himself in the head.

The victim in the downtown shooting was Gloria Leonidas. She was a business woman, married with two teenaged daughters. Stawicki, who'd suffered with mental illness most of his adult life, wanted her car. He shot her in the head to take it. Completely unnecessary.

Only one person shot inside the Café Racer survived. It was the barista who'd agreed to make Stawicki a cup of coffee. He spent months in the hospital, and eventually went back to work at Café Racer.

Stawicki's family said they'd been trying to get treatment for Ian for years. They, and five victims, besides Ian himself, were the victims of a failed mental health system.

29

My phone rang again on a Sunday evening in February of 2014. It was Mark Worstman.

"We're being called to a shooting at 1st Northwest and Northwest 85th Street in Greenwood. There's one dead at the scene."

Greenwood isn't exactly a high crime area of the city. I hadn't been to too many murders in the area.

Rain was falling as I drove north on Interstate 5 to the scene.

The scene was near a supermarket, and next to a fairly new strip mall with trendy stores befitting the area. A half-dozen patrol cars were parked on the street, along with an ambulance. Yellow crime scene tape encircled the lot. Randy Ward was the patrol sergeant.

Randy was a third-generation Seattle Police Officer. I'd worked around his dad, Mike, earlier in my career. Randy's grandfather had been an SPD officer and had been killed in the line of duty.

"The victim's in the back of the ambulance," he said. "He called 911 to report that someone tried to rob him of his cell phone. He was on the phone with the operator, when he said that the guy was coming back. There was the sound of a struggle, and then the phone went dead.

"In the meantime, we got a call of a shooting at this location. My guys arrived and found this guy down. Medics tried to revive him, but they pronounced him dead.

"There was a theft at the Baranof restaurant on Greenwood Avenue just before this came out. Two black males and a white female were in there and stole a bank bag with cash in it. I don't know if it's related, but I have a couple of my guys over there.

"There's video from the Fred Meyer, (supermarket). They have a camera on this side of the building. It doesn't show the shooting, but there's a black male on it that goes west from the scene, and then goes back toward the scene. A minute later, that same guy is seen running northbound on 1st Northwest."

"Good work, Randy," I said. I walked to the ambulance parked nearby. I stepped up inside and looked at the victim. He looked to be a white male in his forties. He'd been intubated, and there was other medical paraphernalia on his body. There was an apparent gunshot wound to the center of his chest. A "ten-ring" shot, as we called them, for the score on targets the police use when a shot is center-chest. He had identification on him. His name was David Peterson, and he lived nearby.

Jeff Baird arrived from the Prosecutor's Office.

The CSI detectives arrived to process what little scene there was.

Dr. Micheline Lubin from the Medical Examiner's Office arrived, along with investigator Stephen LeBellarte.

"How are you tonight, Micheline?" I asked.

"Well, you interrupted Downton Abbey," she said, "so this better be good."

"It looks like we have a real-life innocent victim," I said.

"It looks like he was center-punched," she said.

She and LeBellarte bagged his hands to preserve any trace evidence that may be present; unlikely in this case, but basic protocol in homicides done every time. They then transferred him to a gurney for transport to the Medical Examiner's Office.

Peterson's phone was missing, but we had his phone number from his call to 911 before the shooting.

I called Len Carver, a detective on an FBI Task Force. I gave him the number.

"I need to go up on this phone right away," I said.

Going up on a phone means getting a warrant, and then tracking the phone live to see its current location.

He called me back a couple hours later.

"The phone's been off since the time this came in," he said. "I'll let you know if it comes back online."

The next morning, I was at the autopsy. The gunshot wound to his chest had severed his aorta and his spinal cord. Death had come quickly. Dr. Lubin recovered a nine-millimeter round from his body.

The victim's wife worked in the civil section of the Prosecutor's Office. She told us that her husband was involved in an online game called Ingress, in which participants walked to different landmarks. That's what he was doing the night he was killed.

I got an email from David Simmons, a detective in the North Precinct, the area where this crime occurred. He was assigned the theft case from the Baranof Restaurant, and wanted to make sure he wouldn't interfere with the murder investigation. I told him he wouldn't be but asked him to keep me apprised of anything he found out.

"Why don't you help me on the murder too," I told him.

He was excited to be invited to work on the case.

When I was a young precinct detective, I had a case that ended up being related to a murder, and I helped work on it. I'm always happy to pay it forward with other young, ambitious detectives.

Like any young detective working what he or she would consider a big case, Dave did a lot of good work, interviewing witnesses and trying to get more information about his theft, which in turn would help the murder case.

A couple days after the murder, we received a tip. A young girl who worked at the Fred Meyer store, next to where the murder happened said that she knows of three people who rob people of their cellphones. They are two black males and one white female, just like the description of the people who'd been in the Baranof Restaurant.

She told us that these three subjects were involved in an assault a couple months earlier. She had enough information about that case for me to look it up in the computer system. The three juveniles involved in that case were named Marquis, Jordan, and Claire. They all attended nearby Ballard High School.

A little while later we got some interesting information from the desk officer at the North Precinct. A person called the station. He sounded like a young black male. He wanted to know what was going on in the murder case. The desk officer told the caller he didn't have any information since murders are investigated by Homicide at headquarters and not from the precinct. The caller hung up without identifying himself or explaining why he was asking, but not before the officer wrote down the phone number he was calling from. The officer researched the number. It came back to Claire, one of the people the Fred Meyer employee had called about.

This murder was widely reported on the news. An apparently innocent man had been killed while out for a walk in a relatively safe neighborhood. Consequently, a number of other tips were called in to a tip line over the next two days, mentioning Jordan and Claire. Then another tipster said that the word was that Byron White was the shooter. White was also a student at Ballard High School. He played on the football team, and was known to associate with Marquis, Claire and Jordan.

David Simmons called.

"I found the bank bag that was taken from Baranof," he said. "It was in an empty lot between the restaurant and the shooting scene."

"Good work," I told him.

Later that day, Jeff Baird called.

"I was called by two attorneys," he said. "They represent two people who may have information about this murder. They want to bring them in tomorrow."

"It's probably Marquis and Claire," I said.

The next day, Jason and I went to the Prosecutor's office. We were right. It was Marquis and Claire. We took Claire and her attorney into a conference room first.

"Hi Claire," I said before she had been introduced. Her eyes widened.

After preliminaries, Claire told us her story.

"I was at a house up the street from where the shooting happened with my boyfriend, Marquis, Jordan, and 'B'. We smoked marijuana and decided to walk to the Baranof to get something to eat. We ordered food to go. 'B' said he was going to steal the bank bag. We didn't want anything to do with it, so Marquis and me left and went back to the house. 'B' never came back."

"That was really good," I told Claire. "The only thing wrong is it's mostly bullshit."

I stared at Claire, saying nothing. She stared back at me, doe-eyed. Then tears welled up and she began to cry.

"Can we have a moment?" her attorney asked.

"Sure." I said. Jeff, Jason and I left the room.

When they were ready to speak again, we went back in. Claire admitted she knew a lot more than she'd told us.

Wow. Who could have guessed that?

She said that everything she said about going to the Baranof was true. When they got back to the house, 'B', whom she now admitted knowing was Byron, didn't show up right away. He arrived several minutes later.

"I think I shot someone," he told them, "I tried to steal a cellphone, but I couldn't get it. The guy was on the phone and he saw my face, so I had to shoot him."

"Byron had a phone on him," Claire continued. "He was disappointed that it wasn't even an iPhone."

Claire admitted that she'd seen the phone. It was in a black case.

Next it was Marquis' turn.

He tried to present himself as a very sincere young man.

"I know who you are, Marquis," I told him. "In fact, if you hadn't come in on your own, we were going to go out and get you.

"The only thing you need to know is, we know what happened. Don't even try to sit here and lie to us."

"Oh, I won't," he said. "I'll tell you the truth."

He admitted knowing Byron's name, but everything he said after that was an even a more ridiculous lie than Claire tried to pass off.

"Marquis," I interrupted him, mid-sentence. "Did you even listen to what I said? We know the truth! What you're saying is absolute bullshit."

His attorney, Robert Flennaugh, had his elbows on the table, and put his face in his hands.

"Can we have a minute?" he asked.

Again, we left the room.

When we came back in, Marquis had seen the light.

"Sorry about the misunderstanding before," he said.

Misunderstanding?

He told a story consistent with the story Claire told after we confronted her.

"Byron lives at the house, (that he'd run to) with his uncle. We spent the night there. The next morning, the gun that Byron had was on the counter in the kitchen. Byron took it outside and hid it in a pile of garbage."

He agreed to show us where the house was.

Marquis and his attorney met Jason and I in the neighborhood where the shooting took place. We put them in our car and drove north on 1st Avenue Northwest. Marquis pointed out the house. It was just up the street from where Byron was seen running.

We went back to the office. I prepared an affidavit for a search warrant.

Once I had the warrant, we called the SWAT team. We were going to serve the warrant the next day.

I called Dave Simmons, the North Precinct detective.

"We're serving a warrant tomorrow. Do you want to come?"

"Sure," he said.

"Be at the SWAT office at 2 o'clock for a briefing."

After the briefing the next day we drove to the area where the house was. We stayed back several blocks while SWAT served the warrant using a Bearcat Armored Vehicle. They found two people inside, neither of which was Byron. I had those two transported to the Homicide office for questioning.

I went back to the office while other detectives searched the house.

The man and woman taken from the house claimed to have no knowledge of the murder. They claimed to have not seen Byron in a week or so.

I was doubtful that they were telling the truth about what they knew, but I released them anyway.

We made a press release that included Byron White's photo; we wanted to arrest him for this murder.

The next morning was Saturday. My phone rang at 7:45. It was Bob Vallor.

"Byron White was arrested at the airport," he said. "He was trying to board a flight to Atlanta. They're taking him to the office."

Jason and I met at the office. Byron wasn't there yet.

When he arrived, we put him in an interview room. A little while later, Jason and I went in. We advised him of his rights, and asked some basic questions, before getting to the point.

"Byron, do you know why you're here?" I asked.

"I heard you were going to bust down my door for selling pills," he said.

"You know this has nothing to do with selling pills," I said.

He looked at the floor. I sat in a chair next to him, our knees almost touching.

"Are you sorry this happened, Byron?" I asked.

He continued to stare at the floor, not saying anything at first. Finally, he nodded his head.

"Yes."

"Where did you first see the guy?" I asked.

"I saw him when I was behind Baranofs where the new stores start. He was walking and looking at his phone.

"I walked up and tried to knock the phone out of his hands, but he pushed me back. I thought, 'this isn't worth it,' and started to walk away.

"Then I saw the guy on the phone, talking to the police. Then the guy hung up. I walked back to him and he was rummaging through his pockets. I thought he had a gun, so I shot him in the chest."

"That's really good, Byron," I said. "Except the guy didn't hang up the phone. He was still on the phone when you came up to him. We could hear the scuffle on the recording. He wasn't rummaging through his pockets and you knew he didn't have a gun."

Byron admitted that was true. He admitted running to the house where we'd served the search warrant and telling everyone there what happened. He admitted being upset it wasn't an iphone.

Welcome to my world, where a kid kills an innocent man just out for a walk and is disappointed he didn't even get an iphone.

I spoke to Byron's mother later that morning.

Byron had a nice home. A mother and father who worked hard at their jobs and provided for him. He went to high school and played football. Yet, something happened.

His mother saw the tell-tale signs; grades slipping, attitude changing, and shady-looking friends coming around. She knew he was straying from the right path.

Her brother lived in Atlanta and owned a business. He offered to take Byron and give him a job, hoping to straighten his life out. Byron refused to go.

Suddenly, a couple days ago, Byron called her. He decided he wanted to go to Atlanta and live with his uncle. She was thrilled. Maybe he'd get his life together after all. She bought him an airline ticket.

Her husband took him to the airport that morning. She stayed home. She turned on the news. There was a photograph of her son. He was wanted for murder. She picked up the phone and called 911.

She told the police where they could find Byron.

30

I looked bleary-eyed at the clock on my nightstand: 2:25.

"Shit," I muttered to myself, trying to find the ringing phone in the dark room. I glanced at the LCD screen. Bob Vallor.

"Hello," I said, wide awake now. It's a talent I'd developed over decades of being wakened in the middle of the night.

"There's a shooting at 29th and South King Street," Bob said. "There are two dead at the scene."

Damn it, I thought, dragging my ass out of bed. A gang-bang. I hate those. Nobody knows anything. It's like pulling teeth to get witnesses to cooperate. Nobody wants to tell the police what they saw, even if it's their friend or family killed. It's all part of the "no snitch" culture that permeates urban life and media.

There had been several shootings in that neighborhood in the last couple months.

I tried to get dressed without waking Doreen. It didn't work.

"Did you get called out?" she asked, barely awake. She was also used to the phone ringing at all hours of the night.

"Yeah," I answered. "Go back to sleep."

"What happened?"

She always wanted to know what I was going out on.

"It sounds like a double homicide in the CD," (Central District), I said.

Dressed, I went downstairs, grabbed my badge, gun and car keys. My suburban street was quiet, like it always is when I leave at that hour. Nothing like where I was going.

I switched the police radio in my car to the frequency for the East Precinct, which covers the Central District, flipped on my red and blue lights, and headed to the scene.

There were seven or eight patrol cars blocking the street when I arrived, yellow crime scene tape beyond the cars, several officers standing near them.

"Good morning, father," Casey said as I walked up. He and his partner had been one of the first cars to arrive.

"Good morning," I said. "Tell me the story."

"The lady that lives at that house," he said, pointing to a house just south of the crime scene, "heard multiple shots being fired. She looked out the window and saw a black male standing over here. She saw him reach down and toss something into the vacant lot next to the bodies."

Two black males lay dead in the street.

"She said the guy got into a car and drove off southbound. After he left, she walked outside and found these two guys dead. Matt got a statement from her."

Matt Blackburn was Casey's partner. I don't know many of the patrol officers at most scenes I go to, but because Casey worked this watch in the East Precinct, I'd gotten to know a lot of the officers he worked around.

The Watch Commander stood nearby, along with the Night Duty Captain. We'd all worked around each other at various times in our careers.

"Well, if it isn't 'Mister Homicide,'" the Watch Commander said, shaking my hand.

We were looking at the victims and at the shell casings littering the street. They were 9-millimeter; a lot of them. A baseball cap laid in the vacant lot. Probably what the witness saw the shooter throw. Maybe we could get DNA off the brim.

John Castleton from the prosecutor's office arrived.

"Looks like a gang-bang," I said to him. "These two have multiple head shots, this one has several in the face," I gestured to one of the victims.

My cell phone rang. It was the Chief Dispatcher.

"We got a call in here a few minutes ago," he said. "A man was calling from Federal Way. He said he just got a call from his brother, whom he called Junior. Junior told him he'd just shot a guy in the face and asked him to come pick him up. He said he was along Interstate 5 downtown. We notified the State Patrol."

Sweet, I thought. This may not be so hard after all.

"I think our shooter is somewhere along I-5 downtown," I told Castleton, filling him in about what I'd just learned.

The dispatcher on the East Precinct frequency came on.

"State Patrol is responding to a report of a pedestrian on I-5 near Roanoke Street."

"Let's go," I told Castleton. We jumped in my car and roared off toward the freeway.

We were about a mile away when we got the word. State Patrol was on the scene; this wasn't our guy.

Damn.

I diverted and went to the office.

I had the names of the victims. I ran them on the computer. I wanted their most recent booking photos. There were no photos of either victim.

What the hell? There are always booking photos in gang-bang cases.

I ran them for criminal history. Nothing.

One of the victims, Dwone Anderson-Young, lived a half block from the scene. They were local, so there should be something.

Jason was on the phone with Junior's brother, who'd called 911. Junior had called again and told his brother he'd gotten a ride and was heading to California. The brother tried to talk Junior into turning himself in, but Junior would have none of it.

He gave us Junior's real name and date of birth. We ran him for criminal history. It was extensive, with a previous arrest for murder. He apparently wasn't charged in that case. He had a warrant out for his arrest. Very convenient.

This was our guy.

I put together a bulletin with Junior's photo and information. I sent it out to all Seattle Police units, and then statewide through the state Attorney General's office.

Jason and Al Cruise headed up to Everett, to Junior's last known address. Junior wasn't there, but they spoke to his girlfriend.

A couple hours later, Jason got a call from Junior. He was coming to turn himself in. He'd be in our office in a half-hour.

Sweet.

An hour passed, and then two. No sign of Junior. I wasn't surprised. People tell us they're going to turn themselves in all the time, and then never show. We went home.

I was home about an hour, when Jason called me.

"I just got a call from Junior," he said. "He's outside our building right now."

It was Saturday morning, and no one was at our building. Jason called radio to have patrol respond and pick up Junior. We raced back in.

While we were on our way, Assistant Chief Nick Metz walked up to the front door of headquarters. He saw Junior.

"Can I help you," he asked.

When the man looked at him, Metz recognized him. He'd received the bulletin too. Metz took him into custody.

"I'm surprised you remembered how to arrest someone," I said when I arrived. I'd known Metz since he was brand new and had worked around him when he was a patrol officer. "And I'm really surprised you had handcuffs on you."

We put Junior in an interview room. A while later, we went in.

"I don't know anything about no murder," he said.

"You called your brother and told him you shot someone in the face," I said. "What a coincidence that we're standing at a scene were someone was shot in the face at that moment."

"I didn't tell my brother I shot someone," he said.

We asked him to go over his activities from last night.

"I went to a bar in Everett with my friends," he said. "Then we went to a strip club in Seattle. From there, we went to a casino in Sea-Tac near the airport. I got into an argument with the people I was with and left. That's why I called my brother for a ride. I didn't say I shot nobody."

He said he could call some friends who could confirm his story. We gave him a phone to make the call. After talking with someone, he handed the phone to Jason. I could hear the woman screaming into the phone from across the room. Jason hung up.

An hour later, Junior's "alibi" witnesses showed up. They were a bunch of gang-banging thugs. They wouldn't answer questions or say where he was, but only said he didn't do it.

We kicked them out of the building.

We booked Junior for the federal gun-running warrant he had out for his arrest.

The next day, Castleton and I went to visit Junior's brother. We showed up unannounced. There was a family event going on at his middle-class suburban home. Junior's brother came outside to meet us.

He was a good guy; a family man who worked for Boeing.

We'd gotten copies of his calls into 911. There'd been no ambiguity in what he told the operator. He was a little reluctant to talk at first.

"I've got a family to raise," he said. "Junior's been in trouble most of his life. He always calls me when he's in trouble. I can't deal with it anymore. I don't need that drama in my life. I love Junior, but I've got a family. I don't want that side of him in my life."

He stood by everything he said in the calls.

We asked detectives from the Technical Electronic Support Unit to collect video at the various places Junior said he'd been to the night of the murders. In the meantime, Jason and I decided we'd better seize the car Junior said he'd been in that night, so we could get a search warrant and look for evidence inside. We asked Bob Vallor to take a couple detectives up to Everett and impound the car.

A couple hours later, Bob came back into the office. He had two prisoners. He was exasperated.

"We got there," he said, "and all hell broke loose. (The screaming woman Jason had spoken to) tried to jump in the car and drive off. Her mother got involved, and it turned into a cluster-fuck. We had to call Everett PD for backup. We arrested them for obstructing.

"Every time you send me to look for a car, it turns to shit."

He was referring to the day I sent him to sit on Christopher Monfort's car in Tukwila. He ended up getting into a shooting.

I laughed.

The TESU detectives showed up later with video from the various businesses. We reviewed the recordings.

We watched the surveillance video from the casino in the city of Sea-Tac Junior said he'd been when the shooting took place. One nice thing about casinos: They have a lot of high-quality surveillance systems.

We saw the car we'd just impounded pull into the parking lot. We couldn't see where it parked, but a couple minutes later, we saw the "screaming woman" and her boyfriend walk in the front door of the casino. No Junior.

Sweet.

"Wait, who's that guy?" I asked. We could see a lone man walk across the lot. Then the man walked in the front door of the casino. It was Junior. He was walking in the door of the casino, 10 miles away from the shooting scene, nine minutes before the first 911 call came in.

Shit. He wasn't our shooter.

But what was the call to his brother all about? The only thing I could think of was maybe there's some other person shot in the face that we don't know about.

We were back to square one for our murders. This happens all the time in murder investigations.

In the meantime, we'd learned more about our victims. Both were gay.

Dwone Anderson-Young had been an IT professional. He spoke fluent Japanese and had planned to move to Japan.

Ahmed Said, the other victim, was Somalian and worked in a clothing store.

Said's homosexuality had been a real problem for him. He was Muslim and shunned by other Muslims. He'd been attacked once by other Muslim's for being gay. He declined to assist with the prosecution of those responsible.

We gave both their cellphones to TESU, so they could be "dumped". All the data on the phones was downloaded to a spreadsheet, including call history, texts, photos and contacts. They put the data on a CD.

I reviewed the data on Dwone's phone. I scrolled through his call history, concentrating on the night he was murdered. He'd made a call just after midnight, a couple hours before he was killed.

I ran that number in various databases we have, trying to identify who the number belonged to, but it wasn't listed in any of the systems. I decided to call it.

John answered the phone. He was a friend of Dwone's.

"Dwone called me that night and said he was at R Place," he said. R Place is a gay bar on Capitol Hill. "He wanted me to come over there, so I did.

"When I got there, Dwone was there with Ahmed. I know Ahmed, but not well.

"While we were in the bar, Ahmed was constantly texting. He said he was meeting a friend outside the bar after closing. I think he was using Grindr."

Grindr is a phone app that gay men use to meet other gay men that are near them geographically.

"After closing we went outside. Ahmed's 'friend' was standing next to the grocery store across the street. He seemed weird; he didn't look right.

"Ahmed, Dwone and this guy were leaving. Ahmed offered to give me a ride, but the guy creeped me out, so I didn't go with them. The three of them walked off to Ahmed's car to leave."

What? It had been three days since the murder at that point, and no one had said anything about Ahmed having a car.

John suggested I call another friend, Patrick, who'd been there too. He gave me Patrick's number.

"Call Ahmed's family," I said to Jason. "See where Ahmed's car is."

Jason was on the phone for a few minutes. He hung up and looked at me.

"Ahmed did have a car. They don't know where it is."

"Why didn't they tell us that earlier?" I asked.

They'd given Jason the make and model of the car. We ran Ahmed's name in the Department of Licensing database and found the information on the car.

Jason prepared a bulletin and sent it out to all Seattle Police units. In just a few minutes we got a call: Patrol units found the car on a Rainier Valley street. Dried blood stains made a pouring pattern out the passenger door.

We had the car photographed in place and then towed to the Vehicle Processing Room. I wrote a search warrant for the car. I asked CSI and Latent Prints, the unit that processes evidence for fingerprints, to process it for evidence.

I called Patrick, the guy John told me about. I asked him to come to my office.

"I saw Dwone in the bar," he said after he arrived. "I know Ahmed, but not as well as Dwone. Ahmed was texting someone on Grindr."

He told me about meeting Ahmed's friend outside.

"I tried to be nice. I said hello, but he ignored me."

They offered Patrick a ride home also, but he lived the opposite direction they were going, so he called a cab.

I put Patrick in my car and drove to R Place on East Pine Street. He pointed out the corner where they'd met the guy Ahmed was texting. There was a surveillance camera right above the spot.

"Where was Ahmed's car parked?" I asked.

Patrick directed me north on Boylston Avenue. I noticed another camera over the sidewalk north of Pine on Boylston. Just past that camera, mid-block on the west side of Boylston, there was a parking lot.

"Ahmed was parked right there," Patrick said, pointing to a specific parking spot in the lot.

I looked around but didn't see any obvious cameras pointing to the lot.

I drove Patrick home.

"I want to hook you up with a forensic artist," I told him. "so you can help develop a sketch of the guy Ahmed met."

Once again, I called the Technical Electronic Support Unit. I asked them to recover any video they could find between R Place and the parking lot. I told them about the two cameras I saw.

Later that evening, they came back to the office.

"The one on the corner where they met the guy isn't working," they told me.

Of course.

"We got video from the one on the sidewalk where they walked."

I looked at that video. It captured them walking down the sidewalk. I recognized Dwone and Ahmed from the clothes they wore. The guy that was with them was a black male. He had a backpack, but the view was from above and from behind; there was no view of his face. It wasn't perfect, but it was better than nothing.

I looked at the time stamp on the video. It was 17 minutes before the first call came in to 911. It was about a 12-minute drive to the shooting scene from there. There was no doubt the third guy in the video was the killer.

Later that day, our case got a huge boost.

Amanda Poast is a Latent Print Examiner for SPD. She processed Ahmed's car. On the rear passenger window on the driver's side, she found a palm print. She ran it through AFIS, the Automated Fingerprint Identification System. She got a hit.

The print belonged to Ali Muhammed Brown.

When you find a fingerprint or DNA at a crime scene, it doesn't necessarily mean you've identified the killer. You must eliminate all possibilities that the evidence is unrelated to the crime.

"Let's call Ahmed's family," I told Jason, "and see if they know this guy." It's a Muslim name. Maybe he's a friend or family member.

Jason made the call.

"They've never heard of him," he told me.

We ran Brown in the computer systems to see what we could learn about him. He had a warrant out for his arrest for failing to register as a sex offender.

We discovered that he'd been arrested the previous April in Siskiyou, California, by the California Highway Patrol. He'd been stopped in a Silver Dodge Durango. He'd been smoking marijuana and had no driver's license on him. They booked him in jail and impounded his car.

The next day, Patrick was scheduled to meet with Betty Kincaid to create a composite sketch. I spoke to Betty when she arrived.

"We've identified a possible suspect. I want you to go ahead and get all the parts to prepare the sketch, but before you draw it, I want to show Patrick a montage. I don't want to influence the sketch in case he can't make a pick."

She and Patrick set up in a conference room in my office. I left them alone.

An hour later, Betty came out.

"We've got all the composite parts selected," she said.

"Patrick," I said, "I want to show you a group of photos. The person you saw with Dwone and Ahmed may or may not be included in the group. I want you to look at each of them and see if the person you saw is in the group."

I handed Patrick the stack of photos. He looked at each of them. When he got to the photo of Brown, he set that photo aside, and looked at the remaining photos. When he'd looked at all of them, he picked up the photo of Brown.

"That's him," he said.

"How sure are you?" I asked.

"I'm absolutely sure."

I prepared another bulletin and sent it out state-wide. There was probable cause to arrest Ali Muhammed Brown for murder.

I called Randy Moore at the Fugitive Task Force. He got the ball rolling to find Brown.

Later, I was still in the office working on the case. Bob Vallor came out of his office.

"The sheriff's office called. They're investigating a homicide and they're looking for a Silver Dodge Durango if anyone knows someone with one."

"Who's looking for a Dodge Durango?" I asked.

"Jake Pavlovich at the Sheriff's office," he said.

Jake is a friend of mine. I called him.

"You're looking for a Silver Dodge Durango?" I asked.

"Yeah. We've got video of one related to a homicide we're investigating that happened in Skyway back in April."

"I just identified a suspect in a double homicide from the CD," I told him. "He's been known to drive a Silver Dodge Durango.

"What kind of weapon was used in your murder?" I asked.

"It was a 9-millimeter."

"Ours too." I told him.

"I'll be right over."

The Sheriff's Major Crimes Section, who handle homicides in the county, is housed across the street from Seattle Police headquarters.

Jake came over along with his partner, Chris Johnson. Jake told me about his case.

"Our victim was walking from the Skyway Bowl, when a Silver Dodge Durango pulled up. It didn't look like there was any interaction between the victim and the driver of the Durango.

"We found surveillance video. It shows the victim walking by, and then the Durango approaches the victim from behind. Just after the Durango goes out of frame, there are several flashes from the gunfire."

The victim died.

I showed a close-up photo of the head stamp on one of the casings we recovered at the scene. It was the same brand of ammunition used in their murder.

That in itself doesn't necessarily mean much, but it's a start.

They'd submitted their casings to the crime lab.

I called Brian Smelzer, a scientist in the lab's ballistics section. I asked him to compare the casings from our case with the ones from the County's. He'd get back to me, he said.

It didn't take long. The casings in both our murders had been fired from the same weapon. They were probably fired from a Smith & Wesson M+P 9 mm.

Randy Moore from the Fugitive Task Force called. He'd gotten a tip from an informant; Brown may be staying at his sister's condo in North Seattle, near the Four Freedoms house. (I just can't get away from that place.)

He'd set up surveillance on the place. The Silver Durango was there. His guys would sit on the place and see what happened.

He called again the next morning. A woman he thought was Brown's wife left in the Durango along with two kids.

Jake Pavlovich went to the address where the Durango was registered in Tacoma. It was parked there. He was setting up surveillance on that location. Jason drove to Tacoma to help with that. I prepared an affidavit for a search warrant to enter Brown's sister's condo.

I had detectives from the Intelligence Unit help with surveillance of the condo. I asked Bob Vallor to call SWAT; we'd need them for this warrant.

SWAT deployed to the parking lot of a shopping center around the corner from the condo. John Castleton rode with me when I went there, search warrant in hand. I handed it to the SWAT commander, Lieutenant Matt Allen.

There's no way to have a full SWAT deployment and not attract a crowd, with several patrol cars, command vehicles, armored vehicles and the like. The place was abuzz with gawkers. We stayed out of sight of the condo complex, so no one knew why we were there.

We didn't know if there were kids in the condo. We decided to wait until someone left the unit. We could then snatch them up and get some intel as to who was inside.

In just a little while, a woman left the condo with some kids. Intelligence detectives snatched them up and took them to an office in the condo. It was Brown's sister and her children.

Bobby O'Donnell was a detective in the Intelligence Unit. He came on the police department a few months before I did, and we worked around each other in patrol early in our careers.

Raised in Brooklyn, Bobby has a strong New York accent. He'd been undercover for years, deep undercover for a couple of them, infiltrating a local organized crime group. He posed as a New York hit man. His look and demeanor assured that no one doubted his role. He was going to retire in just a couple months.

"Dat fuckin' bitch!" he said when I walked up. "She's callin' us all fuckin' infidels and says we're all goin' to hell. I told her, 'I'll see you there, bitch!'

"She said Brown's not there. She said the only one in her condo now is her mother, who's old and sick."

Bobby always made me smile. Whenever we had a murder-for-hire case I always asked him to play the hit man. He was really good at what he did.

I went up to Brown's sister. She wore a full hijab. Her eyes sliced through me.

"When's the last time you saw Ali?"

She just stared.

"Look, if you don't want to talk we can just lob tear gas and stun grenades into your condo before the SWAT team goes in."

"He's not there," she said. "I haven't seen him in weeks." She told me that her mother was in a bedroom and was bedridden. No one else was in the unit. I relayed that information to the command post.

SWAT made a slow and deliberate entry, eschewing the tear gas and stun grenades. She'd told the truth. An old woman laid in a bedroom. She didn't even move or acknowledge anyone's presence.

I called Pavlovich and updated him on the situation at the condo.

"Brown's wife drove away, and we followed her," he said. "The brake light in the rear window was burnt out. So was the one on our suspect vehicle in the shooting.

"The next time she leaves, we're going to stop her."

It was time to turn up the pressure on Brown. We put out a press release with his photo, letting the public know there was probable cause to arrest him for the murders of Dwone Anderson-Young and Ahmed Said. We intentionally didn't mention the Skyway murder.

Randy Moore kept looking for Brown, following up on other leads.

A day later, my office phone rang. The caller was Clint Daniel, a detective with the Point Pleasant, New Jersey Police Department. Point Pleasant is a coastal community on the Jersey Shore.

"We had a guy try to carjack another guy a couple days ago," he said. "But the victim's car was a stick-shift and the suspect didn't know how to drive one. He got out and ran into a nearby store. I got a surveillance photo of him.

"I found out that this guy was in a restaurant here the night before. He didn't have money to pay the bill. He gave the waitress a phone number. She called and spoke to the guy's brother, who gave her credit card information over the phone.

"I went to the restaurant. They still had the number. I called and BS'd his brother into giving me the guy's name. He told me it was Ali Muhammed Brown. I did a Google search and holy shit! I found out that he was wanted for murder in Seattle."

That was good work on Daniels' part.

"Can you send me the surveillance photo?" I asked.

He emailed it. Sure, as shit, it was Brown.

"You know," he said. "There was a murder the other night in West Orange, New Jersey. A 19-year-old kid was shot and killed for no apparent reason. I wonder if it could be him?"

I looked up that case online.

Nineteen-year-old Brendan Tevlin was home after his freshman year at the University of Richmond in Virginia. He'd been at a friend's house playing video games. He'd texted his mother to let her know he was on his way home. He never made it.

A call came in of shots fired in an intersection, but when the police arrived, they only found shell casings in the street.

A little while later, they found Tevlin's car parked about a mile up the road in the parking lot of an apartment complex. Brendon's body was crumpled on the passenger side floor. He'd been shot several times.

I called the Essex County Prosecutor's Homicide Task Force, who was investigating the murder. I spoke to a detective. I told him about the three murders in Seattle, and that we knew Brown was in New Jersey.

"The MO in our murders was similar," I said.

"We're pretty certain this was a robbery gone bad," he said.

"Do you know what kind of weapon was used in your murder?" I asked.

"It was a Smith & Wesson M+P," he said.

"That's what was used in our murders," I told him. "When the whole robbery thing peters out, give me a call." I gave him my phone number.

A week later, I got a call from the Newark Police Crime Lab.

"Can you send us a few casings?" they asked.

"Sure," I said. I called the Evidence Unit and asked them to ship some of the casings.

Later, Brian Smelzer from the crime lab called.

"NIBIS shows that these casings were fired from the same gun," he said, referring to my murders, and by extension, the Skyway murder, and the New Jersey murders. He agreed that we should send some to New Jersey to verify the findings.

A few days later, I heard from the New Jersey lab.

"There from the same gun."

On July 18th, I was at the scene of a homicide/suicide in North Seattle. I was standing over a woman's body when my cellphone rang. It was Randy Moore.

"Ali Muhammed Brown was arrested in New Jersey," he said.

This murder, tragic as it was, was a slam-dunk.

I went back to the office and made arrangements to fly to New Jersey the next morning.

Jason was out of town, so Al Cruise was going with me. Jake Pavlovich and John Castleton were also going.

In the morning, we were on a flight to Newark.

When we arrived, we met with the detectives working the Tevlin murder. They were great guys and shared everything they had on the case with us. They drove us around to the murder scene and all the relevant places involved in the murder. We went to the apartment complex where Tevlin's body was found. One of the suspects they had in custody along with Brown, in the robbery case lived there.

I didn't buy it. Brown was a loner. Why would he be with a bunch of gang-bangers in New Jersey? But it wasn't my case.

We wanted to interview Brown. I assumed we'd bring him back to their office and do it there. That wasn't going to happen.

The Homicide Task Force was housed in a building that wasn't secure. Our offices in Seattle are in police headquarters. Our interview rooms are hardened and equipped with electronic locking systems. We can bring prisoners over in a tunnel and up an elevator directly to the interview rooms, so even ultra-high security prisoners can be moved with no problems.

The bosses in Essex County considered Brown a high-risk prisoner. So did I. They didn't want him brought back to their offices. We had to go to the jail to interview him.

I make it a point not to interview prisoners in jail, particularly murder suspects. Jails don't usually have adequate interview rooms, and there are often other distractions. Sometimes, though, when I travel to other cities to interview murder suspects, I've had to do it in jails.

One time in Redwood City, California, Jason and I were literally in a closet interviewing a murderer.

Another issue with interviews: I don't want more than two detectives in the room. No one wants to talk about terrible things they've done in a crowd. The New Jersey detectives had a serious interest in what Brown had to say, and normally, they would watch the interview through one-way glass, or over a video feed. Since the interview would occur in a jail, none of those options were available.

The jail staff were very accommodating, but a jail is a jail. It's not a police station or a detective's office.

They led us to a long, narrow room. Me, Pavlovich, Al Cruise, John Castleton and three New Jersey detectives were there. Not ideal at all.

Pavlovich and I conducted the actual interview.

When Brown was brought into the room, he looked around at all the people like I knew he would; I hoped it wouldn't shut him down.

"I'm Cloyd Steiger," I said to him. "This is Jake Pavlovich. We'd like to talk to you."

Like most interviews of murder suspects, we soft-peddled ourselves at first.

Pavlovich advised Brown of his rights.

Brown was a little reticent.

"You guys come in here and bombard me like this," he said.

We let him carry on for a few minutes.

"We came here from Seattle. We just want to speak with you a bit," I said.

"Go ahead and speak. What do you want to talk about?" he asked.

When he was arrested, he said his name was Muhammad Ali Abdulla.

"Is that the name you want to go by?" I asked.

"Yes," he said.

I asked basic background questions, both to see how he communicated and see if he had any obvious delusional issues.

He told me he was born in Seattle, but then moved to Oklahoma before ultimately returning to Seattle.

"Have you been a Muslim all your life?" Pavolvich asked.

"Yes," he said.

"Is that a pretty strict religion to follow?" Pavlovich asked. "I don't know much about it."

"I wouldn't necessarily call it strict," he said. "because there's no compulsion in my religion. No one's being forced to do anything."

"But there are certainly rules of conduct in Islam," I said, "like any other religion."

"Of course."

"Have you always been this devout?" I asked, really meaning radical. "Or is this something that came up later in adulthood?"

"What do you mean by devout?"

"I mean seriously following your religion. When you're a teenager, people mostly just go through the motions, because their family is, until you mature a bit and really get to know what it's about. Have you always been serious about your religion?"

"I decided to start seeking knowledge about my religion," he said, "and as I developed knowledge…you're going to apply religion more because you know more."

"So how long have you been seriously studying your religion, do you think?" I asked.

"Seriously studying?" he asked.

"Yeah, seriously studying."

"Deeply, about four years now."

"To tell you the truth," I said, "this thing we're investigating, and you know what we're talking about. It looked like you were trying to send a message. It seems clear to me, anyway, that that's what you were trying to do.

"So, we're just here to give you an opportunity to tell us what your message is. We just want to know what's going on."

"My religion is the religion of truth, and it's the religion that...it's as simple as this: Islam is what the world needs.

"Islam is what has always...has always been governing the entire world. For over 1300 years until the year 1924 when the Caliphate collapsed. And now, Islam is coming back. Islam is coming back."

"Tell me what Islam can do for the world; what the world needs Islam for," I said.

"Bring the world peace," he answered. "I want to ask you a question now."

"Yeah, sure," I said.

"Where are you coming from as far as a statement?"

"It seems to me that this incident was, and maybe I'm wrong, but I think you were trying to make a statement," I answered.

"What incident?" he asked.

"Well, we're talking about the incident that happened at 29th and South King Street, with the two guys from the club down on Pike Street.

"Let me tell you right up front," I continued. "Your fingerprints were all over the inside of that car. We've got video of you walking with them to the car. It's not an issue. We didn't come here to get you to tell us anything, because that doesn't matter. It's a done deal. But it does seem like you wanted to make a statement or send a message, and maybe it's about Islam.

"We know about meeting up outside the club, we know about walking to the car, and we know that you drove away in the car. Some people saw you out there. When you picked up that hat and tossed it into the lot, people saw that. They saw you. We have your fingerprints inside the car. That's how we know your name. You used the same gun to kill them that you were arrested here with.

"It's not like we said, 'Let's go see Muhammad and see if he'll tell us something so we can nail him.' You're already formally charged with two murders in Seattle, so it's not an investigation anymore, but we want to give you a chance, as a man, to tell us what this was all about. I've seen a lot of things in my career, and when I look at this, I think, 'Muhammad's trying to send a message.' Well, this is your opportunity to tell us what that message is.

"Maybe you're reluctant to tell us what that message is, but if you're a true believer in the message, you have to have the courage to tell us what that message is. Maybe I'm completely wrong, but if I am, you have to tell me."

"I think it's a worthwhile story," Pavlovich added. "It's kind of interesting, learning about you and the religion and if that's got something to do with it or not, I don't know."

"My religion has everything to do with it," Brown said.

"So, if you're sending a message, and it's because of your religion…"

Brown interrupted me.

"It wasn't about sending a message. It was just about following the commands of my lord."

"That's what I thought," I said.

"And I'm speaking in general," Brown said.

"That's fine."

"My life is based on living in the cause of the law. Living in the cause of the law. To live by the law, to die for the law.

"This is what my life is about. What's important to me.

361

"And the things that I do, people may not understand, but it's the path that I've chosen to take."

"I'd like to understand it," Pavlovich said. "That's why we came out."

"You're talking about God's law, of course," I added.

"God's law," Brown repeated.

Pavlovich leaned in close.

"What are the literal, the most important ones? What does God teach you?"

"You know; I'm not trying to make some statement. I'm not trying to expose my actions, expose myself or put myself out there, you know what I'm saying? Look at me, what I'm doing now.

"My actions are solely for the sake of the law."

"If you're following this," I said, "and you're following God's law, then you have to have the courage to say before men what you're doing. You're not boasting, and I'm not asking you to boast, but now everyone knows about the deed."

"Is that what your religion would tell you is a righteous deed?" Pavlovich asked.

"If it wasn't, I wouldn't have done it," he said.

"And what about it made it a righteous deed?" I asked.

"Moving in the path of the law," Brown said. "It's not about punishing someone. Not looking to punish someone for some law that they have broken. It's not my intention."

"So, it's moving off the path, not following the path," Pavlovich asked. "Is that what you're saying?"

"Not even saying that," Brown said.

"What are you saying then," I asked, "Without us putting words into your mouth, what do you think?"

"Just as simple as this," Brown said. "Jihad training."

"Have you been to Jihad training?" I asked.

"Yeah."

"I heard that you went to a camp down in Oregon at some point." I said.

"Yeah," Brown said. "I was there, actually.

"Human beings have absolutely no morals," Brown added, "Human beings have no guidance, no instruction, no nothing."

I moved on to the murders.

"One of the victims was Muslim and gay. Ahmed Said. Is that what set you off?"

"No," Brown answered, "It's not a hate crime. It's not that I hate gay people. You can love a person and hate the act. No one with any type of morals about themselves is not going to like what gay people do. It's absolutely against nature.

"Everything in the creation of the Almighty has balance, from the creation of the heavens and the earth, from the animal kingdoms, from the ecosystems, everything following its path. Even the animals, everything in the creation of the Almighty follows a path. That God the Almighty has fixed for it. But what about the human being? What makes a human being different?

"The God Almighty has set a code for the human being, and the code is the moral code. And as you can see what happens when the human beings don't follow that code. They throw off the balance of the creation of the Almighty God, he tells the Holy Koran, the scripture, he says that God has set a balance, so do not upset the balance.

"So you have these human beings who are wilding out like crazy. You guys shouldn't be worried about a couple of simple crimes, or whatever. Don't you guys need to be cleaning up the entire city?

"Allowing men and women, I mean same sex marriages, then allowing those same sex couples to adopt children so those children can be raised with their minds screwed up. With their moral understanding all thrown off balance. It's not my fault, or anyone's fault. It's your government's fault, allowing all this fitnah, all this evil to fester and grow instead of cleaning it up. There's no way a man should marry a man, or a woman should marry a woman. This is man-made law. It's not God's law."

Brown told us his plan was to travel to the Middle East and join his brother Muslims. Perhaps a group like ISIS.

He spoke more specifically about the Seattle murders.

"Something needs to be done. Because out there, in those streets in Seattle, you have gay bars everywhere.

"The people need new governance and the only thing that's going to bring things back to normal is Islam and the Caliphate governing the world like it used to."

Pavlovich moved the conversation to the Skyway murder he was investigating. At first, Brown denied any knowledge of that crime.

"Why would it be," Pavlovich said, "that the gun you were caught out here with and the gun that was used in their murder was the same gun used to kill this guy?"

"Are you saying this guy is dead?" Brown asked. "That's between him and his maker."

"Yeah," Pavlovich said, "but neither one of them can talk to me right now."

"There's people dying by the millions, in Afghanistan, in Syria, in Iraq, in Somalia, by the hundreds of thousands. And you guys are worried about just these couple of people?

"It happened to them because God wanted it to happen.

"The Prophet Muhammad said, 'When you see evil, change it with your hands. If you're not able to do that, then speak out against it. And if you're unable to do that, then at least hate it in your heart. This is the weakest.

"So what you have to do is just throw your weapons down, give up and let the Muslim's take over because that's the only way we're going to have peace is that we establish Sharia; Islamic law; the Caliphate."

The interview lasted a couple hours, and then we left him in the jail.

A few weeks later, the New Jersey detectives called. Brown asked to speak with them again. During their conversation, he confessed to killing Brendan Tevlin. He described how he did it and placed himself in a nearby restaurant waiting to commit the crime. They went to that restaurant and saw him on the surveillance video, alone.

He also got into more details about the Seattle murders.

Brown was charged with the Skyway murder. Like the murders of Dwone Anderson-Young and Ahmed Said, the charge was Aggravated Murder, which could potentially result in the death penalty.

He was charged in New Jersey with the murder of Brendan Tevlin. Despite Brown's insistence that he acted alone, and video of him alone shortly before the murders, they charged the two people they had suspected tried to rob Tevlin from the beginning. I guess someone in the food chain just couldn't give that up and admit that Brown acted alone. The charges against those two were later dropped and an added charge of Terrorism was filed against Brown; the first use of that charge by the state.

During our interview with Brown, he continually railed about wanting peace, but all the while he was out killing innocent people at random.

The irony was apparently lost on him.

31

I pulled my unmarked detective car up to the curb, behind about ten patrol cars that blocked the street.

I was tired. I'd gone to bed at midnight on a Saturday; my phone rang at 2 o'clock in the morning, summoning me to this West Seattle address.

A body laid in the middle of the street, blue tea lights dispersed around it, marking various pieces of potential evidence located by the first arriving officers.

It was October, but still warm. I didn't bother donning a jacket and walked into the inner scene.

"Good morning, Detective Steiger,"

It was my number two son, Landon. Smart ass. He and his partner had been one of the first patrol cars to arrive.

"What's going on here, Land?" I asked.

"There's one dead here. A second victim was transported to Harborview. He's in pretty bad shape too. The shooter's a guy named Nigel.

"Is Nigel in the wind?" I asked.

Landon nodded.

"The dead guy's brother is here. He witnessed the shooting. I'll have him tell you what happened."

A young, well-dressed black male approached from a group of officers. I shook his hand.

"I'm Detective Steiger from Homicide," I told him. "What happened here?"

"I was downtown at a club," he said through tears. "Jerome called me. He said he'd been jumped by Nigel. I got in a car

367

and headed down here. When I got here, Nigel was in a car. He jumped out. I thought we were going to fight, but he pulled a gun and pointed it at me. I turned and ran. I heard a bunch of shots, but I didn't see where he was shooting. I got around the corner, and the shooting stopped. I waited and then ran back here. I wanted to find my brother, but the police had the area taped off. I saw a body in the street. It's my brother, Jerome. He works as a chef in a restaurant downtown. He was just on his way home from work."

"Who's Nigel?" I asked.

"We were all friends until a couple years ago, but we've had an ongoing fight for a while. I never thought this would happen."

"I'm going to need to take a formal statement from you later," I told him. "Someone will take you downtown to my office in a few minutes."

Another stupid murder about nothing.

I walked up to the yellow tape and ducked under. A young officer held a crime scene log.

"Name and serial number?" he asked.

"Steiger, four three one three."

Jerome laid in the street, a yellow police blanket covering his body. Blood spatter patterns around him; arterial spurting. Death came quickly.

I pulled back the blanket. His half-open eyes were cloudy, in a death stare. Medics had tried in vain to save him; he was intubated, and EKG stickers were attached to his chest.

Fired shell casings surrounded the scene. A lot of rounds had been fired. They were .40 caliber. Based on the primer strike mark, the murder weapon was a Glock. Their firing pins are unique; that mark was on the casings.

I stood in the middle of the scene by myself when it occurred to me: This could be my final murder as the primary detective. I'd been investigating murders most of my adult life. It's a part of me; it defines me, at least professionally. I'd never really thought about that ending.

An officer walked up to me.

"There's a witness over there who doesn't want to stick around."

Fuck that, I thought. I walked over to him.

"I'm Detective Steiger. I'm going to need to get a quick statement from you. Why don't you have a seat in my car." I motioned to the car, parked a few feet away. He sauntered over to it.

"Get in the front," I said.

I asked him his name and address. He told me.

"I'm not comfortable doing that," he said.

"Here's the deal," I told him. "You can give me a quick recorded statement here and be on your way, or I can have you taken downtown. That could take hours."

"I don't trust the police," he said.

I had no patience for this bullshit. I got out of my car and motioned at the witness.

"This guy goes downtown," I told the officers. They put him in a car and left.

I walked back to the scene.

Ron Lavell was the Night Duty Captain.

"The shooter lives just a few blocks away," he told me. "I have SWAT standing by. Do you want them to drive by the house and see if his car's there?"

"Sound's good," I said.

Ron's a good guy. A captain who still gets it.

A little while later, he approached again.

"SWAT says the car is there."

I jumped in my car and rushed downtown to my office. I needed to write a search warrant, so we could go in Nigel's house. Mister "I don't trust the police" can cool his heels in my office for a while. I guess he should have just given me the statement in the car.

Twelve hours after my phone first rang depriving me of a night's sleep, we had the shooter in custody, recovered the murder weapon and put this case to bed. I went home.

I'd already missed my grandson Kai's soccer game. His older brother Keaton had one at 3.

I sat down in the recliner in my family room for a minute before heading to Keaton's game.

I looked up at the clock. Six o'clock. I'd fallen asleep. Doreen went to the game without me. This job is really bad for family life.

I'm way too old for this shit.

The Washington State Attorney General's Office has a unit called the Homicide Investigation Tracking System. Staffed with retired homicide detectives, it tracks every murder in the state, entering information into a database, hoping to link related murders across jurisdictional lines. They also help agencies with murder investigations, particularly small agencies that don't have a dedicated Homicide unit, or whose detectives aren't as experienced in those types of investigations.

I'd been asked on several occasions to go with them to various agencies around the state to review murder investigations and suggest how to proceed.

Marv Skeen was the Chief of that unit. He told me he was retiring. He knew I was contemplating retirement from SPD and suggested I consider applying for his job or another investigator job that was opening, since my old partner Gregg Mixsell, who'd gone to work for them after retiring from SPD, was retiring again.

I told Marv I'd think about it.

I decided I would apply for the job. I was fairly confident I could get hired.

I was on call on December 13th, 2015. I'd let everyone know I'd be taking a couple months off around Christmas, and I didn't plan to come back.

My phone rang again early that Sunday morning, just after 3 o'clock. After getting the location of the murder, I sat up in bed.

"Did you get called in?" Doreen asked, barely awake.

"Yeah."

"You know, this could be the last time," she said.

"I was just thinking that."

Most of my adult life, that phone rang in the middle of the night. I was an EMT before coming on the police department and was wakened to go on calls. When I worked as a patrol officer, I worked until 4 in the morning, and frequently had to get up after only a couple hours sleep to go to court, work an off-duty job, or go to a family event. I was called out in the Sex Crimes unit to reports of rapes, now officer-involved shootings and hundreds and hundreds of murders since I'd been in Homicide. Sleep deprivation is a way of life for me.

Once again, I raced down the deserted freeway, red and blue lights piercing the night to the downtown address I was called to. I pulled my detective car to the curb in front of a building.

The scene consisted of a blood spot on the sidewalk. A security guard in a building heard gunshots. He looked out and saw a car race away, but nothing else. He called the police.

The patrol officers arrived and saw what they thought was a transient asleep on the sidewalk. They checked on him; he'd been shot. Medics rushed him to Harborview, but he was dead.

Guy Pratt, a new sergeant in Homicide, pulled up. The area was ensconced in yellow tape. A very anti-climactic scene on which to end my career.

The entire shooting had been captured on surveillance video. The victim was just walking by. There was no disturbance before he was shot. Another stupid murder for no reason.

This wasn't my case. CSI was on the way to process the scene. I walked up to Pratt.

"There isn't anything for me to do here," I said. "I'm going home."

I got in my car and drove away, the yellow tape fluttering in the wind in my rear-view mirror.

The suspects were arrested and charged a couple days later.

My last day at work was December 23rd, 2015. It was a bittersweet day; a clear turning point in my life and career. Mike Ciesynski and I went to lunch at F.X. McCrory's Fish House, near Century Link Field, home of the Seahawks. We had the manager take our picture together afterward.

I loaded everything from my desk into a couple boxes and dropped the keys to my police car on the lieutenant's desk. Jason gave me a ride home.

During my two-month sabbatical, I couldn't completely stay away. I reviewed cold case murders for American Investigative Society of Cold Cases, a nonprofit who'd ask me to consult with them on cold cases from all over the country. I communicated constantly with other members of the group.

Murder is in my DNA.

I applied for the job with the Attorney General. I arrived at their office, one block north of Seattle Police Headquarters for an interview in January of 2016. I knew the three people interviewing me very well. Lana Weinmann had been a King County Prosecutor as had Scott Marlowe. Marv Skeen was the third person in the room. I'd worked closely with him for years.

"I haven't been to a job interview for 37 years," I said. I was very relaxed.

"Why do you think you're the best candidate for this job?" they asked; the last question in the interview.

"Well, I don't want to sound arrogant," I said. "But I think I'm probably the most experienced Homicide detective in the State of Washington."

Lana called me a couple weeks later.

"I want to offer you the Chief Investigator job," she said.

I took the job and put in my retirement papers for SPD. It was the perfect fit. I'd still be helping investigate murder all over the state, but I knew I'd go home every day on time.

And they never call me at two in the morning.

Made in United States
Troutdale, OR
07/09/2024

21128476R00216